THE

VICTORIAN CRITIC
AND THE
IDEA OF HISTORY

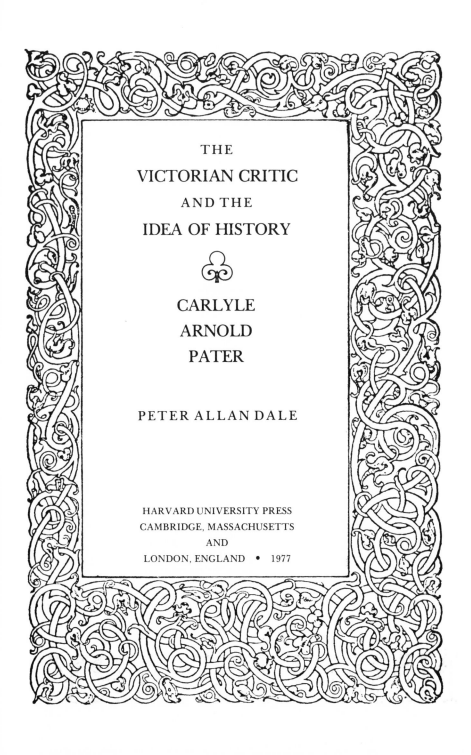

THE
VICTORIAN CRITIC
AND THE
IDEA OF HISTORY

CARLYLE
ARNOLD
PATER

PETER ALLAN DALE

HARVARD UNIVERSITY PRESS
CAMBRIDGE, MASSACHUSETTS
AND
LONDON, ENGLAND • 1977

Publication of this volume has been aided by a grant from the
Andrew W. Mellon Foundation

Library of Congress Cataloging in Publication Data

Dale, Peter Allan, 1943-
    The Victorian critic and the idea of history.

    Includes bibliographical references and index.
    1. Criticism—Great Britain—History.
2. Historicism.   I. Title.
PN99.G72D34   801'.95'0941   77-5936
ISBN 0-674-93581-0

TO EVELYN

ACKNOWLEDGMENTS

It is impossible to express adequately my obligation to the many people who have helped me with this book, first, because it is always difficult to account for all the things tangible and intangible that one owes to one's friends and colleagues in the course of researching and writing, and second, because one does not want to embarrass those same friends and colleagues with too much complicity in a work that must, after all, ultimately be the author's own responsibility. Perhaps the safest place to begin is where the debt is greatest and the likelihood of embarrassment least, with my wife, Evelyn, who has contributed to the making of this book at every stage, sacrificing more hours than I like to mention to what I know must have been pretty tedious work. Much is owed as well to the great kindness and wise guidance of those who read and commented on the manuscript at various points in its development: to Graham Hough, who supervised my doctorate at Cambridge, and to Barry Bullen, who did his best to keep an alien's spirits up at that great institution; to Walter Jackson Bate, Jerome Buckley, and David Perkins, all of whom contributed their time and experience to helping me improve the final version when I arrived at this other Cambridge. Finally, I cannot, I feel, close my list without recognizing the influence of one other friend and teacher, Andor Gomme, who, while he has not advised me on this particular study, has in many ways provided its principal inspiration. I hope it may at least approach his own high standards of critical discussion, though I fear it must inevitably fall short.

Acknowledgment is due as well to the following publishing houses for permission to quote from their authors' works: George Allen and Unwin, Ltd., for H. P. Rickman's translation and editing of *Meaning in History: Wilhelm Dilthey's Thoughts on History and Society;* G. Bell and Sons, Ltd., for F. Osmaston's translation of G. W. F. Hegel's *The Philosophy of Fine Art;* Oxford University Press for E. Wilkinson's and L. Willoughby's translation of J. C. F. Schiller's *On the Aesthetic Education of Man;* The University of Michigan Press for R. H. Super's edition of Matthew Arnold's *Complete Prose Works.*

Cambridge, Massachusetts
1977

CONTENTS

THE
VICTORIAN CRITIC
AND THE
IDEA OF HISTORY

When I look at this age with the eyes of a distant future, I find nothing so remarkable in the man of the present day as his peculiar virtue and sickness called "the historical sense."

—*Nietzsche*

HISTORICISM
AND CRITICISM

This is a study at once in nineteenth-century English criticism and intellectual history. It assumes at its outset that there is a necessary connection between a person's opinions on literature and art and his opinions on life in general and that such connections are well worth tracing. In particular it deals in substantial detail with this connection as it is found in the work of three of the Victorian period's most important and influential writers on critical matters, Thomas Carlyle (1795-1881), Matthew Arnold (1822-1888), and Walter Pater (1839-1894).

Each of these men had, of course, a quite distinctive intellectual outlook and with it a distinctive approach to literature and/or art, and I have tried throughout to do justice to the complexity and the uniqueness of each's position. At the same time, it has seemed clear that all three as well as many of their contemporaries, both English and Continental, were influenced by a single pervasive intellectual concern that significantly draws together their separate philosophical and critical opinions and gives to their work a kind of unity deriving from the "spirit of the age" and making for a characteristically Victorian approach to literary and artistic problems. This approach so far as I am able to tell has not yet really been adequately defined. The chapters which follow may not, in the end, succeed in supplying that adequate definition, but I hope that they will have gone further in this direction than much that has been written to date on the criticism of the period, or that, at the very least, they will suggest fruitful possibilities for future study of that criticism.

The pervasive intellectual concern that I mention and that has seemed to be at work throughout the critical writing of these three men and of the mid and later nineteenth century is, very briefly, the concern with the historical process and its philosophical meaning. In this short introduction I propose to describe in general outline, first, exactly what that concern amounted to and, second, how it affected literary criticism.

That the nineteenth century was dominated as no period before or since has been by the "historical sense" is a truth of intellectual history sufficiently well established to need no extended reiteration here. V. F. Storr has made the point as well as anyone:

> Among the new influences which were to shape the thought of the nineteenth century, the foremost place must be given to the historical method. . . . The eighteenth century witnessed the birth of this method at the hands of Lessing and Herder, but it was the following century which fashioned it into a powerful method of critical research, and showed how by its aid the long story of humanity's development might be rendered intelligible.[1]

In England one may first begin to see this new preoccupation with history taking vigorous hold on the national mind in the late twenties.[2] By 1830 Carlyle was proclaiming with good reason that history has "perhaps never stood higher than in these times of ours":

> Poetry, Divinity, Politics, Physics, have each their adherents and adversaries; each little guild supporting a defensive and offensive war for its own special domain; while the domain of History is as a Free Emporium, where all these belligerents peaceably meet and furnish themselves; and Sentimentalist and Utilitarian, Sceptic and Theologian, with one voice advise us: Examine History, for it is "Philosophy teaching by Experience."[3]

A year later J. S. Mill was noticing the same phenomenon: "The idea of comparing one's own age with former ages," he wrote, had occurred to philosophers in the past, "but it never before was itself the dominant idea" of the age.[4] This sense of the triumph of Clio over every branch of human thought continued virtually unabated down to the end of the century when Lord Acton told a Cambridge audience (1895) that the great lesson of their times had been that "philosophy is only the amended sum of all philosophies, that systems pass with the age whose impress they bear . . . that history is the source of philosophy, if not quite a substitute for it . . . [that all things are subjected] to that influence for which the depressing names historicism and historical mindedness have been devised."[5]

Of the various manifestations of this nineteenth-century phenomenon of "historical mindedness," I shall be concerned with one peculiarly relevant to the question of poetics, what may loosely be called the *philosophical* manifestation of the historical sense. Involved here is not simply an interest in the past and a desire to resuscitate it but an attempt to think seriously about the *meaning* of historical process.[6] One wonders, that is, about such things as the cause of history, its pattern, and the end toward which it is moving; about one's inevitable involvement in the "web" of the past; about the nature of historical knowledge; and, above all, about the cultural relativity that Acton is talking about above, about the possibility that all values and beliefs are relative to the age in which they occur. I shall call this serious or philosophical thinking about history historicism, following common modern usage.[7] Some of its principal characteristics and tendencies are worth noting.

The first thing to be observed about nineteenth-century historicism is that it began by setting up historical process not as in itself a sufficient explanation of experience but as the most likely venue to such an explanation. Not through physics or metaphysics could one best discover the meaning of life, but through history. For the theistically or idealistically inclined this meant that history became the revelation of God's or Absolute Spirit's providential design for mankind.[8] For the more positivistically inclined, history was nothing so magical as a revelation, but it was, nonetheless, a very important key to the meaning of life. G. H. Lewes could scorn Carlyle's notion of history as "philosophy teaching by example," but this did not prevent him from seeing rather large possibilities in the "scientific organization of history." "For the first time a mission is assigned to the study of the past, worthy of fulfilment: this mission is to exhibit the evolution of humanity, and to form thereby a social science." To form a "social science" meant for Lewes, as for the positivist tradition in general, to approach the study of history as one would that of physics in search of *laws:* "the art of history will be thoroughly dependent upon the laws of social development," and mankind will accordingly know just where it is.[9]

Regardless of the philosophical basis from which the nineteenth-century thinker approached history for the key to knowledge, he was likely to find in history a logical pattern or law and an overall goal that gave it the same gratifying intelligibility that scientists and philosophers of an earlier century imagined they had found in nature. It is precisely this faith in the intelligible design and purpose of history, this belief that historical process could fall neatly into phases of thesis, antithesis, and synthesis and that it was going somewhere in particular, which K. R. Popper has singled out (and criticized) as the essential quality of historicism.[10] The historicist concepts of historical patterning and of historical teleology were various, and some of the more important of them I shall be dealing with in greater detail in the chapters that follow. My point here is that although they were no doubt accepted by their advocates as true interpretations of the nature of historical process, their source, after all, was not in the data of history itself but in quite ahistorical assumptions about God or the Absolute, about psychology or natural law, in short about any number of things that were not in themselves specifically historical modes of knowledge.

The function of these various explanations of historical pattern and purpose was twofold: to enable the historicist to interpret and to rationalize what for most thinking men from 1830 onward was the disconcertingly confused spectacle of the "modern age." We are confronting, Matthew Arnold told an Oxford audience in 1857, a "copious and complex present," "an immense, moving, confused spectacle, which . . . perpetually baffles our comprehension." Deliverance from this confusion lies ultimately in the study of the past: "To know how others stand, that we may know how we ourselves stand . . . that is our problem."[11] Beyond this desire to learn from the pattern of the past where we ourselves stand, the nineteenth-century historicist outlook characteristically had a rather more ambitious objective: by revealing the recurring pattern or necessary direction of human affairs this study of history became, in fact, the study of the future. Carlyle's expectations are characteristic: "Unspeakably precious is [our 'Letter of Instruction' from the past]. . . . Only he who understands what has been, can know what should be and will be."[12]

So far I have spoken of the nineteenth century's philosophical use of history as the main intellectual road to wisdom, as the means of discovering God's Providence and interpreting scientific law, as the means of comprehending the present and predicting the future, as the means, in sum, of approaching every problem, religious, philosophical, moral, scientific, aesthetical, confronting the mind of man. This discovery of a new means of knowing things, however, is not quite what Friedrich Meinecke, one of the foremost twentieth-century historical thinkers, had in mind when he spoke in his classic study, *Die Entstehung des Historismus* (1936), of the rise of historicism as "one of the greatest revolutions that has ever taken place in Western thought."[13] What Meinecke meant was a revolution in thought that led not simply to a new *means* of knowing but to a new principle of reality; he meant that philosophy had begun to move toward an understanding of history not as a means to knowledge but as the *end* of knowledge, as a complete knowledge in itself beyond which the human mind could not and need not go.[14]

To clarify this point one may look back to Hegel's crucial distinction in the introduction to his lectures on the philosophy of history (1822-23) between the nonhistorical processes of nature which are governed by natural law and the processes of history which are governed by thought. With this distinction, says R. G. Collingwood, "history steps out full-grown on the stage of philosophical thought."[15] For Hegel it is thought or reason which produces history, and there is no history but that which is the expression of thinking beings. Reason is the "sovereign of the world"; it is also the "Infinite Energy" of the universe, which is not simply content passively to speculate on things but which produces acts which in turn produce things; these acts and things, these material manifestations of Reason in the world, are history, and history is nothing else but these. "That this 'Idea' or 'Reason' is the True, the Eternal, the absolutely *powerful* essence; that it reveals itself in the World [through History] and that in that World nothing else is revealed but this . . . is the thesis, which . . . has been proved in Philosophy."[16] Hegel imagined himself ultimately to be engaged in the rational proof of God, and what he calls Reason here he regards as anchored in Absolute Spirit, which is his version of God.

Those who later followed his thought on the rational or idealist basis of history—Croce, Collingwood, Ortega, and with qualification, Wilhelm Dilthey and Meinecke—detached the Reason or Spirit which is history from this anchor in the Divine and made of history a thoroughly human process. For them history became the expression of humanity's composite mind or consciousness developing through time, and that composite mind was the source and arbiter of all knowledge and all value. This identification of history and philosophy amounts to the denial of any existence or truth except what belongs to the history of man's spiritual development. Beyond the realm of history there is no Divine realm of spirit at all.[17] "[H]istorical judgment," writes Croce, "is not a variety of knowledge, but it is knowledge itself; it is the form which completely fills and exhausts the field of knowing, leaving no room for anything else."[18] Thus reality, in the end, consists of the historical manifestations of thought or the cultural systems by which man literally makes himself. For the complete historicist, there is no God, no Absolute, no fixed human nature, no permanent concept

7

at all, only the continuous historical development of man's thought about himself. In Ortega's rather startling words, "man . . . is brought up against himself as reality, as history. And for the first time, he sees himself forced to a concern with his past, not from curiosity nor in the search for examples which may serve as norms, but because it is all he *has*."[19]

Here one has the resolution of the great nineteenth-century historicist movement. Its implications present from the very beginning have been accepted, stoically by Ortega, far more exuberantly as welcome freedom by Meinecke and Croce. Through most of the nineteenth century such a resolution as this, with its apparent acceptance of the historical relativity of all values and concomitant reduction of reality to a precarious stream of tendency called human culture, would not have been in the least welcome. Certainly in nineteenth-century England there were very few prepared to carry historicism to this length. Carlyle with his exaltation of the clothes-making—that is, culture-making—capacity of man came close, but he stopped short of accepting a complete historicism. Matthew Arnold was not even tempted but instead "refuged" himself from the *Zeitgeist* in the ahistorical bosom of Spinoza. Only in Pater does one find the adoption of a complete historicism. However, his position was so conscientiously skeptical and so highly colored by aestheticism that one might almost miss in him what is, in fact, a very significant shift from history as variety of knowledge to history as complete knowledge.

The historicist outlook, as Acton's remarks above suggest, saturated all aspects of contemporary intellectual life, including thought on poetry and art. People who think seriously about literature do not, any more than people who think seriously about any other significant human problems and activities, confine themselves to their own special intellectual preserve labeled "aesthetic" or "critical." Inevitably they wander afield and more likely than not find their critical thought the richer for the excursions. Modern criticism, for instance, few would deny, has gained immensely from its practitioners' explorations in linguistics, psychology, and anthropology. The Victorian critics were in general very much concerned with history and historicism, a fact particularly true of the three men on whose criticism I have chosen to concentrate. Carlyle, although he began as a literary critic, eventually became one of the foremost historians of his age.[20] Arnold, always preeminently the critic, was the son of another of the great early Victorian historians and from him imbibed not only a sense of the extreme importance of history but, more significantly, the philosophy of the principal eighteenth-century forerunner of the historicist movement, Giambattista Vico. Pater, for all his reputation as an aesthete, was well versed in Hegel and at least as interested in tracing with Hegel the progress of the Idea in art as he was in burning with a hard gemlike flame. The thought of each of these men on the nature of poetry and art cannot, in the end, be easily disengaged from their thought on history. It is precisely these historicist concerns that impart a degree of intellectual continuity to their various critical positions, linking them together in ways not generally recognized and extending beyond them into the critical writings of many of their contemporaries.

The particular effects of contemporary historicist preoccupations upon poetics may be seen in a number of ways, which I shall, of course, be treating in greater detail as I go along. Here, however, I want to suggest the general nature of the issues that will arise in this study. The first and most obvious way one would expect historicism to affect critical thought would be in the development of a thoroughly genetic approach to criticism, in the fulfillment, that is, of Mme de Staël-Holstein's program announced at the outset of the century: "I wished to demonstrate the connection that exists between the literature and the social institutions of each country; and this had not yet been done in any known book."[21] Mme de Staël is exaggerating the originality of her enterprise. The genetic approach to criticism in its most general form, the desire to trace the relation between historical or cultural factors and art, had been around long before she wrote.[22] The differences found in the nineteenth century and particularly after the Romantic era of triumphant "individual genius" are both quantitative and qualitative. On the one hand, what had always before been a minor motif in criticism had become a dominant assumption; from 1830 onward few English critics would have considered it possible to talk meaningfully of poetry without taking into account the "age." On the other hand, the main tendency of the nineteenth-century genetic approach, at least in England, was to focus not, as in the eighteenth century, upon geographical, racial, or sociological influences so much as upon spiritual or intellectual ones. Above all, as would be expected in a period preoccupied with the decline of religious belief, nineteenth-century critics wanted to know what the age gave the poet to believe in and how that belief found expression in his poetry.

A second principal type of critical issue raised by the historicist outlook has to do with the other side of the relationship between poetry and society, the side on which poetry influences, rather than is influenced by, society. With the growing awareness, in Carlyle's words (borrowed from Schiller), that "Truth immer WIRD nie IST," the critic became increasingly interested in the role of poetry and of art in general either in making some new belief prevail or preserving an old one.

A third, and surely the most difficult critical problem raised by historicism, is that of aesthetic value. One may see this in two ways. On the one hand, the interpretation of the modern age, which the study of historical "patterns" gives the critic, may materially influence certain critical preferences, Arnold's classicism in aesthetical matters, for instance, has not a little to do with his Viconian-inspired belief that history had come round again to a "classical" condition. More significant was the challenge posed by historicism to the concept of aesthetic value as such. None of the critics I am concerned with was prepared to adopt the thoroughly historicist position that to admit the necessary relation between literature and cultural background is to deny the possibility of any but relative or historical values. All in their different ways accepted in principle that there were what Arnold (following Aristotle) called "real estimates" to be made in criticism. At the same time, all sought to discover grounds for such estimates that would take into account their new realization that truth, again is always becoming.

A final word should be said about my reasons for concentrating on the three men that I have chosen. I have sought, in the first place, to choose men who have produced a significant body of critical writing. Each of my main figures, I hope it will be granted, ranks as one of the two or three most important critical thinkers of his generation of the Victorian period. My second reason for selecting these writers lies in the great breadth and seriousness of the intellectual interests they have brought to the study of literature, the extent to which they have attempted to comprehend the best that was thought and known in their day and to integrate it into their literary discussions. Among other critics writing in this period one would be hard pressed to find any to exceed these three in their sensitivity to the main movement of contemporary thought, not only in England but on the Continent as well. More specifically, there were no other major critical thinkers, with the possible exceptions of J. S. Mill, G. H. Lewes, and Leslie Stephen, so intelligently alert to the implications of the historicizing spirit of the times. These exceptions, who by both my criteria it might seem should be included in this study, lead me to a third and I think the most important criterion for my choice. Carlyle, Arnold, and Pater were trying in their different but not unrelated ways to make poetry or art a viable substitute for a religious belief which had been thoroughly undermined by the historicist spirit. From one standpoint, the study of the influence of historicism on poetics is a study of the attempt to find in aesthetic experience something to compensate for the dissolution of religious belief under pressure of the contemporary Zeitgeist. From Carlyle's introduction of Schiller's aesthetic to English criticism, through Arnold's application of Spinoza's religious thought to poetics, to Pater's concept of "aesthetic morality," a continuous effort to make of poetry a variety of religious experience may be discerned. In the positivist school of critical thought, in which Mill, Lewes, and Stephen may be included, there is no such expectation of poetry. Their critical thought represents quite a different intellectual tradition and one which, though very interesting in itself, is, because of its relative detachment from the whole religious problem, rather less central to the mainstream of Victorian concerns.

THOMAS CARLYLE

I have known many who on the wide ocean of
human history imagined they had lost that
god, whom on the firm ground of natural
knowledge they beheld with their mental eye
in every stalk of grass, in every grain of dust,
and adored with overflowing heart.

—Herder

1

THE METAPHYSICS
OF WILL

Compared to his reputation as a sage, Carlyle's reputation as a literary critic is slight. Some have made rather large claims for him. Alfredo Obertello, for instance, writes that his "real critical output is very small" but that its importance is "inestimable."[1] What Obertello means by "real critical output" is not clear, but if one considers output simply as essays designed specifically as critical reviews — as against fictional, social, and historical writing — this output is, in fact, fairly substantial. It comprises some thirty lengthy articles, eight critical prefaces, two translations, one full-length critical biography, and a series of lectures on the history of European literature. Even by Victorian standards this is a fair showing. As for the importance of Carlyle's criticism, although it is certainly not negligible, to call it "inestimable" is to exaggerate. In terms simply of nineteenth-century England, Carlyle's critical contribution is very much overshadowed by that of the great Romantics before him, Wordsworth, Coleridge, and Hazlitt, and the great Victorians after him, Ruskin, Arnold, and Pater. A more realistic estimate of his significance as critic would place him as the best of his generation, that is, the first generation of the Victorian period, which would include such critical writers as

H. H. Milman, J. G. Lockhart, Macaulay, H. Coleridge, J. Sterling, and Mill. As far as influence is concerned, he may certainly claim preeminence, for far more than any of these others he made his critical thought felt on later poets and critics, men such as Tennyson, Browning, Lewes, Ruskin, Arnold, Morris, and up to the very threshold of modernism, Arthur Symons.[2]

As for his distinctive contributions to English criticism, two things seem to me to give him a position of significance. First, there is his introduction of German Romantic literature to England: "Carlyle as an interpreter of German literature," writes René Wellek, "is immeasurably superior in knowledge and insight to all his contemporaries."[3] Second, there is the application of his ideas on historical process to the study of poetry. It is this latter area with which I shall be particularly concerned, and to a degree Wellek points the way here also, for he recognizes as one of Carlyle's major contributions that he was the first to bring serious historicist concerns to nineteenth-century English criticism.[4] Wellek, however, sees this as essentially a matter of Carlyle's interest in literary history. My own concerns will have to do more with theoretical problems regarding Carlyle's concept of the nature of poetry and poetic value and the relation of poetry to the "spirit of the age." To begin with, I want to consider what seems to me the real basis of Carlyle's claim to significance in the development of English criticism—his movement from what may be called a dialectic of being to a dialectic of becoming in his interpretation of the metaphysical nature of poetry.[5]

Carlyle's "Aesthetic" Criticism: The Dialectical Orientation

It must inevitably seem odd to speak of Carlyle's *aesthetic* criticism, for if he has one grave shortcoming as a critic, it is precisely his lack of interest in and sensitivity to what one normally considers the aesthetical qualities of poetry, those of form and those of sensuous and emotional effect. Carlyle characteristically dismisses the whole question of artistic form as beneath the serious critic's concern. This is partly because he believes that form follows on automatically from meaning and is not therefore something one ought to be self-conscious about: "the grand point is to *have* a meaning, a genuine, deep, and noble one; the proper form best suited to the subject . . . will gather round it almost of its own accord."[6] Still more important is his Calvinistic tendency to associate the love of form with insincerity, lack of natural feeling, and ultimately with unbelief. Form is mere "sleight-of-hand" (*Critical and Miscellaneous Essays,* I, 384), "dead artificial cold splendor, as of polished metal," as against the "manifold soft summer glories of Nature" (*Critical and Miscellaneous Essays,* I, 452). The grand arbiter of form is *taste,* and taste is what one believes in only after having disposed of God, as in the case of the Enlightenment, upon which Carlyle is always ready to heap Hebraic invective. "Over all Europe the reign of Earnestness had now wholly dwindled into that of Dilettantism. . . . No Divinity any longer dwelt in the world; and as men cannot do without a Divinity, a sort of terrestrial-upholstery one had been got together, and named TASTE" (*Critical and Miscellaneous Essays,* II, 424).

If Carlyle has a moral aversion to a criticism that occupies itself with formalistic questions, that aversion is scarcely less pronounced in his attitude toward the discussion of poetry's effect on the "sensibility," a critical approach which he associates with another aspect of the previous century's spiritual bankruptcy, the "mechanistic" philosophy of empiricism. "Poetic beauty, in its pure essence" can have nothing to do, he writes, with what "all our [English aesthetic] theories" from Hume's to Alison's concern themselves with; it is not

> derived from anything external, or of merely intellec-
> tual origin; not from association or any reflex or remi-
> niscence of mere sensations; nor from natural love,
> either of imitation, of similarity in dissimilarity, of ex-
> citement by contrast, or of seeing difficulties overcome.
> . . . [One must abandon] the hypothesis, that the ulti-
> mate object of the poet is to please. Sensation, even of
> the finest and most rapturous sort, is not the end, but
> the means (*Critical and Miscellaneous Essays,* I, 55-
> 56).[7]

Carlyle's reputation as a critic has understandably suf-
fered from his prejudices against what, as I say, most would
consider the real aesthetical issues. As early as 1911 George
Saintsbury was condemning him for his "estrangement from
the [critical] task" and associating him with the "general
critical poverty of [his] period."[8] There has been no lack of
modern comment continuing this theme,[9] and although the
easiness of the target may be regretted, I am afraid this line
of attack is, after all, unexceptionable. One simply does not
go to Carlyle for the discussion of the specifically aesthetical
issues with which the best criticism has always concerned itself. Still, when Carlyle began at last to make his way in the
literary world, in the mid 1820s, he did see himself as something of a revolutionary in critical matters, and, what is
more to the point, he tended to see his contribution as that
of introducing the British to the "aesthetical" criticism that
he had learned, or half-learned, from his mentors across the
North Sea. It is worth starting, then, with an examination of
what the term aesthetical meant to Carlyle.[10]

Using German aesthetic theories of the previous forty
years as authority, Carlyle called upon his countrymen to
cease their frivolous reviewing and develop a "new science of
criticism" such as was to be found among their intellectually

more profound and earnest Teutonic cousins (*Critical and Miscellaneous Essays,* I, 52). Most of this was bluff. Carlyle, in fact, never had anything but the very slightest understanding of German aesthetical thought as such. He dropped most of the relevant names — Baumgarten, Herder, Winckelmann, Kant, Goethe, Schiller, Schelling, and Hegel; he brought these men before the English eye; but nowhere in his work does he show any evidence of ever having grasped, or even of having tried to grasp, their specifically aesthetical doctrine. On the contrary, in the cases of Goethe and Schiller, whose work he knew better than that of any of the others, he seems to have gone out of his way to ignore what they were saying about the nature of the aesthetical.[11] What this new aesthetic criticism coming out of Germany meant to him was, to begin with, simply the philosophical upgrading, the exaltation, of artistic and, in particular, literary activity. As a younger man, before his discovery of German writers, he was an omnivorous reader of scientific, philosophical, and historical works and had always been somewhat apologetic about his literary interests. "It was foolish, you may think," he writes to a friend in 1818, "to exchange the truths of philosophy for the airy nothings of [poetry]: but I could not help it."[12]

Following his discovery of the Germans (ca. 1821), however, he began to find literature and the study of literature invested with a new, intellectual importance. "The character of a Poet," he writes in 1827, ". . . stand[s] higher with the Germans than with most nations," and, accordingly, for them the study of poetry is no mere dilettantism; it is a "science" springing "from the depths of thought, and remotely or immediately [connecting] itself with the subtlest problems of all philosophy" (*Critical and Miscellaneous Essays,* I, 55). What has happened is that Carlyle has had enough exposure to German thought on art to realize that it is everywhere the tendency of that thought to elevate aesthetical activity into one of man's most important spiritual accomplishments.[13]

What exactly was it about poetry that was so philosophically interesting? The answer to this question directly reveals the single most important way in which German aesthetics influenced Carlyle's critical thought. The object of the new criticism, he observes, is not "external" considerations of form and effect; its object, rather, is the *essential nature* of poetry, its "soul," its "spiritual existence," its "pure essence."

> Criticism stands like an interpreter between the inspired and the uninspired; between the prophet and those who hear the melody of his words, and catch some glimpse of their material meaning, but understand not their deeper import. She pretends to open for us this deeper import; to clear our sense that it may discern the pure brightness of this eternal Beauty, and recognise it as heavenly (*Critical and Miscellaneous Essays*, I, 52).

In short, the "aesthetic" critic's principal function is to direct attention to the *metaphysical meaning* of poetry and the relation of that meaning to absolute truth. The nature of the connection here with German aesthetics is not difficult to see. The great post-Kantian aestheticians, Schiller, Schelling, Solger, Hegel, as well as their less philosophically inclined contemporaries, Goethe, the Schlegels, Jean Paul Richter, and Novalis, were all in some important degree metaphysical or idealist theorists of art, which means simply that they all regarded art as in some sense the expression of the Absolute, the spiritual One underlying and governing all experience. In the words of Hegel with which Bernard Bosanquet concludes and epitomizes his discussion of what he calls the post-Kantian "revolution" in aesthetical

thought, "[In] art we have to do with no mere toy of plea
sure or of utility, but with the liberation of the mind fror
the content and forms of the finite, with the presence an
union of the Absolute within the sensuous and phenome
nal."[14] Carlyle almost certainly knew nothing of Hegel
Ästhetik. Hegel's aesthetical thought derives from Schiller
however,[15] and Carlyle knew and wrote of Schiller's views o:
art as early as 1824. "Literature [according to Schiller] in
cludes the essence of philosophy, religion, art; whateve
speaks to the immortal part of man. The daughter, she i
likewise of all that is spiritual and exalted in our character
(*Schiller,* p. 200). In Schiller's friend and (in some ways
continuator J. G. Fichte, Carlyle also found the high meta
physical view of literature: "Literary Men [according tɩ
Fichte] are the appointed interpreters of [the] Divine Idea; ɛ
perpetual priesthood, we might say, standing forth, genera
tion after generation, as the dispensers and living types oʃ
God's wisdom" (*Critical and Miscellaneous Essays,* I, 58).
What the Germans taught Carlyle was that poetry was a
route to the Divine or to Truth itself and that the critic wa‹
best occupied in guiding the philistine along this route.

An important qualification is necessary, however. What
one gleans from these passages and many others similar to
them throughout Carlyle's work is a very one-sided version
of the German aesthetic. He has virtually ignored the insistence of that aesthetic, from Kant through Hegel, upon the
peculiarly *sensuous* or *finite* nature of the artist's embodiment of the Absolute and upon aesthetic experience as
something that has at least as much to do with "play" and
immediate pleasure as with spiritual transcendence. For
Schiller — whom I single out not only because his views on
this subject are seminal and bear remembering with a view
toward developments in English criticism after Carlyle but
also because he is the German critic/aesthetician whom

Carlyle knew most about — art is not distinctive for its "pure essence" or its expression of the Idea. It is distinctive for its harmonious balancing of man's impulse for the spiritual with his impulse for the sensuous.

> In the enjoyment of beauty, or aesthetic unity, an actual union and interchange between matter and form, passivity and activity, momentarily takes place, the compatibility of our two natures, the practicability of the infinite being realised in the finite hence the possibility of sublimest humanity, is thereby actually proven.[16]

Carlyle was not unaware of these views of Schiller's (see *Critical and Miscellaneous Essays,* II, 213). He simply refused to accord them any serious attention, and this, of course, is of a piece with his refusal to recognize the worth of formalistic and affectivist issues in criticism. It is no doubt to Carlyle's credit that he was occasionally troubled by a sense that something had been left out of his account of the "aesthetic." "I wish I could define to myself the true relation . . . of Religion to Poetry. Are they one and the same, different forms of the same; and if so which is to stand higher?"[17] He never was quite able or perhaps interested enough to solve the difficulty. Poetry remained for him significant primarily as an expression of the Divine or of the spiritual Absolute, in other words as a variety of religious experience.

One might call Carlyle's aesthetic criticism, then, a sort of spilt Romanticism. He has imbibed, largely through the Germans, a central Romantic tenet that the highest poetry is the expression of the Absolute, the One Life. But his is spilt Romanticism in the sense that, unlike the best of the Romantic theorists, whether German or English, he has virtually eliminated questions of form and effect from the business of criticism and focused almost exclusively on that "grand point" of *meaning*, which for him, again, is ultimate metaphysical or religious meaning.

Carlyle was by no means alone in this general approach to the function of criticism. What may be called the essentially "dialectical" orientation of his criticism seems to me to be characteristic of English criticism from 1830 down to the mid century.[18] Few other critics of this period shared Carlyle's grand and increasingly mystical expectations of poetry, but most agreed with him that it was the primary function of poetry to talk about the great questions, about the ultimate philosophical or religious meaning of life.[19] Criticism, writes Henry Taylor in 1834 in an important statement of the period's shifting concerns, must cease to worry over the "graces and charms," the mere "external embellishments of poetry" and must turn instead to "an appreciation of its intellectual and immortal part."[20] Asked why this shift in critical orientation occurred, one may hypothesize that it was directly related to the growing fears intelligent men and women had, fears nowhere more impressively stated than by Carlyle himself, that all the accustomed philosophical, religious, and political certainties were fast coming unmoored. In the face of such a crisis all intellectual energy that was not devoted to securing a coherent meaning to life, all energy spent on mere aesthetic embellishment, was energy criminally wasted. It is no doubt proper to deplore this development, as Saintsbury does, as an "impoverishment" of criticism, and no doubt Carlyle must come in for a lion's share of the blame. What I propose to do, however, is to take this dialectical preoccupation of Carlyle's as it is, without further regret for its inadequacies, and consider how in its interpretation of poetry it moves intellectually beyond English Romanticism to become a necessary adjustment in assumptions about the metaphysical status of poetry, pre-

liminary to the renewal of genuinely aesthetical concerns in
the criticism of the later nineteenth century.

The Nature of the Idea in Poetry:
Carlyle's Transitional Position

Romantic poetic theory, as M. H. Abrams has argued in
The Mirror and the Lamp, is an expressive theory which
sees poetry as the manifestation of the inner life of the poet
rather than an imitation of realities outside him.[21] The distinction is clear enough when the inner life consists of subjective emotions, memories, and perceptions of the external
world. When one comes to the question of the transcendent
Idea, the question of ultimate metaphysical truth, that
Romantic theory characteristically says is poetry's business
to embody, the neatness of the distinction between imitation
and expression, as Abrams is well aware, begins to break
down. Up until and including the eighteenth century, he
says, idealist (dialectical) poetic theory considered the Idea
or spiritual truth in poetry not as a subjective expression at
all but as linked to the one unchanging, objective spiritual
Reality, religious or metaphysical, that was seen to underlie
the entire cosmos. "Whether these ideas are held to be repli-
cas of transcendental archetypes or, as in Reynolds, are defined as the abstraction of like elements from a class of sensible particulars, they maintain their theoretical grounding in
the nature of the external universe." With the advent of
Romanticism the status of the transcendent Idea became
much more problematical; to the concept of external or objective reality was added a new emphasis on the creative
power of the subjective imagination. "[The doctrine] most
characteristic of the . . . [Romantic] generation of critics,
[was] that the content of art has an internal origin, and that
its shaping influences are not the Ideas or principles inform-

ing the cosmic structure, but the forces inherent in the emotions, the desires, and the evolving imaginative process of the artist himself."[22]

Two quite different conceptions of the power of the human mind are being considered here. Very briefly and very simply, beginning with the basic idealist assumption that all material experience or "phenomenon" is but an appearance or "veil" which is underlain by a spiritual principle or "noumenon," which is ultimate reality, the human mind's relation to that spiritual reality may be conceived in two ways. There is the view that the mind's highest power consists of a fundamentally passive capacity to see through the veil of phenomena and know something of the spiritual world itself. In such a view this spiritual world or principle is understood to exist absolutely independently of and uncontingent upon the mind that perceives or knows it. I shall call this view the Neo-Platonic view, for convenience's sake.[23] The other view sees the human mind's highest power as active, creative, capable of actually forming its own highest spiritual reality and participating by its creative, imaginative activity in the gradual self-realization of spirit. The difference is a crucial one; historically, it is Kant who marks the transition from one conception to the other. In opposition to what I have called the Neo-Platonic outlook, Kant denied the mind's power to know the spiritual reality in itself and in the process delivered a devastating blow to traditional idealist metaphysics. At the same time, he affirmed that the mind in the very act of perception did partially create or form the external reality it perceived. Thus he raised the possibility — which he himself denied — of constructing a new metaphysics based on the mind's active powers of creation. The realization of this possibility was the work of men such as Schiller, Fichte, Schelling, and Hegel, in other words, of the post-Kantian idealist movement in Germany.

Abrams' belief is that the English Romantics were moving toward the post-Kantian side of this line of demarcation I have roughly drawn. In my own view, it is not at all clear that, except in the case of Coleridge, the major English Romantics had, in fact, made the transition from the concept of the transcendent Idea as perceived to that of the transcendent Idea as in some sense created by the subjective mind, although Abrams has succeeded in demonstrating the beginning of a certain confusion about the ontological status of the Idea. By and large English Romantics remained in the essentially Neo-Platonic position of believing that the poet perceives and embodies in his poetry an objective transcendent Idea rather than creates the Idea by his own mental activity. Shelley's position in the essay *On Life* seems to me fairly characteristic of the English Romantic position in general. "That the basis of all things cannot be . . . mind, is sufficiently evident. Mind, as far as we have any experience of its properties . . . cannot create, it can only perceive."[24] Coleridge's theory of the imagination, however, presents a significant exception to my generalization, precisely because Coleridge was more aware than any of the other English Romantics of the thought of Kant and the post-Kantians and was, accordingly, better able to go beyond the traditional Neo-Platonic assumption of the passivity of mind with regard to the transcendent Idea.

Carlyle's own position on this question of the source of the transcendent Idea is what I would call significantly ambiguous. Generally, he is taken by present-day scholars to be thoroughly Neo-Platonist in poetic theory. This is certainly Abrams' interpretation of him; it is as well the interpretation of most of the writers who have attempted an analysis of his criticism. As Alba Warren has put it: "The poet proper [for Carlyle] . . . is a 'seer,' a man who reveals the ideal in the actual, the spirit of beauty in the world which is also its truth. . . . Poetry is what the poet 'sees' with his extraordinary powers of intellection and passion."[25] Carlyle's criticism gives ample ground for such an interpretation. Like his Romantic predecessors he commonly uses the metaphor of the Aeolian harp to describe the operation of the poetic faculty, and when he does so, the intent is always to suggest the passive or receptive nature of the poet's correspondence with the transcendent Idea. The mind, like the harp, receives the Idea from the realm of objective spirit and transmutes it into poetry (*Critical and Miscellaneous Essays,* I, 24). The logical extension of the metaphor is the concept of poetry as the bodying forth of the "invisible" music of the spheres; hence Carlyle's well-known comparison of poetry to music:

> If your delineation be authentically *musical,* musical not in word only but in heart and substance, in all the thoughts and utterances of it, in the whole conception of it, then it will be poetical. . . . —Musical: how much lies in that! A *musical* thought is one spoken by a mind that has penetrated into the inmost heart of the thing; detected the inmost mystery of it. . . . The meaning of Song goes deep. . . . A kind of inarticulate unfathomable speech, which leads us to the edge of the infinite, and lets us for moments gaze into that! (*Heroes,* p. 83.)

Again the metaphor assumes that the poet's mind in its relation to the Idea, or what Carlyle calls here the Infinite, is a penetrative or seeing power, not a creative one. Perhaps the most explicit expression of this side of Carlyle's critical thought comes in an essay on Jean Paul (1830) where, using the Kantian formula (he had begun reading Kant by that time), Carlyle gives literature a quite un-Kantian power: literature is the "eye of the world" "unfolding to us things themselves" (*Critical and Miscellaneous Essays,* II, 133).

This Neo-Platonic interpretation is one way of treating Carlyle's understanding of the Idea in poetry, but it is far from the only way. Coleridge, who began with the Neo-Platonic concept of the imagination's powers, had second thoughts after studying Kant in 1801, as his attack on Newton of March of that year illustrates. "*Mind* in [Newton's] system is always passive. . . . If the mind be not *passive,* if it indeed be made in God's Image, and that too in the sublimest sense, the Image of the *Creator,* there is ground for suspicion that any system built on the passiveness of the mind must be false."[26] Contrasting Coleridge's developing concept of the active or creative powers of the human mind with Wordsworth's outlook, H. W. Piper comments:

> For Wordsworth the One Life was pre-existent — "a soul divine with which we participate": for Coleridge it was the product of the creative soul (though that soul or state of feeling was, of course, the image of the Creator). . . .
>
> It is pointless now to discuss which of the two metaphysical views was true; it is sufficient to note that they were different, and that the differences . . . issued from what were now fundamentally different concepts of the relationship of Nature to man's soul.[27]

With his fundamentally religious point of view, Coleridge did not pursue the implications of his Kantian-inspired insight in the manner of the post-Kantian idealists. To begin with, he denied Kant's premise that the human mind was incapable of knowing something of the ultimate spiritual reality. More importantly from my present standpoint, he carefully qualified his concept of the poet's creative imagination by describing it as merely a reflex of the Divine Mind's creative principle, a "repetition in the finite mind of the eternal act of creation in the infinite I AM." In other words, Coleridge scrupulously insisted upon the subordination of the finite mind to the Divine Mind. Moreover, the creativity allowed the subjective mind was only an artistic or illusory creativity, not, as it were, a real one. Coleridge approached the substitution of the creative human mind for the Divine Idea, but he clearly and quite self-consciously held back from such a position.

One who was not so scrupulous about preserving the objectivity of the Divine Idea was Coleridge's German contemporary Johann Fichte. In the *Wissenschaftslehre* (1794) Fichte effectively made self or ego the basis of all philosophy. Kant's concept of the transcendental ego, which for Kant had been merely a logical condition of the unity of consciousness, was given an ontological status by Fichte, became the spiritual reality which posits all experience. Thus the critical philosophy was transformed into a pure idealism. In the process the concept of a transcendent Absolute independent of the human mind went by the board and in its place came that of the creative subjective human will striving to achieve absolute freedom from nature and necessity. To all mystical notions of passive communion with the One Life, Fichte was resolutely hostile. Bertrand Russell has splendidly described what this meant for the history of philosophy:

> The concept of "truth" as something dependent upon facts largely outside human control has been one of the ways in which philosophy hitherto has inculcated the necessary element of humility. When this check upon pride is removed, a farther step is taken on the road toward a certain kind of madness — the intoxication of power which invaded philosophy with Fichte, and to which modern men, whether philosophers or not, are prone.[28]

Fichte has committed the "cosmic impiety" of substituting mind for "things-in-themselves."

The aspect of Carlyle's thought which will be most important to me in this study is his reaction against what he took to be the "Hindoo-like" passivity of the English Romantics (Coleridge especially annoyed him: "His cardinal sin is that he wants *will*" [*Letters*, III, 90]).[29] Conversely, Carlyle responded warmly to the prominence given man's striving spiritual force or will in the work of two post-Kantian idealists, Russell's despised Fichte, whose "bold and lofty" principles Carlyle was admiring as early as 1827, and Schiller, who in many ways anticipated Fichte's exaltation of the human spiritual will and whom Carlyle was reading closely at least as early as 1823. This positive reaction to the tendency of post-Kantian Idealism to emphasize the power of human will to create its own spiritual reality discloses the basis of a quite new development in English poetics. Here Carlyle departed most decisively from English Romantic tradition and introduced some of the key assumptions of Victorian poetics.

Germany and the Metaphysics of Will

In 1822 Carlyle wrote to Jane Welsh of his plans for a novel. It was to be about a "poor fellow" of

> a very excellent character of course . . . but tired out . . . with the impediments of a world by much too prosaic for him, entirely sick of struggling along the sordid bustle of existence where he . . . found so much acute suffering. . . . At length . . . he speaks forth his sufferings — not in the puling Lake-style — but with a tongue of fire — sharp, sarcastic, apparently unfeeling, yet all the while betokening to the quick-sighted a mind of lofty thought and generous affections, smarting under the torment of its own over-nobleness, and ready to break in pieces by the force of its own energies (*Letters*, II, 229-30).

It does not take a great deal of perspicuity to recognize in this "poor fellow" a self-portrait. Carlyle's early letters and notebooks reveal that he had an enduring image of himself as fairly bursting with pent-up energy and, at the same time, locked in a titanic and lonely struggle with adversity. Beyond this, if one considers the nature of the men he admired and wrote about in his early works — Schiller, Samuel Johnson, Jean Paul, his own father — one will find a close family resemblance between his interpretation of their characters, their "burning energy of soul," and that of the "poor fellow" above.[30] Consider as well his first great work, *Sartor Resartus* (1833-34), where Diogenes Teufelsdröckh epitomizes all the poor fellows Carlyle ever wrote about:

"My Active Power (*Thätkraft*) was unfavourably hemmed-in; of which misfortune how many traces yet abide with me! . . . Thus already Freewill often came in painful collision with Necessity; so that my tears flowed, and at seasons the Child itself might taste the root of bitterness, wherewith the whole fruitage of our life is mingled and tempered" (*Sartor,* p. 78).

Or *The French Revolution* (1837), where the poor fellow has become an entire oppressed people:

Great meanwhile is the moment, when tidings of Freedom reach us; when the long enthralled soul, from amid its chains and squalid stagnancy, arises, were it still only in blindness and bewilderment, and swears by Him that made it, that it will be free! . . . Freedom is the one purport, wisely aimed at, or unwisely, of all man's struggles, toilings and sufferings, in this Earth. Yes, supreme is such a moment . . . first vision as of a flame-girt Sinai in this our waste Pilgrimage. . . . Forward ye maddened sons of France! (*French Revolution,* I, 183-84.)

Finally, consider *Heroes and Hero Worship* (1840), the work in which more than in any other Carlyle tries to synthesize what he believes in. Here the poor fellow has been apotheosized into the Hero; his immense energy, now under control, is brought to the business of transforming the "languid" "unbelieving" times into a new order, or at least some order whatsoever:

> I liken these common languid Times, with their unbelief, distress, perplexity . . . impotently crumbling down . . . towards final ruin — all this I liken to dry dead fuel, waiting for the lightning out of Heaven that shall kindle it. The great man, with his free force direct out of God's own hand, is the lightning.

In Hero-worship is the

> adamant lower than which the confused wreck of revolutionary things cannot fall. . . . It is the eternal cornerstone, from which [these ruined times] can begin to build themselves up again. . . . [It is] the one fixed point in modern revolutionary history, otherwise as if bottomless and shoreless (*Heroes,* pp. 13-15).

In short, there is no more important problem for Carlyle than the nature of human spiritual energy, its crying need for self-expression, and its power, in the end, both to destroy and to save society.

No doubt Carlyle's fascination with spiritual energy or will in all its many forms was rooted in his particular psychological make-up. No doubt it also had something to do with the Victorian frame of mind.[31] What most concerns me at the moment, however, is that this fascination found significant intellectual support in the fruits of the German Idealist movement and in this it moved quite beyond the biographical and sociological contexts to participate in a larger revolution in European thought.[32]

It seems a fair generalization to note that the Idealist movement in Germany, from its progenitor Kant on through Schiller, Fichte, and Hegel, may be characterized by its preoccupation with precisely that struggle of free will against necessity which Carlyle in *Sartor* will call the "meaning of life"—or put another way—with the endless striving of the human spirit to escape the constraints of natural causality and to achieve complete freedom and self-realization.[33] Of the four great German thinkers I have named Carlyle made fairly free use of Kant's name and tended to think of German philosophy of the period in the aggregate as "Kantism," but he, in fact, had no real understanding of Kant's philosophy as he himself appears to have recognized: "Alas! I have only read 100 pages of his works. How difficult it is to live! How many things to do, how little strength, how little time to do them!" (*Notebooks,* p. 100.)[34] Of Hegel Carlyle seems to have known virtually nothing.[35] With Schiller's thought, with his poetry, plays, histories, aesthetical and philosophical writings, Carlyle was thoroughly familiar, and, although less well acquainted with Fichte, he seems certainly to have known *Über das Wesen des Gelehrten* (1805), probably *Grudzüge des gegenwärtigen Zeitalters* (1805), and possibly something of the *Wissenschaftslehre* (1794).[36] In Schiller and Fichte he would have found ample support for his own native sense of the primary importance of the active heroic will in coping with life and rendering it intelligible. He would, by the same token, have found quite another outlook on experience from what he found in the more mystical Neo-Platonist and/or religiously oriented German writers who influenced him, Goethe, Friedrich von Schlegel, Jean Paul, and Novalis. Let us look at what he seems to have taken from his studies of Schiller.

Although Schiller was the subject of Carlyle's first major literary effort (*The Life of Schiller,* 1823-24), the influence of the German poet/philosopher/historian on his thought has not received the sort of attention it deserves.[37] It is not my intention to produce a thoroughgoing account of that influence here, but I do hope to make clear what the fundamental nature of the influence was. It is true, as I have said, that Carlyle ignored one of Schiller's most important insights, his concept of the aesthetic state. The aesthetic condition, however, was not Schiller's only, or, for that matter, even his principal theme. At least as important to him was the desire to vindicate man's spiritual freedom in the face of contemporary materialism and determinism; in this he was following the philosophical lead of his master Kant, for whom the idea of spiritual freedom was the "keystone" of philosophy.

> The concept of freedom, in so far as its reality is proved by an apodictic law of practical reason, is the key stone of the whole architecture of the system of pure reason and even of speculative reason. All other concepts (those of God and immortality) which, as mere ideas, are unsupported by anything in speculative reason now attach themselves to the concept of freedom and gain, with it and through it, stability and objective reality.[38]

Writing of the central importance of the idea of moral freedom to Schiller and of Schiller's debt to Kant in this matter, R. D. Miller has observed that

> the idea of moral freedom, fundamental in Kant, is scarcely less important in his disciple Schiller; and the group of associated ideas which cluster round this main idea — freedom of will, the power of reason to liberate man from his own sensuous nature, man as an end in himself, the principle of autonomy, and the supreme importance of the human personality — all of these Kantian ideas are wholeheartedly accepted by Schiller.[39]

34

What Schiller means by moral or spiritual freedom, as this quotation partially suggests, is essentially two things. First, he means the power of man's mind to transcend nature and the natural causality to which the empiricist philosophy would subject it:

> Nature deals no better with Man than with the rest of her works; she acts for him as long as he is as yet incapable of acting for himself as a free intelligence. But what makes him Man is precisely this: that he does not stop short at what Nature herself made of him, but has the power . . . of transforming the work of blind compulsion into a work of free choice, and of elevating physical necessity into moral necessity.[40]

Second — and this is a more specifically historicist point — he means the power of mind to release itself from bondage to empty cultural "forms," that is, belief systems which have ceased to be relevant to it and are consequently restraining its full self-expression:

> The independence of [man's] character must first have become secure, and submission to external forms of authority have given way to a becoming liberty [anstandigen Freiheit], before the diversity within him can be subjected to any ideal unity.[41]

Two things about Schiller's doctrine of freedom are particularly important to bring out. One, there is the fact that Schiller saw his age, the closing years of the eighteenth century, as a corrupt and oppressive one, not only in a political sense but, more fundamentally, in a moral sense. *Über die Ästhetische Erziehung des Menschen* (a work Carlyle greatly admired [*Schiller,* p. 111]) was written largely from Schiller's conviction of the impending moral collapse of European civilization in the aftermath of the French Revolution.[42]

At the present time material needs reign supreme and bend a degraded humanity beneath their tyrannical yoke. Utility is the great idol of our age, to which all powers are in thrall and to which all talent must pay homage.

. . . . .

What a figure [man] cuts in the drama of the present time! On the one hand, a return to the savage state; on the other, to complete lethargy: in other words, to the two extremes of human depravity, and both united in a single epoch.[43]

Second, and directly related to this outlook, was Schiller's pronounced missionary zeal for reform, a desire to bring about a new spiritual order. Thus he writes in a letter from which Carlyle later quotes (*Critical and Miscellaneous Essays,* I, 58) that the great artist must descend upon a corrupt age, "terrible like Agamemnon's son, to cleanse and purify it"; he must rouse it from its "slumber" and prepare "the shape of things to come."[44] With this zeal for reform went a scorn for mysticism and quietism, a "revolutionist" insistence that the realization of freedom is a continuous battle against circumstances and not an escape from them.[45]

Reason has accomplished all that she can accomplish by discovering the law and establishing it. Its execution demands a resolute will and ardour of feeling. If Truth is to be victorious in her conflict with forces, she must herself first become a force and appoint some drive to be her champion in the realm of phenomena; for drives are the only motive forces in the sensible world. If she has hitherto displayed so little of her conquering power, this was due, not to the intellect which was powerless to unveil her, but to the heart which closed itself against her, and to the drive which refused to act on her behalf.

. . . . .

Not for nothing does the ancient myth make the goddess of wisdom emerge fully armed from the head of Jupiter. For her very first action is a warlike one. Even at birth she has to fight a hard battle with the senses, which are loath to be snatched from their sweet repose. The majority of men are far too wearied and exhausted by the struggle for existence to gird themselves for a new and harder struggle against [intellectual] error.[46]

I have quoted enough at this point to indicate the nature of Schiller's influence on the young Carlyle. Almost certainly it was from Schiller that Carlyle first learned to elevate his personal sense of frustrated spiritual energy into a kind of metaphysical significance and, beyond this, to "historicize" that sense into his well-known vision of a morally depraved, ignoble "present time." The very language he uses to describe the circumstances of his age seems at times to echo Schiller. "Not Godhead, but an iron, ignoble circle of Necessity embraces all things; binds the youth of these times into a sluggish thrall, or else exasperates him into a rebel. Heroic Action is paralysed" (*Critical and Miscellaneous Essays,* III, 30). (Compare Schiller's "tyrannical yoke" of the present and his reduction of modern men to the "lethargic" and the "savage.") In addition Carlyle seems to have taken up with a vengeance what I have called Schiller's revolutionist doctrine and mission; he has taken up the notion that the essence of man's life is an endless struggle against material and conventional oppression and toward the total realization of his spiritual freedom *in the world.* This is most clearly seen in his treatment of Diogenes Teufelsdröckh. The more one reads *Sartor,* the more one recognizes that the central point about Teufelsdröckh is the "strange contradiction" in him between passive and active principles. On the one side, he is of "an almost Hindoo character," a "man without Activity," a "No man" (*Sartor,* p. 81); on the other,

37

he comes to learn that contemplation and passivity must be overcome and that thought must be transmuted into action. Thus he anticipates, as he is "getting under way" as a young man, the key to his future deliverance. "A strange contradiction lay in me; and I as yet knew not the solution of it; knew not that spiritual music can spring only from discords set in harmony; that but for Evil there were no Good as victory is only possible by battle" (*Sartor,* p. 102).

The principal movement of Teufelsdröckh's mind, then, the one which Carlyle is most concerned to bring out, is toward the recognition of the need to transform mere thought into activity or, in Schiller's terms, "theoretical culture" into "practical culture." "Conviction," Carlyle's German sage comes to realize, "were it never so excellent, is worthless till it convert itself into Conduct" (*Sartor,* p. 156). The constant emphasis throughout the book on the need to adopt a warlike stance toward life culminates in what Carlyle calls the "Gospel of Freedom," Teufelsdröckh's final interpretation of the meaning of life and the essence of his "Everlasting Yea":

> "Our life is compassed round with necessity; yet *is the meaning of Life itself no other than Freedom,* than Voluntary Force; thus have we a warfare; in the beginning, especially, a hard fought battle for the Godgiven mandate, *Work thou in Welldoing,* lies mysteriously written, in Promethean Prophetic Characters, in our hearts; and leaves us no rest, night or day, till it be deciphered and obeyed; till it burn forth, in our conduct, a visible acted Gospel of Freedom" (*Sartor,* p. 146; first italics mine).

(Compare again Schiller's "tyrannical yoke" and his description of wisdom's first action as "warlike," a "hard battle.") Teufelsdröckh having learned this lesson leaves the haven of

Weissnichwo ("know-not-where") and sets out (the editor suspects) to make a revolution in his own times, for he was "not without some touch of the universal feeling, a wish to proselytize." In future works Carlyle drops the Teufels-dröckhian mask and speaks directly in his own voice: The famous doctrine of Heroes, the keystone of his "philosophy," is a thoroughly revolutionist doctrine, for Carlyle's Hero is a Hero only insofar as he is prepared to transform passive insight into a new world order.

> Universal History, the history of what man has accomplished in this world, is at bottom the History of the Great Men who have worked here. They were the leaders of men . . . all things that we see standing accomplished in the world are properly the outer material result, the practical realization and embodiment, of Thoughts that dwelt in the Great Men sent into the world (*Heroes,* p. 1).

The Hero here in the mature Carlyle, as in the earlier case of Teufelsdröckh, it seems to me, is, in the end, simply Carlyle's version of Schiller's man of powerful will who must come like "Agamemnon's son" to assert the transcendence of the spiritual principle and thus rescue the age from moral collapse.

What Carlyle learned from Schiller would have been reiterated a fortiori by his reading of Fichte. Unlike the later Schiller, Fichte never shows the least interest in the way the human spirit might achieve a sort of reconciliation, a momentary pause in its constant struggle against matter, a reconciliation which he called the aesthetic state. For Fichte the expression of human spirit is always an *active doing,* and "absolutely nothing else";[47] there can be no question of an aesthetic relaxation of spiritual energy. Nature or "Non-

Ego" can never be more than an obstacle, against which spirit must endlessly strive in its desire for freedom.

> In this idea of the obstructions which surround Existence in Time, we have, when it is thoroughly seized and pondered over, the idea of the objective and material world, or what we call Nature. This is not living and capable of infinite growth like Reason, but dead — a rigid, self-enclosed existence. It is this which arresting and hemming in the Time-Life [of mankind], by this hindrance alone spreads over a longer or shorter period of time that which would otherwise burst forth at once a perfect and complete life. Further, in the development of spiritual existence, Nature itself is interpenetrated by life; and is thus both the obstacle to and the sphere of, that activity and outward expression of power in which human life eternally unfolds itself.[48]

Prominent also in Fichte is a Schillerian preoccupation with the decadence of the modern age. It is *"the Age of absolute indifference towards all truth, and of entire and unrestrained licentiousness:—the state of completed sinfullness."*[49] Fichte is rather more explicit about the cause of the age's decline, however. The old religious beliefs have been overthrown by new philosophy and new science; in their place has come only the pathetic pseudoreligion of the Utilitarian happiness principle, "that I should *be* and *be* happy." "The Old Time has passed away, and we stand above its grave, amid an intricate and wonderful concourse of new elements . . . but what this concourse of elements may signify, and to what it may tend, cannot be understood . . . [except] by deeper insight."[50]

He is also more specific about remedies. What is needed now is new religion, not the Christian religion of the past but the true religion of metaphysics, and in particular the metaphysics of will. "The philosophical and scientific Knowledge of the Age overthrows the form of Superstition which is thoroughly recognised and understood by the Age, but cannot as yet establish True Religion in its place."[51] The antieudaemonism, the looking forward to new religious belief even while standing on the grave of the old, even the vatic intensity with which Fichte speaks of these things in his popular lectures seem to have been absorbed by Carlyle: "Cease [Voltaire] . . . for the task appointed thee seems finished. Sufficiently hast thou demonstrated this proposition . . .: That the Mythus of the Christian Religion looks not in the eighteenth century as it did in the eighth. . . . But what next? Wilt thou help us to embody the divine Spirit of that Religion in a new Mythus, in a new vehicle and vesture, that our Souls, otherwise so like perishing, may live?" (*Sartor,* p. 154.)

Finally, Fichte insists, as did Schiller before him, that human intelligence or spirit is worthless unless transformed into duty and action. The new religion can come about and be made to prevail only by an active exertion of the human will. "To impress its image on the surrounding world is the object for which the living Idea dwelling in the true Scholar seeks for itself an embodiment. It is to become the highest life-principle, the inmost soul of the world around it; — it must therefore assume the same forms which are borne by the surrounding world."[52] This impressing of the Idea upon the world, Fichte calls "Industry." Industry, he maintains, is the necessary complement of the scholarly "Genius" that at first only passively conceives the Idea, and this Industry takes various "modes," political, philosophical, religious, scientific, and artistic. Fichte's Industry has almost certainly become Carlyle's doctrine of *work,* another way for Carlyle of expressing the imperative need to transform spirit into action, while Fichte's several modes of Industry probably lie behind Carlyle's several interpretations of the heroic vocation in *Heroes and Hero Worship.*

The central question raised by both Schiller's and Fichte's account of human life as an expression of the will to spiritual freedom, is the question that I earlier noted of the ontological status of the Idea, which the men of heroic will must seek to apply to life. Is that Idea something received from Heaven, as it were, and simply *acted upon* by the hero, or is it—and this is a very different proposition—in some sense created by the very activity of the hero? Both Schiller and Fichte answer that it is the latter, that the Idea is in an important sense *self-creating.* This is especially clear in the case of Fichte, who shows a greater philosophical interest in the question than does Schiller. There exists, he says, an absolute unchanging Divine Idea which is the "foundation of all appearance," but that Idea manifests or reveals itself only in time, through the agency of man's "learned culture":

> The Divine Life in itself is absolute, self-comprehending unity, without change or variableness. . . . In its manifestation . . . it becomes a self-developing existence, gradually and eternally unfolding itself, and constantly progressing onward in the everflowing stream of time. . . . This living manifestation we call the human race. The human race is thus the only true finite existence.[53]

The Divine Idea is continuously unfolding itself. There is no one known dogmatic expression of truth, only a process of developing truth; that is, while truth *in itself* is a *Being,* permanent, complete and all-comprehending, it is in its earthly manifestation (the only form in which man can know it) a *Becoming.*

But how does it become? This is the great problem for

Fichte. To begin with, there is a fundamental metaphysical Force grounded in the Absolute Divine Idea which acts as an instinct in man impelling him toward the progressive realization of the Divine Idea; this is what Fichte means by Genius, the "impulse towards an obscure, imperfectly discerned spiritual object," the *"supernatural* instinct in man attracting him to a *supernatural* object."[54] In addition to this metaphysical Force connecting man with the Absolute there is the specifically human quality of Industry which is necessary if the vague spiritual Force of Genius is to take the form of specific ideas.

> The question has often been raised, whether Genius or Industry is most essential in science [science being the progressive development of mind]. I answer both must be united: the one is but little worth without the other. Genius is nothing more than the effort of the Idea to assume a definite form. The Idea, however, has in itself neither body nor substance, but only shapes itself an embodiment out of the scientific materials which environ it in Time, of which Industry is the sole purveyor. . . . [T]he embodiment of the Idea is then for the first time completed in him [the matured Scholar] . . . the point where the Scholar passes into the free Artist [that is, creator] is the point of perfection for the former.[55]

Fichte is saying that the Idea, whatever its ground in the Absolute, is not "perfect" until it has in some significant sense been formed and embodied by the essentially human, naturalistic powers of industry and creativity. Carlyle in *Sartor* has, it seems to me, picked up this central point of Fichte's.

> "A certain inarticulate Self-consciousness dwells dimly in us; which *only our Works can render articulate* and decisively discernible. Our Works are the mirror where-

in the spirit first sees its natural lineaments" (*Sartor*, p. 132; my italics).

. . . . .

"But indeed Conviction, were it never so excellent, is worthless till it convert itself into Conduct. Nay properly Conviction is not possible till then; *inasmuch as all Speculation is by nature endless, formless, a vortex amid vortices: only by a felt indubitable certainty of Experience does it find any centre to revolve round and fashion itself into a system"* (*Sartor*, p. 156; my italics).

The consequences of this Fichtean outlook in *Sartor* are very significant indeed in the context of nineteenth-century English intellectual history. As A. J. LaValley in his study of Carlyle's relation to the "modern" has recognized, *Sartor* is primarily a book about man's awesome responsibility as the creator of his own highest spiritual reality. "Within this self [represented by Teufelsdröckh] both the Ideal, the power of being, as well as the impediment, the threat of nonbeing, exist. Hence it is this self which alone must fashion the new myth for the society to be reborn in the Phoenix deathbirth."[56] In *Sartor,* as throughout his post-1830 works, Carlyle shows himself ever more taken up not by the human mind's power of seeing into the heart of things but by its power of subduing all experience to its own spiritual will, and, above all, its power of producing the very belief-systems, the religious myths by which it lives and by which it interprets and knows the Infinite. The Clothes Philosophy, the history of the French Revolution, the doctrine of Hero Worship, all are for Carlyle expressions of this metaphysical power of human will; all, like the smith whom Teufelsdröckh finds in the Schwarzwald, preach the "Gospel of Freedom, the Gospel of Man's Force, commanding, and one day to be all-commanding (*Sartor*, p. 56). In sum, Carlyle's work seems to be the clearest expression in early nineteenth-century English letters of one of the most essential strands of the German Idealist movement in philosophy — the tendency to make the absolute ground of belief, the basis of a new "religion" for the modern age, out of man's will to spiritual transcendence.

What, then, has all this to do with my central theme, historicism? LaValley has emphasized, I believe unduly, the Zarathustrian isolation of Teufelsdröckh (and Carlyle) in this struggle of the self to forge meaning — "By stressing energy, force, self-realization in action, the self becomes so aware of its own process of self-realization that any hold upon dogma, history, continuity is lost."[57] This seems to me to be giving Carlyle a little more modernity than he can bear. I do not see him as having reached the stage of Nietzschean disillusionment with history and the essential continuity of humanity. On the contrary, I see him as joining the post-Kantians in their enthusiasm for history as the unifying, corporate process by which man gradually achieves his desire for spiritual freedom. For all the great German idealists history is the field on which philosophy traces the ongoing progress of mind in its struggle with matter and, at the same time, receives assurances of the meaningfulness of that struggle. Thus Fichte points out that

> freedom becomes apparent in the collective consciousness of the Race . . . — as a true and real fact; — the product of the Race during its Life and proceeding from its Life, so that the absolute existence of the Race itself is necessarily implied in the existence of this fact and product thus attributed to it.[58]

While for Schelling:

> History as a whole is an ongoing, gradual, self-unveiling revelation of the Absolute. . . . Mankind through

its history conveys a continuing proof of the existence of God, a proof, that can, however, only be achieved through history in its entirety.[59]

And Hegel:

Universal History . . . is the exhibition of Spirit in the process of working out the knowledge of that which it is potentially. . . . The History of the world is none other than the progress of the consciousness of Freedom.[60]

From very early on in his career Carlyle showed a deep interest in this question of the development of spirit through history. In one of the earliest notebook entries (March 1822) he makes a characteristic observation on the progressive or historical nature of truth. "Nine-tenths of our reasonings are *artificial* processes, depending not in [sic] the real nature of things but on our peculiar mode of viewing things, and therefore varying with all the variations both in the kind and extent of our perceptions. How is this? Truth immer WIRD *nie* IST?" (*Notebooks*, p. 4.) Some five years later, having read Fichte's *Über das Wesen des Gelehrten,* he takes up the notion that the Divine Idea requires a different expression or form in each historical age. "For each age, by the law of its nature, is different from every other age, and demands a different representation of the Divine Idea, the essence of which is the same in all" (*Critical and Miscellaneous Essays,* I, 58). And a year later, citing J. Müller, Schelling, and Herder as authority, he finds "it is a common theory among the Germans, that every Creed, every Form of worship, is a *form* merely; the mortal and ever changing *body,* in which the immortal and unchanging *spirit* of Religion is . . . expressed to the material eye, and made manifest and influential among the doings of men" (*Critical and Miscellaneous Essays,* I, 143).

It is not, however, until he comes to *Sartor* (composed

1830-31) that this interest in the historical development of religious creeds and social ideas or *forms* of belief is taken up as his primary intellectual concern. From *Sartor* onward Carlyle becomes pre-eminently the historian of the human spirit's efforts to construct cultural formulas by which to live. While it would perhaps be going too far to claim that *Sartor* is itself ultimately a philosophy of history, it is true that the Clothes Philosophy that it presents is very much a philosophy about man's dependence upon historical or cultural forms and his sole responsibility for creating those forms. Clothes in Teufelsdröckh's understanding of the word, elevate man from his original animal nakedness.

> "Clothes, as despicable as we think them, are so unspeakably significant. Clothes, from the King's mantle downwards are Emblematic, not of want only, but of a manifold Victory over Want. On the other hand, all Emblematic things are properly Clothes, thought-woven or hand-woven; must not the Imagination weave Garments, visible Bodies, wherein the else invisible creations and inspirations of our Reason are, like Spirits, revealed, and first become all-powerful" (*Sartor,* p. 57).

Clothes are either hand-woven, that is, the products of man's lower, technical, and economic activity, or they are thought-woven, the products of his higher, rational, and spiritual faculty. Both modes of activity are important to Carlyle, but obviously the latter is far more so. " 'Of Man's Activity and Attainment the chief results are aeriform, mystic, and preserved in Tradition only: such are his Forms of Government, with the Authority they rest on' " (*Sartor,* p. 137). Of these thought-form clothes the highest, higher than art or philosophy, is religion. " 'Highest of all Symbols are those wherein the Artist or Poet has risen into Prophet, and all men can recognise a present God and worship the same: I mean religious Symbols' " (*Sartor*, p. 178).

What Teufelsdröckh's spiritual deliverance consists of ultimately is the recognition that it is within man's power to re-create new spiritual forms of belief which can order the chaos of experience and elevate humanity to the ideal. Thus he writes a philosophy not about man's communion with God or with Nature, or even with himself, but about man's capacity to make civilizations and symbols and (particularly in the third book) about the way these products of his own spiritual activity grow, mature, and die in continuous cycles through time. It is to that spectacle of progressive spiritual activity that Teufelsdröckh and Carlyle both look, like Fichte, Schelling, and Hegel, for the final revelation of truth. " 'Is not Man's History, and Men's History, a perpetual Evangel? Listen, and for organ music thou wilt ever, as of old, hear the Morning Stars sing together' " (*Sartor*, p. 202). With so high an estimate of history, it is not surprising that from *Sartor* onward Carlyle increasingly directed his attention to historical subjects and historical problems.

Carlyle As a Historical Thinker

The years 1830-1832 were years in which Carlyle was beginning at last to discover his vocation as a historian after almost a decade of writing literary reviews. Early in 1830 he began a history of German literature at Francis Jeffrey's suggestion. The writing of this work gave him so much trouble that he never finished it,[61] but in the process of researching he evidently revived an interest in history which had been with him since his early (1819-1821) enthusiasm for the great English Enlightenment historians, Hume, Gibbon, and Robertson. By the summer of 1830 he was asking himself the crucial question "Do I really like Poetry?" and answering that perhaps he did not (*Notebooks*, p. 151). At the same time he was writing his first theoretical essay on history in which he recommends that his age "search more and more into the Past," for it is here that is found "the true fountain of knowledge; by whose light alone . . . can the Present and Future be interpreted or guessed at" (*Critical and Miscellaneous Essays,* II, 89). In 1831 he and Jane moved from the Weissnichwo of Craigenputtock to London, and his notebooks, letters, and published works of this year show an almost total absorption in the social crisis which he found in the metropolis: all Europe is in a state of revolution, the "whole frame of society is rotten and must go for fuelwood" (*Notebooks*, p. 184). No doubt the spectacle of Reform London and Revolutionary France in this period did much to encourage in him a growing sense of the unreality, the uselessness of mere imaginative, "fictive" writing and to make him wonder about more practical means of bringing about essential social and moral change. What one sees from "Characteristics" (1831) onward is a gradual disengagement from strictly literary subjects and a movement toward historical ones. By early 1833 he had produced in "Count Cagliostro" a strange transitional genre, half history, half fiction, or perhaps better, history written in the manner of *Sartor,* and by 1834 he had begun research toward the *French Revolution.*[62] Thereafter, all his major works with the exception of *Chartism* (1839), *The Life of John Sterling* (1851) and *Latter Day Pamphlets* (1850) were, either in large part or entirely, historical studies. Moreover, with the significant exceptions of the *Lectures on the History of Literature* (1838) and the lecture on "The Hero as Poet" (1840), he did not return again to primarily literary topics. It is apparent as Carlyle's shift of intellectual focus in these years is followed that the turning to history was made in the conviction that it was in history rather than in either the writing or the criticism of "fictive" literature that truth was to be found, the sort of truth that would at once explain the catastrophe of the modern age and deliver mankind from it.

As I have indicated, the study of history was for Carlyle ultimately an exercise in discovering Divinity. History is as "infinite in meaning as the Divine Mind it emblems; wherein he is wise that can read here a line and there a line" (*Critical and Miscellaneous Essays,* III, 253). The overall meaning of history, in this sense, was a foregone conclusion; history was the revelation of God's will on earth. Carlyle wanted to know more than this about history, however. He wanted to know the secondary causes behind historical change and the patterns according to which history moved; he wanted to know something of what may be called the *intrinsic* meaning of history, the meaning of history in and of itself apart from any external or religious interpretations. Finally, he wanted to know these things because he believed they could tell him about the condition of his own society and its prospects for the future. History is the "most profitable of studies" because "only he who understands what has been can know what should be and will be" (*Critical and Miscellaneous Essays,* III, 169). Carlyle was very much a historicist in Popper's sense of the word as one who approaches the study of history with the assumption that "*historical prediction* is [its] aim" and that "this aim is attainable by discovering the 'rhythms' or the 'patterns', the 'laws' or the 'trends' that underlie the evolution of history."[63]

Strictly speaking, it would be a mistake to call Carlyle a *philosopher* of history; he never produced a thoroughgoing, systematic account of the meaning of history in the manner of, say, Vico or Hegel. Still, he did view history philosophically in the sense that he was, as historian, not interested simply in the empirical data of the past but in the overall pattern of the historical process as well as the metaphysical forces behind it. He always took great pains to distinguish between the sort of history that is not worth writing, history in the "narrower vulgar sense" as "mere chronicle," and the sort that is — "universal history" in which past events are viewed through "philosophical spectacles" and seen to comprise a "magic web" of meaningful progress (*Critical and Miscellaneous Essays*, II, 175).[64] In all this, Carlyle was one of the earliest and most important of English historical thinkers to feel and transmit the impact of the new continental historicism, that search for the laws and the meaning of history, that, according to Duncan Forbes, "was beginning to revolutionize English historical thought" between 1820 and 1840.[65] He was not, of course, alone. Inspired by German sources as well (in this case primarily by Niebuhr) and by the Italian Vico, the "Liberal Anglican" historians, Thomas Arnold, Julian Hare, Connop Thirlwall, and Henry Milman were paralleling Carlyle's efforts.[66] Beginning from quite different presuppositions, Carlyle's friend J. S. Mill was, with the aid of Auguste Comte, working out his own synthetic interpretation of history.[67]

What, then, did the "philosophical spectacles" through which Carlyle viewed history reveal to him? To begin with, his concept of historical process is, as against Mill's, for instance, completely idealist. All history for him is the product of spirit emanating from man working according to the will of God. "Every Society, every Polity, has a spiritual principle; is the embodiment, tentative and more or less complete of an Idea; all its tendencies of endeavour . . . are prescribed by an Idea, and flow naturally from it, as movements from the firing source of motion (*Critical and Miscellaneous Essays*, III, 13-14). The highest expression of this "spiritual principle" or "Idea" is, again, religion. I have already mentioned Carlyle's view that religious Ideas are constantly developing through time. Let us now consider briefly his view of the cause of this development, the rhythm or "laws" according to which it moves, and its relation to social "health."

When a religious mythus is vital in society, that is, commands widespread and unself-conscious assent, then, says Carlyle, that society is healthy; it is at harmonious unity with itself, and each individual shares in this feeling of repose and unity. "Life from its mysterious fountains, flows out as in celestial music and diapason" (*Critical and Miscellaneous Essays*, III, 2). But the religious belief of society, and hence the whole fabric of society, are subject to decay. "Inquiry," the "first symptom of disease," sets in and the "vital union of Thought" is lost. "Thus Change, or the inevitable approach of Change, is manifest everywhere" (*Critical and Miscellaneous Essays,* III, 21). In this continuous change there is for Carlyle one central rhythm, which is simply the dialectical alternation of Belief and Unbelief. " 'As in longdrawn Systole and longdrawn Diastole, must the period of Faith alternate with the period of Denial; must the vernal growth, the summer luxuriance of all Opinions, Spiritual Representations and Creations be followed by, and again follow, the autumnal decay, the winter dissolution' " (*Sartor,* p. 91).

With the concept of endlessly alternating epochs of Belief and Unbelief goes that of palingenesis, the Phoenix Death-Rebirth of society. "Thus is Teufelsdröckh content that old sick Society should be deliberately burnt . . . in the faith that she is a Phoenix; and that a new heavenborn young one will rise out of her ashes!" (*Sartor,* p. 189).[68] Where this metaphor for historical change seems most to have caught Carlyle's Calvinist fancy is in its suggestion that the unbelieving society dies not quietly and naturally but with a vast retributive conflagration produced by the release of irrational forces held in check only by religion. This conflagration, of course, takes the form of social revolution, which for Carlyle is a sort of naturalized apocalypse. His earliest efforts at historical writing were aimed at describing the cause and outbreak of the greatest revolution of the modern epoch, and he is, as L. M. Young has said, pre-eminently the historian of revolution.[69]

What causes these continuous revolutions of history? The answer depends upon what side of the cycle one looks at. On the negative or down side, the cause of historical movement, the decay of a given civilization, lies in the proliferation of the spirit of "inquiry" or "self-consciousness," in a word, philosophical skepticism about the truth of the prevailing contemporary religious mythus, a skepticism such as Carlyle believed he saw growing everywhere around him and which he was fond of tracing back to Hume and Voltaire. On the positive or up side, historical movement comes from the intervention of the Hero, the Great Man, with his "flowing light-fountain" of "native original insight, of manhood and heroic nobleness," who "enlightens" the "darkness of the world" (*Heroes*, p. 2). As even these limited quotes indicate, Carlyle's emphasis is on the active, almost impulsive moral will of the Great Man and his independence from the sophistical thought of his day. The Hero who is "at the bottom of History" is, above all, an unself-conscious, indeed, to a degree an anti-intellectual conveyor of the Idea, whose primary characteristic is a driving will to make his Idea a power in the world and thus bring society back to an era of belief.[70]

Finally, there is the question of whether history has a goal toward which it is tending. Like most of his contemporaries, Carlyle accepted the prevailing myth of progress.[71] Mankind does not simply move in endless cycles of belief and unbelief but moves *forward*. Every man "invents and desires somewhat of his own." "No man whatever believes, or can believe, exactly what his grandfather believed: he enlarges somewhat, by fresh discovery, his view of the Universe" (*Heroes*, p. 118).

Having said this, one is bound to note, however, that what is characteristic of Carlyle's outlook is the strong element of gloom or pessimism which he brings to the concept of historical development. He was, to say the least, skeptical of the progressivist optimism of Enlightenment historiography, as found, for instance, in Gibbon and Voltaire.[72] And one suspects that he had little use for Macaulay's continuation of that optimistic or "Whig" tradition in history.[73] What is distinctive about Carlyle in this context of contemporary progressivism is his belief that the progress of the race periodically receives colossal setbacks, epochs of unbelief in which whole societies decay and collapse, and he was far more preoccupied with these than he ever was with the Idea of Progress.[74] He thus found himself very much in the tradition of Coleridge before him and, in his own generation, the "Liberal Anglicans" (Thomas Arnold et al.).[75] All these men held cyclical rather than linear concepts of historical movement; they saw various civilizations as moving through recurring patterns of rise and fall rather than in a constant line of development for the better. Although they did believe that ultimately, despite its cyclical setbacks, the human race was moving forward, their concept of historical rise and fall allowed scope for their more pessimistic convictions that their own age, far from representing an improvement over the past, was a period of decadence. Thus, though progress in the long run was never denied, what was denied and vigorously was the healthiness of their own modern age. In Carlyle's case his pessimism grew blacker, and his rage against the rotten fabric of society more bitter as he went on in his career without receiving any clear sign that the spiritual state of man was, in fact, getting better rather than worse.

Historicism versus Religion

A man's religion, Carlyle was fond of saying, is the most important thing about him. Certainly no account of Carlyle's own intellectual make-up can be complete without something said about the relation between his concern with the metaphysics of will and with the historical process, on the one hand, and his religious outlook, on the other. What is immediately noticed here, as with Schiller and Fichte, is that the two strains of thought are not by any means entirely compatible. The post-Kantian German Idealist movement with which I have been seeking to associate Carlyle's thought worked ultimately against the religious interpretation of the Idea or the spiritual. This was not, to be sure, the intention of the Idealists; on the contrary, with the exception of Schiller, they all imagined themselves engaged in the rational proof of religion. But the fact is, as Frederick Copleston has pointed out, they showed a "marked tendency to substitute metaphysics for faith and to rationalize the revealed mysteries of Christianity, bringing them within the scope of the speculative reason."[76] At the heart of their irreligious tendency lies the merging of the finite human mind's power for spiritual self-realization with the Divine.

My emphasis throughout has been upon Carlyle's participation in this exaltation of human will and spiritual self-determination, but now I must place things somewhat more in perspective; there is a danger, after all, of over-Germanizing Carlyle. His thought does, in the end, stand apart from post-Kantian Idealism in two significant ways. First, he was interested in what he called the "scientific rigor" or rationalism of German philosophy only at a distance; temperamentally he was always inclined to abandon reason and system altogether in favor of a distinctly mystical approach to the Absolute.[77] Thus he produced in "Characteristics" (1831) what is probably the most impressive onslaught of his time against the "self-conscious" reason and enshrined the "unconscious" intuition of the Divine as the highest form of knowing. The second important point at which he departed from the Idealists was in the care he took to insist that, in the end, man's clothes-weaving activity takes second place to the creative activity of the Deity. Man cannot, he writes, "by much lifting, lift up his own body"; metaphysics and heroic exertion can only be an aid to the Divine, not the Divine itself (*Critical and Miscellaneous Essays,* III, 43). The Hero is a "natural luminary," but one that shines only "by the gift of heaven" (*Heroes,* p. 2). In both these ways Carlyle is, as he says of Teufelsdröckh, "still-scenting out Religion" (*Sartor,* p. 229), still trying in some way to retain the fundamental attitudes toward God and man with which he had grown up.[78]

The unique interest of Carlyle's position in the context of nineteenth-century intellectual history seems to me to lie precisely in the interplay in his thought of the two idealist impulses I outlined at the end of the previous chapter, the more conservative, Neo-Platonic, and/or religious impulse looking back toward Coleridge and the English Romantics, and the "Kantist" impulse looking forward to Nietzsche's elimination of God in favor of placing the "whole drama of fall and redemption" within the spiritual power of man's finite will. It may be said that Carlyle's outlook is fundamentally religious, but immediately it must be added that in Carlyle this fundamentally religious position found itself under significant pressure — more significant, it seems to me, than in the case of any of his English Romantic predecessors. The English Romantics, skeptical of dogmatic religion, sought Divinity outside the church and its formularies, as Abrams has said,[79] in the self, but just as characteristically they sought Divinity outside the self in an objective physical nature, for the Divinity in self was not enough for them unless substantiated by a corresponding impulse from the vernal wood.

For Carlyle the search for God in nature was no longer viable as an intellectual alternative to established religion. He turned, rather, to society and the development of society which is history for the earthly revelation of God. But to look for God in history, as the remarks from Herder which I have quoted as epigraph for this chapter suggest, was a somewhat more dubious enterprise than looking for God in nature. To seek God in Nature was still to seek him outside man and in something man did not make. However, history, as Carlyle and the Germans saw it, was the product of man's own heroic endeavors. To seek God there, accordingly, was to run the danger of finding simply oneself. To protect himself from this danger Carlyle developed the strategy of "clothes"; clothes are the historical garment of the Divine which one knows ultimately as particular religious beliefs. But these particular and transitory beliefs must be regarded ironically, for they are artificial and unreal in comparison to the Idea they body forth, which alone is real and permanent. Something of the Platonic distinction between archetypal form and particular, temporal appearances is at work here. Except in Carlyle's version, appearances include the very belief systems by which men live and which, like clothes, they are constantly putting on and taking off. The division implied between the Idea itself and particular beliefs in time is, however, a precarious one. The tendency of nineteenth-century thought was ever toward the collapsing of this division, that is, toward substituting the *historical* belief-system, or mythus, for the Divinity or Idea itself which it putatively clothes.

Carlyle retained, as I say, his fundamentally religious disposition, but the pressures toward a complete historicism in which one dispenses with the saving notion of a permanent Idea behind the flux of changing beliefs, are, nonetheless, strongly felt in his work. This is nowhere more evident than in what one might call the general rhetorical bias of Carlyle's writing. He was, after all, always more interested in talking about Clothes and Clothes-making than about the Divinity itself. What fascinated him was the power of human cultural creativity, the battle of Mind with Nature or with outmoded cultural forms. He did not want, as Coleridge, for instance, did, to trace the metaphysical complexities of union with God. Nor did he want, as did so many of his contemporaries, to construct an apology for the Christian religion. What he wanted to do, above all, was to vindicate man's existential capacity to *act* and to *make* in the face of a hostile universe. The reservations about man's subservience to Divine power often seem, in the end, no more than pious afterthoughts. It is the human miracle of Clothes, not the glory of God, that is agitating and inspiring this "poor fellow" from Nowhere.

2

POETRY AND THE
GOSPEL OF FREEDOM

Obertello has argued in his book on Carlyle's criticism that Carlyle's critical principles owe very little to his experience of German literature and philosophy.[1] This is a position which might be challenged from any number of directions. One might point, for instance, to Carlyle's probable debt to Friedrich von Schlegel for his notion of the mythic function of poetry, to Jean Paul for his concept of the humorous in literature, to Novalis for the view that art is the expression of the unconscious.[2] Above all, I believe, one must consider the post-Kantian Idealist preoccupation with man's spiritual freedom and with the realization of that freedom in history as having had a very substantial effect on Carlyle's understanding of the nature of poetry and of literature in general.

The Metaphysics of Will Applied to Poetics

On the broadest level, the application of the metaphysics of will to poetry produces in Carlyle the formula — very different from the Neo-Platonic formula I noticed earlier —

that poetry, the "sole poetry possible" is "precisely this same struggle of human Freewill against material Necessity, which every man's Life, by the mere circumstance that the man continues alive, will more or less victoriously exhibit" (*Critical and Miscellaneous Essays,* III, 44-45). The "music," which in Carlyle's view it is poetry's highest business to express, seems, then, to be not only the Neo-Platonic music of the spheres that comes from seeing into the heart of things but also another sort of spiritual music: the music that Teufelsdröckh learns springs only from the discord of human will striving against the enclosing ring of necessity.

It is possible to be still more precise about the German source of this concept of the poetic. In Schiller's essays on aesthetics, particularly the earlier ones (1791-1793), a recurrent theme is the interpretation of art in terms exactly of this struggle of free will and necessity. Thus, for example, he praises Johann Winckelmann's account of the conflict of intelligence with nature in the Laocoön and concludes that two elements contribute to the "sublime" effect of this particular piece and, beyond that, of art in general. "*First,* we recognise this irresistible natural force as terrible, by comparing it with the weakness of the faculty of resistance that the physical man can oppose to it; and *secondly,* it is by referring it to our will, and recalling to our consciousness that the will is absolutely independent of all influence of physical nature, that this force becomes to us a sublime object."[3] Reading Carlyle's discussion of Schiller's plays in *Schiller,* one cannot help but be struck by the extent to which he has interpreted and approved these works precisely in terms of what their author has called the "sublime" struggle between heroic will and necessity. Thus he remarks on Schiller's portrayal of Joan of Arc's mission to the French nation: "It seems the force of her own spirit, expressing its feelings in forms which react upon itself. The strength of her impulses persuades her that she is called from on high to deliver her native France; the intensity of her faith persuades others . . . all bends to the fiery vehemence of her will" (*Schiller*, p. 157). Schiller's concept of the sublime, it seems, has been instrumental in forming Carlyle's earliest articulate notions of what constitutes the highest poetic expression.

In Carlyle's developing criticism there are essentially two ways in which this concept of man's struggle for spiritual freedom finds its way into the interpretation and judgment of poetry, ways which I shall call (1) ethical and (2) historicist.

The first of these may be dealt with fairly summarily. Here Carlyle sets up a criterion for poetry which exalts the expression of manly or heroic force. According to this criterion, all the major English Romantics, other than Byron, are simply dismissed for their *"un-Kraft"* or weakness. Shelley, for instance, is "weak in genius, weak in character (for these two always go together); a poor thin, spasmodic, hectic, shrill and pallid being."[4] On the other hand, the poets Carlyle most admires are those who he feels express the transcendent dignity of man in his efforts to overcome a hostile universe. Aeschylus, for instance, is preferred to Sophocles and Euripides because he is a "gigantic man" like his own suffering Prometheus.[5] The *Nibelungenlied* is "by far the finest poem of the Middle Ages" down to Dante himself because of its "old heroic German spirit" (*Lectures*, p. 70), Dante is remarkable as a poet for "that grand, natural, moral depth . . . that grandeur of soul" (*Lectures*, p. 79). Coming down to Carlyle's own times, Ebeneezer Elliot is cited—however implausibly—as proof that contemporary poetry, so long without strength, may at last be on the way toward better things: "Here is a voice coming from the deep Cyclopean forges, where Labour . . . beats with his thousand hammers . . . doing personal battle with Necessity" (*Critical and Miscellaneous Essays,* III, 138). Tennyson, at the same time, is admired for his "right valiant, true fighting victorious heart,"[6] and Browning is urged to "gird up [his] loins again; and give us a right stroke of work."[7] Everywhere Carlyle can be heard calling for a poetry of manliness, nobility, force of "spirit"; in a word, he is establishing a criterion of *strength* in poetry that was to plague Victorian criticism for many years to come.[8]

The second, more interesting, and critically far more attractive way in which Carlyle's preoccupation with the metaphysics of will finds expression in his poetic is in his belief that poetry embodies the spirit of the race in its historical realization of the Divine Idea. Here again Schiller is very important. The first clear evidence that Carlyle is thinking of poetry as the expression of Zeitgeist comes in a notebook entry of spring 1823 where, referring to his current reading in Schiller, he observes that a "poet should preach or poetise for his age [,] should elevate and beautify the ideas which are current in it" (*Notebooks,* p. 48). In his biography of Schiller, begun in the same year, he continues the point: poets are "the last forlorn outpost[s] in the war of Mind against Matter." "They are the vanguard in the march of mind; the intellectual Backwoodsmen, reclaiming from the idle wilderness new territories for the thought and activity of their happier brethren" (*Schiller,* p. 43).

Fichte, although not especially interested in poetical matters, was probably no less instrumental than Schiller in leading Carlyle toward the concept of poetry as the expression of developing Spirit through history with his notion of the "scholar as author." The author's chief business, he comments (in a way, incidentally, that strongly suggests Carlyle's remarks in *Sartor Resartus* on symbolism) is to clothe the Idea in language: "The Idea must have become in [the author] so clear, living, and independent, that it already clothes itself to him in words; and, penetrating to the inner spirit of his language, frames from thence a vesture for itself, by its own inherent power."[9] This Idea, again, is Spirit making itself known to men historically "through the learned culture of the day." Consequently the Idea that the author expresses is necessarily the Idea of his age: "he has not only recorded *his* knowledge alone, but also the fixed and settled character of a certain age in its relation to that knowledge."[10]

According to this criterion, the criterion I am calling specifically historicist, poetry must, then, express something more than a mere unarticulated will or impulse to freedom. It must also express the intellectual and spiritual systems, the Ideas of the World that ultimately grow from that original impulse. Hence Carlyle's famous injunction to close one's Byron and open one's Goethe (*Sartor,* p. 153). Byron is the poet of mere strength, mere unformed energy of revolt, while Goethe is the poet of synthetic wisdom, the poet who draws upon and comprehends the latest knowledge thrown up by the Zeitgeist and incorporates it into his poetry. In him "we are reading the poetry of our own day"; the "light, the science, the skepticism of the age are not hid from us" (*Meister,* p. 28); in him we have "the Wisdom which is proper to this time," the triumphant union of "clear knowledge" and religion (*Critical and Miscellaneous Essays,* I, 208). In this expectation that the poet will stand at the head of the march of mind and embody the highest Idea of his period and even in the use of Goethe as the preeminent modern exemplar of how this is done, Carlyle sets an important pattern for future Victorian criticism. Arnold, for example, characteristically insists that the poet express the "modern spirit." Thus Heinrich Heine, Goethe's "continuator" is a "soldier in the war of liberation of humanity";

while Pater in an essay on Winckelmann, whom he sees as the great teacher of Goethe, maintains that an artist must express, as Goethe does, the spiritual and intellectual conditions proper to his age.

By 1831 Carlyle had developed his concept of poetry as the expression of Zeitgeist to the fullest degree and had, in fact, ceased to show much interest in poetry except insofar as it expressed Zeitgeist. Historically considered, poetry

> is the test how far Music, or Freedom, existed [in a man]; how far the feeling of Love, of Beauty and Dignity, could be elicited from that peculiar situation of his, and from the views he there had of Life and Nature, of the Universe, internal and external. Hence, *in any measure to understand the Poetry, to estimate its worth and historical meaning, we ask as a quite fundamental inquiry: What that situation was?* Thus the History of a nation's Poetry is the essence of its History, political, economic, scientific, religious. With all these the complete Historian of a national Poetry will be familiar; the national physiognomy, in its finest traits, and through its successive stages of growth, will be clear to him: he will discern the grand spiritual Tendency of each period, what was the highest Aim and Enthusiasm of mankind in each, and how one epoch naturally evolved itself from the other. He has to record the highest Aim of a nation, in its successive directions and developments; for by this the Poetry of the nation modulates itself; this *is* the Poetry of the nation (*Critical and Miscellaneous Essays,* II, 341-42; first italics mime).

This must certainly rank as one of the pivotal statements in the history of English criticism. It amounts to the formulation of a principle that was in various forms to become the most characteristic and pervasive of Victorian assumptions about the function of criticism and the nature of poetry.

From the 1830s onward it was accepted by the majority of critics as never before in English letters that "in any measure to understand" poetry and "to estimate its worth" there must be a substantial knowledge of its cultural or historical background. Considered as a methodological principle, this meant that the Victorian critic must bring to his work the knowledge of a historian and sociologist, just as the Romantic critic characteristically brought to his a knowledge of epistemology and psychology, or, as the modern critic brings to his a knowledge of, or at least a sensitivity to, for example, linguistics or "deep structure." Examples of such a historicist or sociological approach may be picked from any of the major critics that followed Carlyle down to the 1870s—Lewes, Ruskin, David Masson, Arnold, Pater, Sidney Colvin, John Morley, J. A. Symonds, Stephen.[11] As Stephen put it at the very end of Victoria's reign in a lecture before the University of Oxford, the "adequate criticism must be rooted in history," for

> the material upon which [the artist] works is the whole complex of conceptions, religious, imaginative and ethical, which forms his mental atmosphere. That suggests problems for the historian of philosophy. He is also dependent upon what in modern phrase we call his "environment"—the social structure of which he forms a part, and which gives a special direction to his passions and aspirations. That suggests problems for the historian of political and social institutions.[12]

Any critic, that is, who has kept abreast of modern knowledge must recognize that artists, like all individuals, are inevitably conditioned by their age and must adjust his method of discussing poetry accordingly.

Of course Carlyle's enthusiasm for the relationship between poetry and the age goes well beyond the question of critical methodology. The "grand spiritual Tendency" of the age, he repeatedly says, is of the very essence of poetry; indeed, it is in itself a sort of poetry. Recurring to my earlier discussion of the dialectical bias of Carlyle's criticism, it is apparent that Zeitgeist, the movement of the spirit of Idea through time, has become for him nothing less than the principal dialectical dimension of the poetic. From this it follows that poetry comes to have for him no meaning and no value apart from its expression of the "highest Aim," "political, economic, social, and [above all] religious" of each successive stage of humanity's historical development. A major theoretical frontier, it seems to me, has been crossed — or perhaps better, bearing in mind Carlyle's lingering penchant for the Neo-Platonic outlook, is in the process of being crossed in English criticism. Let us consider some of the principal implications of this development.

Poetry and the Weaving of the Cultural Garment

In precisely what sense does the poet participate in the developing march of mind? The Romantic response would be that the poet having received his vision of the Idea from "out there" becomes society's most significant spiritual leader, whose duty it is to write a poem that will express the Idea and thus deliver men from their misapprehensions and oppressions. Schlegel was one of the earliest to give significant critical expression to this view of the poet's function. In his *Gespräch über die Poesie* (1800) he calls upon the poet to use his skill with symbol and allegory to create a new mythology.

> We have no mythology. But . . . it is time that we earnestly set to work together to create one.
> . . . . .
> The new mythology, in contrast [to the old ones] must be forged from the deepest depths of the spirit; it must be the most artful of all works of art.[13]

What Schlegel is recommending here Romantic poets both English and Continental were everywhere putting into practice in the first quarter of the nineteenth century; René Wellek has observed, "All the great Romantic poets are mythopoetic . . . whose practice must be understood in terms of their attempt to give a total mythic interpretation of the world to which the poet holds the key."[14] From the Romantic point of view, the poet's participation in the Zeitgeist amounts to conveying the new Idea for the times in concrete "mythical" form.

Carlyle participates in this Romantic view of the mythopoetic function of the poet to a great extent. Is it not, he asks in *Sartor* after quoting Goethe and Shakespeare on the power of poetry to make worlds, in the "far region of Poetic creation" that the religious rebirth of "Human Society" "appears possible, is seen to be inevitable?" (*Sartor*, p. 214.) If he had asked the question of himself some three or four years earlier the answer would probably have been an unequivocal, Romantic "yes." As it is, it is by no means certain that yes is the intended answer here, for by the 1830s Carlyle had developed considerable skepticism about the poet's mythopoetic vocation. The reason for that skepticism has to do with the question of how much and what sort of a role the poet himself is to be seen as having in the production of the Idea. Carlyle's problem, paradoxically, is that he was more inclined than were his Romantic predecessors to take literally the notion that the poet actually *creates* new belief. For the Romantics the poet's mythopoetic function rested ultimately not on his *art* but on his *vision* of an objective spiritual reality outside himself, and it was this reality that underlay and gave authority to his vision.[15] For Carlyle, however, there is always the question of whether the vision behind the art is, in fact, genuine and objective or whether it is simply an elaborate fabrication of the poet's subjective imagination with no real spiritual authority at all. The poet's principal means of fabrication, as Carlyle sees it, is his special cunning with language, which leads Carlyle to the nascent recognition that language has the ability to create the Idea or belief and that it may therefore lie at the very basis of man's will to spiritual self-realization. A brief consideration of this distinctly modernist tendency in Carlyle's thought will serve better than anything else to open the way toward an account of his mature view of the relation between poetry and Zeitgeist.

Writing of Carlyle's relation to German philosophy, Hippolyte Taine has drawn attention to his most characteristic way of receiving and expressing ideas. "He translates German philosophy in a poetic and religious style. Like Fichte he speaks 'of the Divine Idea of the world, the Reality that underlies all appearance.' Like Goethe he speaks 'of the Spirit that eternally weaves the living garment of God.' He borrows their metaphors; only he takes them literally."[16] The immense importance of imagery, metaphor, symbol, and the "style poétique" in general for Carlyle, his tendency to take his tropes and figures somewhat literally, has been noted by more than one critic since Taine, but no one has more thoroughly explored the subject than has John Holloway. The use of figurative language, he notes, was probably the most important of the methods Carlyle employed to put across his philosophy. "In order to say what he wished to say, Carlyle had to remould and modify a quite appreciable part of the language. On a scale not fully recognized, he created language."[17]

What Holloway has perhaps not sufficiently emphasized is the extent of Carlyle's self-consciousness about this language-making power and the relation of that self-consciousness to his clothes-philosophy concept of developing belief systems. To a degree not generally appreciated, Carlyle seems to me to have been approaching an understanding that the absolute basis of man's spiritual pretensions, his will to self-realization, lay in his power to create symbols and, in particular, verbal symbols. On this side of his thought, he went some ways toward anticipating the dominant modern understanding of man as *homo significans,* as a being whose distinctive characteristic is his ability to make linguistic symbols. As Ernst Cassirer has put it, "Man has, as it were, discovered a new method of adapting himself to his environment. Between the receptor system and the effector system, which are to be found in animal species, we find in man a third link which we may describe as the *symbolic system.* This new acquisition transforms the whole of human life."[18] Signs or symbols are not for Carlyle the ultimate reality they are for Cassirer; he continues to want to believe in the existence of a God behind the signs. But he does show, for his time, an extraordinary awareness of them as the fundamental "terrestrial" building blocks of man's belief-systems.

This self-consciousness about the power of language emerges as early as 1829, when he writes in his notebook that "all language but that concerning sensual objects is or has been figurative. Prodigious influence of metaphors! Never saw into it till lately. A truly useful and philosophical work would be a good *Essay on Metaphors.* Some day I will write one!" (*Notebooks,* p. 142.) Three years later, having produced in *Sartor,* if not exactly an *Essay on Metaphors,* at least a magnificent experiment in the power of figurative language to create belief, Carlyle received from Gustave d'Eichthal a letter requesting his opinion of the St. Simonians. To the positivist d'Eichthal, who was more interested in Carlyle's ideas than his metaphors, Carlyle responded that the positivists' new "religion of humanity" was all very well except for a crucial lack of adequate symbols.

> In all cases, there must be *some* symbol to offer itself to the worshipper; for hereby alone is Imagination, the true organ of the Infinite in man, brought to harmonize with understanding, the organ of the finite.[19]

And the point is elaborated later in *Heroes:*

> Idol is *Eidolon,* a thing seen, a symbol. It is not God, but a Symbol of God. . . . And now in this sense, one may ask, Is not all worship whatsoever a worship by Symbols, by *eidola,* or things seen? Whether *seen,* rendered visible as an image or picture to the bodily eye; or visible only to the inward eye, to the imagination, to the intellect (*Heroes,* p. 121).

The most important modern purveyor of these symbols, which are the sine qua non of worship, Carlyle goes on to say, is literature. Literature is the true Church of England, the art of writing the "most miraculous of all things man has devised" (*Heroes,* p. 160).

The relation between Carlyle's preoccupation with the miracle of language and his concept of poetry is fairly straightforward. Poets have the faculty of "insight" with which they, like all heroes, apprehend the Divine Idea. But they also have a peculiarly symbolic and linguistic power, an "emblematic intellect" as he calls it in reference to Goethe, by which they express the Divine Idea. This emblematic intellect involves a "perpetual never-failing tendency to transform into *shape,* into *life,* the opinion, the feeling that may dwell in [the poet]." In Goethe one can find this faculty "in the very essence of his intellect; and trace it alike in the quite cunning epigram, the allegory, the quaint device. . . . Everything has form, everything has visual existence; the poet's imagination *bodies forth* the forms of things unseen his pen turns them to *shape*" (*Critical and Miscellaneous Essays,* I, 244). The power of language, which Carlyle most admires is seen by him to be the special province of the poet. The great poet is a consummate master at making the symbols that make belief, and poetic imagination is not so much the organ of insight into the absolute as it is the faculty of "bodying forth" in living language.

Had Carlyle been able to maintain an unqualified faith in the miracle of poetic language he would have been saying, as I have suggested, something quite modern about the special nature of the poet's participation in the march of mind. He would have been saying that in his power of making language the poet is the greatest hero in mankind's self-creative process. This would, in one sense, have been similar to what his Romantic predecessors had been saying about the poet's mythopoetic function. It would also have been radically different precisely because of his tendency to rest the power of creating belief more on the poet's purely linguistic genius or "cunning" rather than upon his intuitive grasp or vision of the Divine Idea itself.

Carlyle did not, in the end, have any such unqualified faith in the miracle of poetic language or the poetic myths erected upon that language. There was another, still more dominant side of his thought, that regarded this special power of language with extreme skepticism, perhaps because he himself was so accomplished a master of it and, at the same time, so constantly uncertain of whether, after all, he had any substantial belief behind the verbal façade. This skepticism caused him to depart from Romanticism in quite another way than the modernist, linguistic one I have suggested.

When Carlyle is not admiring the miracle of poetic language for its own sake, he is likely to be treating it in a rather pragmatic way as a very effective means of getting people to do or believe the things one wants them to, that is, as a good rhetorical device. He tends to emphasize in this case the way poetic language can literally seduce people, especially the masses, or as Caryle puts it, the "general level," into belief. One of his spokesmen in the unfinished novel *Wotton Renfreid* (written 1827-28), having raised the problem of the age's need for a symbol to satisfy its "longings for the Infinite" and suggested the poet as the source of that symbol, remarks revealingly on the poet's special powers:

> "The gifted soul instinct with music, discerned the true and beautiful in nature, and poured its bursting fulness in floods of harmony, *entrancing* the rude sense of men; and song was a heavenly voice *bearing wisdom irresistibly with chaste blandishment into every heart.*"[20]

And elsewhere:

> Art also and Literature are intimately blended with Religion; as it were, outworks and abutments, by which that highest pinnacle in our inward world gradually connects itself with the general level, and becomes accessible therefrom (*Critical and Miscellaneous Essays*, II, 94).

With this heavily rhetorical interpretation of poetic myth and symbol, Carlyle looks forward obliquely to Arnold's Spinozan distinction between speculative truth suitable only to the elect and emotional truth that appeals to the masses. To both Carlyle and Arnold poetry has become a religion, but a religion in the quite special linguistic sense that it produces concrete symbols of Divinity, which because of their direct appeal to the heart and imagination exercise an extraordinary moral power on the individual and, beyond that (it is hoped), on a society that looks like approaching anarchy as its old religious symbols cease to work. If one becomes sufficiently self-conscious about the merely rhetorical power of poetic language, one can very easily grow skeptical of the poet's grand mythopoetic mission as envisioned by the Romantics. This is precisely what happens in the case of Carlyle.

When poets propose to create symbols for belief, ordinary people will be excused for fearing that they are being imposed upon. "The poet," as Jeremy Bentham has observed, "always stands in need of something false."[21] To which that other seminal mind of the nineteenth century, Coleridge, would reply that poetic illusion is "that *negative* faith, which simply permits the images presented to work by their own force, without either denial or affirmation of their real existence by the judgment."[22] Between Bentham and Coleridge, Carlyle's sympathies on this issue would probably have fallen, in the end, with the former.

From the beginning of his career Carlyle had serious misgivings over the unreality of poetry and of imaginative writing in general. There is obviously, for instance, sympathy on his part with the movement he describes in Schiller from a preoccupation with literature, the "dreamy scenes of the Imagination," to the "love of knowing things as they are," in this case the love of history (*Schiller,* p. 84). As I have said, he himself was eventually to reproduce in his own career essentially the same movement of mind that he is attributing to Schiller. His "realist" misgivings lead him to question the whole concept of poetic myth-making. This is seen nowhere more clearly than in *Sartor* which Abrams has, I believe not quite accurately, understood as Carlyle's continuation of the Romantic myth-making enterprise, a sort of logical successor to the *Prelude* and *Hyperion*.[23] There is no question but that Carlyle has created Teufelsdröckh in the image of Romantic myth-makers; no doubt but that the autobiographical fragments and the clothes philosophy present themselves as a sort of mythus for the modern age. But the presentation is quite deliberately ironical, undercut at every point by the quixotic character of the German sage and his somewhat mystified and definitely skeptical editor who keeps reminding his reader that there is reason to suspect that the sage of Know-Not-Where may be a quack.

> Here, indeed, at length, must the Editor give utterance to a painful suspicion which, through later chapters, has begun to haunt him; paralysing any little enthusiasm, that might still have rendered his thorny Biographical task a labour of love. It is a suspicion grounded perhaps on trifles, yet confirmed almost into certainty by the more and more discernible humoristico-satirical tendency of Teufelsdröckh . . . that these Autobiographical Documents are partly a mystification! What if many a so-called Fact were little better than a Fiction (*Sartor,* p. 161).

It is not that the editor does not want to *believe* — at times he does come close to believing and thus collapsing the ironical situation Carlyle has so carefully constructed; it is just that he never quite succeeds. In an important sense, *Sartor* is not a mythus for belief at all but a testimony to the difficulty of knowing when one is confronted with a genuine religious myth and when with the mere phantasm of a subjective "poetic" imagination. Faced with the apparent demise of a traditional religious mythus, Carlyle has seemed in the Romantic manner to want to renew belief through the poetic power, but he has, at the same time, quite self-consciously, presented his reader with a formidable problem in verification and, in the process, significantly challenged the mythopoetic powers of the poet. As time went on and the great Romantic mythi failed to save society and the lesser Spasmodic ones continued to multiply,[24] Carlyle became increasingly taken up by the problem of verification and, correlatively, the dangers of quackery. Nothing, he observes by 1833, is more natural to an age of moral decline than the proliferation of quacks.

Skepticism over poetic language and the poetic imagination, I believe, ultimately helped push Carlyle from a literary-critical vocation to the study of history. This does not mean, however, that he abandoned altogether his poetic interests; he simply adjusted them to fit with his growing concern for "knowing things as they are." This new realism in poetic matters may be discerned in two significant ways: first, in an insistence that the highest poetry is that which concentrates on the imitation of reality, specifically historical reality, rather than bodying forth dubious visions and, second, in decidedly un-Romantic assumptions about the necessary dependence of poetry on historical conditions. This latter consideration will lead in turn to what is always the most difficult problem for the critic, the problem of establishing the grounds of poetic value.

History As Poetry's "High Argument"

Against the Pisgah vision of Teufelsdröckh, one may set the "Aesthetical Picklock" of another, less well-known of Carlyle's German personae, Gottfried Sauerteig. Sauerteig, unlike Teufelsdröckh, is not a man of mythic poetic pretensions, he is simply a critic, and what concerns him as critic is the "feigned," the unreal nature of poetry. " 'Fiction, while the feigner of it knows that he is Feigning, partakes more than we suspect, of the nature of lying; and has ever an, in some degree, unsatisfactory character' " (*Critical and Miscellaneous Essays,* III, 49). Poets must inform the finite with a certain infinitude; this is true enough, but at the same time they must make sure they don't overlook that finite altogether. " 'I, for the present, will . . . predict that chiefly by working more and more on REALITY, and evolving more and more wisely *its* inexhaustible meanings . . . will this high enterprise [of poetry] be accomplished, or approximated to' " (*Critical and Miscellaneous Essays*, III, 53). But what kind of reality is the poet to imitate, and what makes that reality peculiarly suitable to poetry? Sauerteig's answer, in effect, is that the reality most interesting to the poet is the one which most interests mankind in general, the reality of History: " 'even in the right interpretation of Reality and History does genuine Poetry consist' " (*Critical and Miscellaneous Essays,* III, 79).

By the "right interpretation" of the reality that is history Carlyle means history viewed through the philosophical spectacles that I discussed in the last chapter. Thus when he writes to John Stuart Mill that he wants to make his *French Revolution* the "grand Poem of our Time," he means that he wants the Revolution to stand as a symbol of the overall pattern or meaning of life.[25] In effect Carlyle has overturned Aristotle and said that history is philosophical and as such not fundamentally different from poetry but informed with the same infinitude or Idea that critics have traditionally expected of poetry.

In this conflation of poetry and history, which Carlyle is putting off as a necessary return from mere fancy to reality, or, as Abrams might say, from expressionist to mimetic principles in poetry, there is, it seems to me, the critical background to a significant shift in contemporary poets' notions about what constitutes the proper subject matter for the highest, the most serious poetry. Carlyle's point that history has at once sufficient reality and sufficient infinitude to provide adequate poetic material and the philosophical interpretation of history that lies behind that point find expression in the characteristically Victorian preoccupation with the writing of poetry about historical subjects and historical process.[26]

I am not concerned, it should be made clear, with the poet's use of historical setting as an escape from the uncongenial modern age, which is one of the most common uses of history in Victorian poetry.[27] What I am talking about, rather, is how the major Victorian poets use history in the way Carlyle says it may best be used, as a philosophical key to the meaning of life in the present. Thus Tennyson conceived of Camelot in *The Idylls of the King* as "everywhere symbolic of the gradual growth of human beliefs and institutions, and of the spiritual development of man."[28] Browning, of all major Victorian poets certainly the most preoccupied by historical subjects, quite self-consciously saw his own great poetic undertaking, *The Ring and the Book,* as a historical/philosophical effort to find the meaning of life through the resurrection of the past:

> . . . man, bounded, yearning to be free,
> May so project his surplusage of soul
> In search of body, so add self to self . . .
> That, although nothing which had never life
> Shall get life from him, be, not having been,
> Yet, something dead may get to live again,
> Something with too much life or not enough,
> Which, either way imperfect, ended once:
> An end whereat man's impulse intervenes,
> Makes new beginning, starts the dead alive,
> Completes the incomplete and saves the thing.
>
> (I. 1. 721-734)

Arnold, to turn to the third of the great early and mid-Victorian poets, was likewise deeply engaged as poet in the interpretation of the past. *Empedocles on Etna* is at least as much a poem about history and historical process as it is about the dialogue of a mind with itself.

In this preoccupation of Victorian poets with history as a source of revelation and consequently as prime subject matter for poetry of the highest philosophical seriousness, one sees an important departure from Romanticism. The Romantics, as I have said, tended to draw on two sources of revelation: the philosophy of nature, which Schlegel argued should be the grounds for a new poetic mythology[29] and which may be seen in various forms underlying the major poetic efforts of English Romantic poets from Wordsworth through Keats; and, equally important, as Abrams has pointed out, intense introspection into the nature of self or, as Abrams calls it, the "theodicy of the private life":

> The Wordsworthian theodicy of the private life (if we want to coin a term, we can call it a "biodicy"), belongs to the distinctive Romantic genre of the *Bildungsgeschichte,* which translates the painful process of Christian conversion and redemption into a painful process of self-formation, crisis, and self-recognition, which culminates in a stage of self-coherence, self-awareness, and assured power that is its own reward.[30]

The Victorian poets were inclined to abandon altogether the Romantic theodicy of nature primarily because the advance of natural science was making the notion of a God in nature increasingly difficult to credit.[31] Although they remained somewhat attached to the Romantic theodicy of the private life (for example, *In Memoriam, Dipsychus,* and a host of Spasmodic productions from 1830 to the mid century), there was a distinct waning of interest in the subject. More specifically, there was a growing suspicion of excessive and irrelevant subjectivism and a consequent movement toward the more objective, *social* theodicy that I have been discussing, the theodicy of history. Carlyle's argument for the fusion of poetry and history stands at the crossroads of this development in English poetics and represents its most significant critical expression. His *Sartor* is itself emblematic of the collapse of the Romantic *Bildungsgeschichte* ("history of individual growth") under the pressure of self-directed irony and the escape of the poet/philosopher from the Weissnichwo of subjectivity to the realm of *Universalgeschichte* ("universal history").

Implicit in Carlyle's skepticism over the poetic imagination and his consequent desire to bring poetry back to mimetic and realistic principles, specifically to the treatment of historical "reality," are certain beliefs about the role of individual genius or inspiration in poetry or, put another way, about the relation of poetry to the age. These in turn lead to questions about the relation between poetry and mankind's developing belief systems, which carry Carlyle quite beyond English Romanticism and into characteristically Victorian concerns.

Poetry and the Believing Age

In English Romantic theory, poetry is conceived of, by and large, as above the age; it is the product of inspiration, and inspiration is not seen to depend in any important way upon the sociological or spiritual conditions in which the poet finds himself. In his earlier work Carlyle was inclined to share the Romantic outlook (see, for example, *Critical and Miscellaneous Essays,* I, 57). But as his historicist interests developed, he responded to the influence of another strain of late eighteenth-, early nineteenth-century critical thought found far more prominently on the Continent than in England, a strain that saw the poet as essentially the product of his age. This approach he would have found in two of his early favorites, Mme de Staël:

I proposed to examine the nature of the influence of religion, customs, and laws on literature.[32]

And Herder:

[An author] wears the fetters of his age . . . he stands in his century, like a tree in the soil, in this he roots himself, from it he draws nourishment.[33]

Thus, as early as 1828 he is doubting the validity of poetic "inspiration":

The age of the Prophets and Theologic Doctors has long since passed away. . . . The wisest, most melodious voice cannot in these days pass for a divine one; the word Inspiration still lingers, but only in the shape of a poetic figure, from which the once earnest, awful and soul-subduing sense has vanished without return (*Critical and Miscellaneous Essays,* I, 200-01).

And partly agreeing with Schiller that the poet is the product of his age (*Critical and Miscellaneous Essays,* I, 217). By 1831-32 the shift to the historicist point of view has become decisive in the sense that henceforth he clearly believes that poetic excellence (however defined in itself) is *crucially* determined by historical factors. The first indication that he is taking this position comes in a notebook entry of August 1831. Here he writes of the great need of the times for spiritual deliverance and asks, "Is it to be done by *Art*—or are men's minds still shut to art and fit only for oratory; not fit for a Meister, but only for a better and better Teufelsdröckh [?]" (*Notebooks,* p. 203.) Again in October of the same year he writes, "For one thing, as I can see, London is fit for no higher Art than that of Oratory, they understand nothing of Art" (*Notebooks,* p. 213).

This is the beginning of what is to become for Carlyle a major theme: the present age is an *unpoetic* one in which it is impossible for the poet to match the magnificent accomplishments of past poets, such as Homer, Sophocles, Dante, and Shakespeare. "The farther we recede from those early days, when Poetry, as true Poetry is always, was still sacred or divine, and inspired (what ours in great part, only pretends to be), — the more impossible becomes it to produce any, we say not true Poetry, but tolerable semblance of such; the hollower, in particular grow all manner of Epics; till at length, as in this generation, the very name of Epic sets men a-yawning" (*Critical and Miscellaneous Essays,* III, 51).

Carlyle's position here is not to be confused with the "primitivist" outlook of the late eighteenth, early nineteenth centuries, which identified the truly poetic with the antique and bardic and which saw the modern age as far too sophisticated for poetry.[34] Thus Carlyle's contemporary Macaulay, an important continuator of this approach (it is of a piece with his progressivist Whig history), concludes that "as civilisation advances, poetry almost necessarily declines," because the growing "light of knowledge" has, fortunately, dispelled the "phantoms which the poet calls up."[35] The difference in Carlyle's outlook is substantial. To begin with, he does not share the primitivist's tendency to regret the poetic age as a dark and barbarous period with the correlative that poetry is a kind of subnormal expression of intelligence, in Macaulay's words, the result of a "certain unsoundness of mind." Nor does he believe with the primitivist that the poetic age is gone forever, but with his cyclical view of historical process sees it as a continuing possibility. What makes an age poetic, in the end is not for Carlyle its primitivism or intellectual backwardness but the vitality of its belief-system.

Belief, that is, *established social belief* shared by poet and audience, is a precondition of both the highest poetical production and the highest poetical enjoyment. The application of this principle may be seen everywhere in Carlyle's comments on poetry after 1831-32. Thus in the *Lectures on the History of Literature* one learns that the *Iliad* is an admirable poem because of Homer's *sincerity* (that is, he believed in the cosmology he presented), and because it was written for a "believing age." Similarly with Aeschylus and Sophocles; but with Euripides "composition" begins to be "diseased" because it is the beginning of an "age of scepticism" (*Lectures,* p. 30). Dante's *Divine Comedy* is a "voice for all ages" because the poet "had belief in every fibre of his mind," in this case, belief in the medieval Catholic church (*Lectures,* p. 91). Shakespeare expresses the organic wholeness of the "glorious" culture of the Elizabethan period, which was the "flowerage" of medieval Christianity, and demonstrates that religion is the "soul of Practice; the primary vital fact in men's lives" (*Heroes,* pp. 102-03). But Milton is the beginning of decadence as belief and its epic embodiment become self-conscious, and the deep religious melody grows thin and intellectualized (*Lectures,* pp. 146-148).[36]

In all this there is a significant reversal of the Romantic notion—a notion, as I have said, shared by Carlyle in his earlier essays—of the poet as a God-inspired genius, a legislator of the world, and a force for social regeneration. One may perhaps underline the point by contrasting Blake's enormous confidence in the bard's powers:

> I will not cease from mental flight,
> Nor shall my sword sleep in my hand
> Till we have built Jerusalem
> In England's green and pleasant land.
> (Preface to *Milton,* ll. 13-16)

with William Morris' thoroughly Victorian view of the poet as one who can do more than strive

> . . . to build a shadowy isle of bliss
> Midmost the beating of the steely sea,
> Where tossed about all hearts of men must be
> Whose ravening monsters mighty men shall slay
> Not the singer of an empty day.
>   (Apology to *The Earthly Paradise,* 11. 38-42)

There is obviously a vast difference between Blake's hopes for bringing about new Jerusalem and the "shadowy isle of bliss" which Morris is trying to salvage from the wreck of modern life. No small part of the difference is owing to precisely that critical revaluation of the poet's independence of the "steely sea" of his times that Carlyle was instrumental in introducing to England.

The Question of Poetic Value

In his enthusiasm for describing the relation between poetry and the Zeitgeist Carlyle tended not so much to overlook as to mute one of the greatest and most obvious problems raised for criticism by the historicist approach. The nature of this problem is perhaps more readily apparent in Stephen's "scientific" formulation of the historicist method than in anything one finds in Carlyle or the earlier Victorians. In proportion as art is seen as the expression of Stephen's historical "atmosphere" and "environment," the traditional notion that it has a transcendent value, one which is valid for all time, becomes increasingly hard to entertain. Art is seen simply or primarily as the product of its age; aesthetic value, insofar as it may be said to exist at all, is not absolute but historical or relative value.

Carlyle was not by any means prepared to accept this implication of his spirit-of-the-age poetic. On the contrary, he was very much concerned to retain in some way the traditional normative function of criticism. His way out of the difficulty is not very thoroughly developed but does suggest interesting possibilities. In a word, he argues that value in poetry depends upon the quality of the age's Idea: the presence in society of a viable religious belief is a necessary prerequisite of poetic excellence. Before dismissing this position as a piece of Victorian moralism, typical of the period's critical "poverty," consider that that pre-eminent modernist T. S. Eliot has argued, after all, along essentially the same lines. What is wrong with Blake, he says, is that he "sadly lacked" a "framework of accepted and traditional ideas"; what is wrong with "modern literature" seems to be about the same thing: it "repudiates or is wholly ignorant of the most fundamental and important beliefs."[37] Carlyle is never particularly explicit about the precise way in which belief makes for aesthetic excellence. As Eliot's discussions of the problem suggest, it is perhaps a subject on which it is difficult to be explicit. But it is clear that Carlyle is not saying, any more than is Eliot, that one must believe literally in the religious and philosophical ideas expressed in a poem in order to approve it. The gods of the *Iliad* are but so much "Superannuated lumber" (*Critical and Miscellaneous Essays,* III, 51); yet Carlyle can still admire Homer's poem. Dante's medieval Catholicism is dead forever; yet Dante's is a "voice for all ages" (*Lectures,* p. 91).

To understand, however partially, the nature of the connection Carlyle insists exists between belief and poetic excellence, one must consider belief not as a series of discursive statements about the nature of the universe but simply as a means by which society is held together in a harmonious whole. For Carlyle society is a "mystic, miraculous, unfathomable Union" (*Critical and Miscellaneous Essays,* III, 11), a *system.* The keystone of this system and what determines its overall quality is religion; when religion is sick, all other spiritual expressions share in the sickness: "the vital union of Thought being lost, disunion and mutual collision in all provinces of Speech and Action more and more prevail" (*Critical and Miscellaneous Essays,* III, 16). This experience of general disharmony inevitably affects the spiritual balance of each individual member of society; all men in an unbelieving society find themselves in a state of inner conflict and anxiety, including, of course, the poet. In such a state of spiritual confusion the poet cannot experience the "pure unmixed life" of "unconsciousness," that is, of naturalness, spontaneity: "always the characteristic of right performance is a certain spontaneity, an unconsciousness" (*Critical and Miscellaneous Essays,* III, 7). A reflection of this belief-inspired social "health," this harmonious unity and spontaneity, one may reasonably infer, is what Carlyle expects of the highest poetry. These criteria, while far from aesthetically specific enough, do in a very general way suggest the organic unity and naturalness that Coleridge is urging in Chapter 14 of the *Biographia.* The great difference (apart from Carlyle's lack of clear aesthetic definition and precise example) is that Coleridge rests his concept of poetic excellence on metaphysical grounds, in an extrahistorical union of spirit and matter; Carlyle rests his on a recurring social or cultural condition produced by the developing Zeitgeist.

The general concept which Carlyle has here introduced to English criticism (I can find no earlier significant expression of it), that poetic excellence depends crucially on the presence in society of a viable system of religious belief and that, moreover, the present age is doomed to be unpoetic because of the absence of such belief, became what is probably the single most important assumption of subsequent Victorian criticism. One sees the theme prominently in Arnold, with the important difference that the concept of belief is deprived for all practical purposes of its theistic import and is grounded on entirely humanistic values. In Pater it appears again and again, much changed from its original formulation in Carlyle.[38] It was the peculiar proclivity of the Victorian poetic that so long as the restoration of public belief seemed possible (and, of course, desirable), the idea of poetic excellence was closely associated with that possibility. As that possibility waned, poetic value became increasingly associated with the merely formalistic and the technical. One ceased, as Roger Fry has put it, to treat art as "crystalised history" and concerned oneself more and more with how it was made and what it did to one's peculiarly aesthetic sensibility.[39]

Inspiriting as his critical, social, and religious thought was to many Victorians, there are two important ways in which Carlyle failed to satisfy the intellectual needs of some of the more advanced minds that followed him. First, there was his tendency toward religious mysticism and anti-intellectualism. "The healthy Understanding, we should say, is not the Logical, argumentative, but the Intuitive; for the end of Understanding is not to prove and find reasons, but to know and believe" (*Critical and Miscellaneous Essays,* III, 5). Such doctrine as this was bound to be disappointing to younger men who were increasingly inclined to follow the more rationalistic guides of contemporary thought—the liberal Christians, Thomas Arnold, F. D. Maurice, Benjamin Jowett, on the one side; the positivists, Mill, Lewes, Herbert Spencer, on the other—and to seek their interpretations of life in the realms of philosophical and scientific thought rather than in intuition and fideism; to look to human nature and human society as the ultimate grounds for belief rather than to an otherworldly Absolute whose existence seemed to them increasingly problematical.

The second area in which Carlyle's thought failed to satisfy the vanguard minds of the succeeding generation was in its lack of appreciation for the specifically aesthetic condition, whether that condition be seen in a metaphysical sense (as in Schopenhauer) as an escape from the driving force of will, or in an artistic sense, as in the case of Schiller's mature concept of the beautiful as a reconciliation of spirit and matter. Carlyle could, as I have said, recognize the value of the disinterested harmonious condition of spirit in which mind is at one with itself and with the outside world, but he did not see this condition as a possibility in his revolutionary times. For him the age was one in which man's sole purpose must be to strive with heroic will against the threatening Abyss, the "Bottomless of Scepticism, Atheism, Jacobinism" (*Past and Present,* p. 139). He must try with all the spiritual energy at his command to reforge some saving belief or — and the tone of desperation becomes increasingly pronounced as the years go by — simply to hold his head above the encroaching chaos. "All work of man is as the swimmer's: a waste ocean threatens to devour him; if he front it not bravely, it will keep its word" (*Past and Present,* p. 199). With such an outlook, such an overwhelming sense of cultural crisis and social responsibility, the aesthetic state of repose could be no more than a very distant ideal; at hand was only endless struggle. Before this strangle hold of will, of *doing,* rather than *being,* could be broken, it was necessary first to concede the possibility that, after all, the struggle nought availeth, that no exertion of heroic will could change the situation in which men found themselves. This admission once made, one became free to consider the value of the aesthetic condition in itself apart from its dependence upon the re-creation of public belief. Matthew Arnold, who considered that Carlyle had led his generation into the wilderness and left it there, began, in effect, by making precisely this surrender of the will to "front" the chaos and ended by opening for Victorians the aesthetic way out of history's all-devouring ocean.

MATTHEW ARNOLD

From now on, then, we must lift our thoughts to the pure concept of human nature; and since experience never shows us human nature as such, but only individual human beings in individual situations, we must endeavour to discover from all these individual and changing manifestations that which is absolute and unchanging, and, by the rejection of all contingent limitations, apprehend the necessary conditions of their existence.

—*Schiller*

3

HISTORY AND THE
BEST SELF

The way into Matthew Arnold's thought, especially as it relates to history, must be through his father, Thomas, Master of Rugby and one of the most eminent historians of his day. I want, then, to begin by outlining very briefly the essential points of Dr. Arnold's concept of history.

Dr. Arnold and Vico's Concept of the Modern

Thomas Arnold, born in the same year as Thomas Carlyle, shared with the latter not only his passion for uncovering the past but his desire to find in history a pattern or "laws" whereby the nature of the present age and its prospects for the future might be judged. It is not enough, he tells an Oxford audience in 1842, for a historian to have a full knowledge of the events and thought of the past; this would be simply "antiquarianism"; only by a philosophical understanding of the inner laws according to which history moves can one hope to make it yield "wisdom."[1] Arnold took his philosophy or laws of history, not so much from the Germans (as in the case of Carlyle) as from their Italian prede-

91

cessor Giambattista Vico whose *Scienza Nuova* (1725) may be regarded as the first significant document in the historicist reaction against Cartesian rationalism in the eighteenth century.[2] Arnold first read Vico in 1830,[3] and in the same year he wrote a very important essay, based entirely on Viconian principles, which he appended to the first volume of his edition of Thucydides. In this appendix he writes that *Scienza Nuova* is a work "disfigured indeed by some strange extravagancies" but "in its substance so profound and so striking, that the little celebrity which it has obtained out of Italy is one of the most remarkable facts in literary history."[4]

Arnold took a number of concepts from Vico's philosophy, but none was so important as that of the cyclical periodization of history. According to Vico, every nation or civilization moves "with the greatest equality and constancy" through a standard pattern of three stages.

> These are: (1) The age of gods, in which the gentiles believed they lived under divine governments and everything was commanded them by auspices and oracles. . . . (2) The age of heroes, in which they reigned everywhere in aristocratic commonwealths, on account of a certain superiority of nature which they held themselves to have over the plebs. (3) The age of men, in which all men recognized themselves as equal in human nature, and therefore there were established first the popular commonwealths and then the monarchies, both of which are forms of human government.[5]

In his appendix to Thucydides, Arnold concerns himself almost exclusively with the transition from the second to the third of these Viconian stages, that is, from the "age of heroes," in which the vast majority of men are enslaved and spiritually suppressed by an aristocratic minority, to the "age of men" or what Arnold calls the modern age, in which all men are recognized as "equal in human nature" and given the opportunity fully to expand their humanity. This is the transition, he says, that Thucydides is describing in his history of the Peloponnesian War: the movement of Greek civilization in the fifth century B.C. from its relatively severe aristocratic phase (associated by Arnold with the Homeric heroes) to its sophisticated modern phase (associated by Arnold with the brilliant intellectual accomplishments of men such as Thucydides himself, Sophocles, Herodotus, Pericles, Socrates, Plato, and Aristotle).[6]

More important, however, than this specific application of Viconian principles to the interpretation of Thucydides is that Arnold, like Vico before him, is emphasizing that the transition from heroic to modern age did not happen in just one civilization, but is a *recurring* phenomenon throughout history. A similar transition, he says, took place in Roman civilization at the end of the Republic, from the first century B.C. to the beginning of the first century A.D. (the period of Julius and Augustus Caesar, Lucretius, Virgil, Horace, Livy, Ovid); and again in European civilization in the sixteenth and seventeenth centuries (in England Arnold associates this latest example of the transition from heroic to modern with the Civil War and the Revolution of 1688).[7] He sums up the point thus:

We shall see that there is in fact an ancient and a modern period in the history of every people; the ancient differing, and the modern in many essential points agreeing with that in which we now live. Thus the largest portion of that history which we commonly call ancient is practically modern, as it describes society in a stage analogous to that in which it now is; while, on the other hand, much of what is called modern history is practically ancient, as it relates to a state of things which has passed away. Thucydides and Xenophon, the orators of Athens, and the philosophers, speak a wisdom more applicable to us politically than the wisdom of even our own countrymen who lived in the middle ages and their position, both intellectual and political, more nearly resembled our own.[8]

It is evident that Arnold considers the transition from heroic to modern age worthy of such special attention because he believes this phase of Vico's recurring historical pattern most closely describes the condition of his own times (which he sees as essentially a continuation of the Revolution of 1688).[9]

It is important to be quite clear on Dr. Arnold's attitude toward this modern age, both in the abstract as a part of the recurring cycle of history and in the concrete as his own Victorian age. For Vico the modern age is the acme of a civilization's development; it is the time at which human nature "crude" in the poetic age, "severe" in the heroic age, becomes at last, "intelligent and hence modest, benign, and reasonable, recognizing for laws conscience, reason, and duty."[10] As for the latest, European phase of the modern age, Vico writes, "today a complete humanity seems to be spread abroad through all nations; and the principal agent dispersing this "complete humanity" is the Christian religion which teaches "an infinitely pure and perfect idea of God and commanding charity to all mankind."[11] Unfortunately, however, the glory of modern ages does not last; they must eventually decline into luxury and effeminacy, and when they do, human nature falls back into a dissolute life, into "all the vices characteristic of the most abject slaves."[12]

Arnold shares with Vico his high opinion of the healthy, fully developed modern age as a stage in the cycle; he clearly prefers it to its less intellectually self-conscious, more feudalistic predecessor. Here the contrast with Carlyle's longing after a more aristocratic and unsophisticated society should be borne in mind, for, as I hope to show, the difference between Thomas Arnold's and Carlyle's concept of the ideal society bears importantly on Matthew Arnold's intellectual outlook. Dr. Arnold, however, cannot share Vico's eighteenth-century optimism about the condition of the present modern age, at least in England. In public he simply emphasizes the critical nature of the transition from "property to numbers" and the grave danger of failing to make the transition or of slipping into decline once the transition is made. In private he is more inclined to express himself with something very like Carlylean pessimism. Thus he writes to a friend in 1831 on the subject of Reform agitation and the general revolutionary mood of the period:

> I believe that "the day of the Lord" is coming, i.e., the termination of one of the great *aiones* [epochs] of the human race; whether the final one of all or not, that I believe no created being can know. The termination of the Jewish *aion* in the first century, and of the Roman *aion* in the fifth and sixth, were each marked by the same concurrence of calamities, wars, tumults, pestilences, earthquakes, etc., all marking the time of one of God's peculiar seasons of visitation.[13]

Dr. Arnold's pessimism about the modern age is, as I say, like Carlyle's, but at the same time it is very different. It is in its way far deeper primarily because Arnold tended to doubt the one firm belief, which more than any other sustained Carlyle, the belief in the transcendent power of the human will. In Arnold there is a distinct strain of fatalism, a stoical willingness to acquiesce in the ineluctable course of events, that provides a little-recognized counterpoint to the far better-known Rugbean exhortations to manly duty. For instance, in a letter of 1840 to Carlyle, Arnold tells him that he is "heartily glad" that he has written on Chartism and asks whether he is not, like himself, utterly overwhelmed by the "fearful evils of our social conditions" and inclined to say with Herodotus' Persian fatalist: *echthisté oduné polla phroneonta medenos kratéein* ["the worst pain a man can have is to know much and be impotent to act"].[14] According to his biographer A. P. Stanley, Arnold loved to dwell with "melancholy pleasure" over the "last decay" of great civilizations.[15] Of course, in his public pronouncements Arnold was still very much the master of Rugby and very much more likely to urge St. Paul's "good fight" than indulge in a lament for the declining age.[16]

Even in public statements, however, Arnold permits himself a degree of doubt about the power of the human will to govern events that is quite beyond anything found in Carlyle. In his last Oxford lecture on modern history (1842), delivered shortly before his untimely death, Arnold first affirms his belief in the validity of the "laws of history" and then tackles the "one great question" remaining, the question whether knowledge of the laws of history can enable us to carry into effect the truths that we value or whether we are, rather, "cursed with that bitter thing, a powerless knowledge, seeing an evil which we cannot escape, and a good to which we cannot attain; being in fact embarked upon the rapids of fate, which hurry us along to the top of the fall."[17] Some answer this question, he says, by holding that great men can control fate, that "there is an energy in the human will which can . . . snap asunder . . . the chain of destiny." (The reference is almost certainly to Carlyle whose lectures on *Heroes and Hero Worship* had been published the year before and whom Arnold had just previously mentioned as one of the pre-eminent historians of the day.) Arnold's own answer is far more pessimistic. There is hope that "good men, working in the faith of God" can do something to amend the "influence of our times," but, on the other hand, we are not to think "that in us or our actions is placed the turning power of the world." On this "great question" of the relevance of human action to historical process, a question to which Carlyle has provided so unequivocal a solution, Dr. Arnold, then, is inclined to end at best with a problem rather than an answer; at worst, with a clear suggestion that the power of individual human will is very limited indeed in determining the course of history.

The Historicist Context of Arnold's Early Poetry

That Matthew Arnold inherited the main points of his father's Viconian concept of history there can be no doubt.[18] It is immediately evident in the early poems that he has assimilated his father's preoccupation with declining civilizations. This is particularly apparent in the *juvenilia* in a poem on the two great epochs of the human race mentioned by his father in the letter to Carlyle, that of Jerusalem:

'Mid the wild eddyings of the whirling storm
Sweeps past no more the Almighty's cloudgrit form,
But unrestrained, round your beleaguered towers,
Borne on the threatening blast, destruction lours.
                                                (1838)[19]

and of Rome:

But then, imperial City! that hast stood
In greatness once, in sackcloth now and tears, . . .
Thou hast gazed, as the world hurried by,
Upon its headlong course with sad prophetic eye.
                                    (1840, *Poems,* p. 4)

as well as on the fall of Constantinople (1839, *Poems,* p. 572), and on the English monarchy in the Civil War (1843, *Poems,* p. 18). These poems, most of them written when Arnold was still at Rugby, read very like illustrations of his father's history lessons. In the more mature poetry of *The Strayed Reveller, and Other Poems* (1849) and *Empedocles on Etna, and Other Poems* (1852), the preoccupation with historical decline is perhaps less obvious, but this only because Arnold has learned to deal with it more subtly and with something like symbolic suggestion rather than explicit statement. In "The Strayed Reveller" the two visions, that of the Gods and that of the poets, tell the same familiar story of doomed civilizations:

> They [the Gods] see Tiresias
> Sitting, staff in hand . . .
> Revolving inly
> The doom of Thebes.
> . . . . .
> They [the wise bards] see the Heroes
> Near the harbour; but they share
> Their lives, and the former violent toil in Thebes,
> Seven-gated Thebes, or Troy.
>
> (*Poems,* pp. 70, 74)

"Resignation" opens with images of "The Goth, bound Rome-wards" and the "Hun, / Crouched on his saddle . . . ," and an important part of the poet's fatalistic vision in this poem is the realization that "great historied lands" and their heroic leaders are bound to pass (*Poems,* pp. 85, 90). The *Empedocles* is explicitly set against the background of that "last decay" of Greek civilization that so fascinated Dr. Arnold. As Matthew Arnold explains in the 1853 Preface, "Greek thought and feeling had begun fast to change character and to dwindle."[20] In summary, it is not too much to say that the evocation of historical process and especially historical decline occupies a place in Arnold's poetry roughly parallel in importance to the evocation of the One Life in nature in the poetry of his English Romantic predecessors, Wordsworth and Coleridge.

Beyond this preoccupation with historical process, the young poet absorbed his father's interpretation of contemporary society as passing through a "modern age" in Vico's sense. Arnold's view of the age as "modern" and hence analogous to Periclean Greece and late Republican Rome becomes evident in the later prose writings; it may be seen as well in the early poetry, particularly in his interest from 1845 to 1852 in two major poetic enterprises, one a tragedy on Lucretius (never completed),[21] the other, the completed poem on Empedocles. Each of these poet-philosophers belonged to what his father regarded as the modern phase of the two great civilizations of the ancient world, Rome and Greece, and in both cases Matthew Arnold is entirely aware of their Viconian modernity. Empedocles lived, he writes, under conditions "we are accustomed to consider as exclusively modern" (*Prose Works*, I, 1); Lucretius' poem and his times bear the "characteristics stamped on how many of the representative works of modern times!" (*Prose Works*, I, 32.) That Arnold as poet has likewise continued his father's tendency to regard the latest, his own contemporary Victorian phase, of the modern with deep pessimism scarcely needs saying. In his poetry he drew some of his period's bleakest pictures of contemporary cultural crisis or what he called

> . . . the strange disease of modern life,
> With its sick hurry, its divided aims,
> Its heads o'ertaxed, its palsied hearts . . .
> (*Poems*, p. 342)

Finally and most importantly, the young Arnold inherits and substantially extends his father's misgivings over the possibility of doing anything to counteract the ineluctable laws of history. Against the spectacle of the "sure revolutions of the world" he sets what is certainly his principal intellectual and moral preoccupation as a poet: the problem of the individual's relationship to the historical processes in which he finds himself caught up. As early as his Newdigate Prize

Poem "Cromwell" (1843), Arnold is developing what is to become with him a characteristic poetic situation. Superimposed upon a given historical spectacle is the sensitive individual consciousness which finds itself called upon to take some position vis-à-vis the historical movement which is unfolding before it — Mycerinus, the Strayed Reveller, the Sick King of Bokhara, the narrators of "Resignation" and of "Obermann," Empedocles, the Scholar Gipsy, and so on.

The problems involved are set out as clearly in "Cromwell" as anywhere and for my present purposes more interestingly because this poem, almost certainly written with an eye on Carlyle's treatment of the Puritan leader as Hero, helps illuminate the crucial ways in which Arnold's own thought, like his father's, departs from Carlyle's.[22] For Carlyle, Cromwell is the "inarticulate prophet," with an "outer hull of chaotic confusion," liable to "visions of the Devil" and "nervous dreams"; but for all this he has a "man's-energy," "a will to *do* and master!" The point about Cromwell's susceptibility to nervous dreams looks very much like being the basis of Arnold's poem, for his "Cromwell" is, after all, an extended nervous dream in which the "hero" as a young man still uncommitted to any particular course of action foresees in a vision the wreck and havoc he will live through and in large part be responsible for. Far from greeting the prospect with the heroic resolution that Carlyle speaks of, he is filled "with a dread no slumber could control." A contrast is sharply drawn — and again this is characteristic of Arnold — between the "peace of childhood" and terrible responsibilities of maturity when the "sterner will" is called upon to "crush" all "soft and fair" remembrances and to act in a world that both stains the conscience and hardens the sensibility. In all this Arnold is obviously raising grave questions about the value of what Carlyle calls heroism, questions that Carlyle himself persistently avoids or dismisses as dilettantism. Most subversive of all is Arnold's conclusion that Cromwell's grand heroic gesture, after all, signifies nothing.

> A daring hand, that shrunk not to fulfil
> The thought that spurred it; and a dauntless will,
> Bold action's parent; and a piercing ken
> Through the dark characters of the hearts of men,
> To read each thought and teach that master mind
> The fears and hopes and passions of mankind;
> All these were thine — Oh thought of fear! — and thou,
> Stretched on that bed of death, art nothing now.
>
> (*Poems,* p. 22)

Again and again in the early poems Arnold returns to essentially the same points that he is making in "Cromwell": to commit oneself to the struggle of life is necessarily to destroy one's inner sanctity and purity of self, and, beyond this, one makes such a commitment without the least assurance that it matters, that anything will be the better for the attempt to manipulate destiny. The following lines from "Resignation," the poem with which Arnold concludes the 1849 volume, perhaps better than any others summarize the prevalent mood of the early poetry:

> Blame thou not, therefore, him who dares
> Judge vain beforehand human cares;
> Whose natural insight can discern
> What through experience others learn;
> Who needs not love and power, to know;
> Love transient, power an unreal show. . .
>
> (*Poems,* pp. 93-94)

This fatalism and this fear of the world's contamination lead Arnold's protagonists away from action and into what is with him a quite self-consciously Lucretian aloofness from the battle of life.[23] The direction of mind in the poems is always toward the assumption of "some high station" from which to survey "with sad lucidity of soul" the "general life that does not cease." In all this, Arnold is saying in effect with Lucretius:

> This is the greatest joy of all: to stand aloof in a quiet citadel, stoutly fortified by the teaching of the wise, and to gaze down from that elevation on others wandering aimlessly in a vain search for the way of life, pitting wits one against another, disputing for precedence, struggling night and day with unstinted effort to scale the pinnacles of wealth and power.[24]

It is worth noting that although Victorian reviewers were quick to complain of the excessive gloom and fatalism in the early poetry,[25] it is precisely these pessimistic, asocial qualities that for the modern reader have tended most to recommend Arnold as poet. Thus Lionel Trilling has admired Arnold's attempt to hide "behind a mask of irresponsibility," for he considers that only by this pose is Arnold able to nourish the truly aesthetic condition. "Misunderstood, hiding behind a mask of irresponsibility, Arnold is free to cultivate that internal, meditative slowly-precipitating part of himself which is to produce poetry."[26] Frank Kermode has broadened the point in his discussion of Arnold's relation to the modern artistic consciousness, a consciousness which he argues rests on the artist's perception of his "necessary isolation or estrangement" from the world of action. The artist must be "exempt from the normal human orientation towards action and so enabled to intuit those images of truth" which the mere intellect misses. What is best in Arnold, according to Kermode, is his devotion to those moments of isolation and aloofness from action, the moments of intense self-contemplation; where Arnold the poet fails is in his inability to maintain this distance between the self and the social-historical world outside self. "Arnold found this solution impossible, suppressed *Empedocles* because it had no action, and set out to reform the world. . . . He plunged into action, into other people's business."[27] What both Trilling and Kermode are saying amounts to essentially the same thing: Arnold's fatalistic withdrawal from action is a necessary preliminary to the discovery of the transcendent value of an inner, specifically aesthetic, as against moral, experience. This seems to me probably the most important thing to be said about Arnold's early Lucretian stance and its relation to his concept of poetry. Up to and including *Empedocles,* Arnold as poet was engaged in a thoroughgoing criticism of precisely that exaltation of human will which, as I argued in Chapter One, found philosophical expression in the Idealist movement in Germany, and, in England, found its greatest popular prophet in Thomas Carlyle. The nature of the positive values that Arnold sought as an alternative to the "metaphysics of will," will be discussed in more detail. For the moment it is enough to note that insofar as Arnold was able to maintain his Lucretian stance and thus to free himself from the tyranny of will, the incessant Victorian demand for action and moral commitment, just to that extent was he able to move toward the discovery of new values, values related to what Kermode has called the "organic sensibility" and what Schiller, whom I have quoted as epigraph to this chapter, called the "aesthetic condition."

At the same time Arnold, even at his most Lucretian, was never, any more than was his father, able to abandon himself totally to fatalism or to give up the notion that good men working together might, in fact, make some difference to "these bad days." In the poems of 1849 and 1852 there is always some embarrassment over responsibilities forgone. The Strayed Reveller in his surrender to Circe's drug is explicitly contrasted to Circe's "favored guest" Odysseus who, of course, never gives up the struggle against adverse circumstances. Mycerinus for all his Epicurean withdrawal from responsibilities of state cannot quite forget his "wondering" people left without guidance; Empedocles must give the philistinic Pausanias some spiritual solace before leaping into Etna, and so on. In other words, Arnold as his father's son and living in mid-Victorian England was never really able to divorce himself entirely from a sense of responsibility to do something more positive about the unfortunate "modern" age.

Beyond Historical Fatalism

As Arnold's career progressed, the sense of social obligation, latent in the early poems but by and large overshadowed by the fatalistic mood, became increasingly pronounced. One can pretty well place the point at which he began to make the transition from aesthetic withdrawal to a greater concern with his responsibilities in the world at about the period in which he completed his philosophical poem *Empedocles,* took up an appointment as an inspector of schools, and was married. In June 1852 he writes to Arthur Hugh Clough, "I am sure . . . that in the air of the present times il nous manque d'aliment, and that we deteriorate in spite of our struggles. . . . *Still nothing can absolve us from* the duty of doing all we can to keep alive our courage and activity."[28]

In the following year he made the momentous decision to suppress *Empedocles,* the product of two years' work and probably the most important poem he was ever to write. He had several reasons for doing this, but most important was the poem's excessive morbidity. Poetry, he writes in the Preface to the *Poems* of 1853, is not justified unless it can be something from which men "can derive enjoyment"; *Empedocles* gives no enjoyment; it expresses, rather, a condition "in which a continuous state of mental distress is prolonged, unrelieved by incident, hope, or resistance" (*Prose Works*, I, 2-3); such a condition is too "morbid" for poetry. Still, *Empedocles* with its morbidity, Arnold continues, is the natural expression of the decadent "modern" condition. The question inevitably arises, then: if one is to suppress the natural expression of the modern age, what is left for the contemporary artist to do? Arnold's answer is a notoriously disappointing piece of Victorian neoclassicism. The modern poet, he says in effect, must be artificial and anachronistic. He must step aside from his own times and imitate the ancients with their "wholesome regulative laws." "In the sincere endeavour to learn and practise, amid the bewildering confusion of our times, what is sound and true in poetical art, I seemed to myself to find the only sure guidance . . . among the ancients" (*Prose Works*, I, 14). Although this view still amounts to an aesthetic withdrawal from the uncongenial times in favor of the magnificent ancients, there is a significant difference from his stance in the early poetry. Here a certain negative power is granted the individual will (in this case, of course, the artist's will); that will may not have the power to express joy, but it can at least suppress morbidity. Henceforth there are to be no more Lucretian laments for the irredeemable misery of men, no more wallowing in historical fatalism.

From this initial resolve to curb his expressions of fatalism and to offer at least some alternative to the unsatisfactory modern condition Arnold began to move toward the assertion of more positive means of "doing all we can to keep alive our courage." Four years after publishing the Preface, he delivered his Inaugural Lecture as Professor of Poetry at Oxford. If there were any doubt that Arnold imbibed his father's Viconian theory of history, this lecture must dispel it. Indeed, the lecture appears almost to have been written with a view toward memorializing his father's own Oxford lectures of fifteen years before. The subject is the modern element in literature. We must, Arnold argues, begin by understanding the "collective [historical] life of humanity" and the nature of the connections that everywhere exist between various ages. We do this in order to understand our own situation and, thereby, to know how to correct ourselves. "To know how others stand, that we may know how we ourselves stand; and to know how we ourselves stand, that we may correct our mistakes and achieve our deliverance — that is our problem" (*Prose Works,* I, 21).

There are, he continues, some epochs of the past that are more interesting to us than others and these are the epochs, called "modern," which, like our own, are characterized by highly complex social arrangements and great intellectual sophistication; they are ages in which the mind of the people is engaged in nothing so much as a critical "endeavour after a rational arrangement and appreciation of the facts" (*Prose Works,* I, 25). Such characteristically modern concerns have been seen in the past in the "age of Pericles" when Thucydides stood as the foremost historian and Sophocles as the foremost poet; and again in Rome from Cicero to Augustus, with its great literary artists, Lucretius, Virgil, and Horace. But — and here he adds to his father's historical thought a distinctively literary twist of his own — the modern epoch of Rome, full and glorious as it was *historically,* was not "adequately" interpreted by its literature. Lucretius, in particular, was an artist in whom the predominance of "modern" anxieties destroyed emotional health and who became "overstrained, gloom-weighted, morbid" and therefore unable adequately to *interpret* his age, for "he who is morbid is no adequate interpreter of his age" (*Prose Words,* I, 34). Arnold in condemning what he now calls the expression of the "modern feeling" in literature, it will be noticed, is essentially continuing the theme of the 1853 Preface. Here as well he argues that there is an alternative to indulging in this modern despair. If one looks to the Greeks, rather than the Romans, one finds that Sophocles' poetry, at once "serious" and "cheerful," did not fill its audience with gloom, but animated and rejoiced them (*Prose Works,* I, 35). The difference between Arnold's position in 1853 and his position four years later in the Inaugural Lecture is that the latter is far more positive about the possibility of the poet's overcoming the adverse consequences of the modern age. Arnold is no longer counseling the poet to evade those consequences by retreating to the imitation of the ancients (advice which in its way bore a certain parallel to Empedocles' retreat to Etna). He is now presenting his audience with two historically analogous modern conditions, the Greek and the Roman; the one has been adequately interpreted by its poets, the other has not.

It evidently lies, then, within the power of the poet, at least in his poetry, to control the consequences of the modern, to transform the chaotic into the intelligible, the morbid into the seriously cheerful — a point of view that seems to me to be giving a good deal more to the poet than was given in 1853. With the background of Romantic mythopoetic expectations of poetry in mind, an important question arises: does Arnold in this lecture go on to argue that the poet's interpretation of the modern age in some way makes a difference for his society at large? There seems to me no question but that at the back of Arnold's thought throughout the lecture, which begins, after all, by emphasizing the modern age's need for deliverance, is the enduring Romantic notion that the poet through his poetry can somehow help bring about this deliverance — or further retard it. Sophocles inspirited and rejoiced his countrymen; Lucretius caused his to despair. In subsequent years, Arnold, like Carlyle before him, turned away from this lingering Romantic tendency to make of the poet some kind of savior for society — or perhaps better, he significantly modified that tendency — but here in the Inaugural Lecture the tendency, though by no means overbearing or even central, is still very much present. The difference between Arnold's position at this point and that of his Romantic predecessors is not so much in the former's social expectations of poetry as in his understanding of the *kind* of deliverance the poet can bring. Even at this early point in his career Arnold is not thinking of the poet's power to produce a new mythus, but of something more specifically aesthetic. What he is thinking of, it seems to me, grows directly out of his early propensity for withdrawal into the self. Although he is not very specific in this lecture about the nature of the poetic experience of deliverance he is concerned with, he does throw out a fairly important suggestion: it touches a condition which he calls the "harmonious development" of "human nature." "Now, the peculiar characteristic of the highest literature — the poetry — of the fifth century [B.C.] in Greece . . . is its *adequacy* . . . it represents the highly developed human nature of that age — human nature developed in a number of directions, politically, socially, religiously, morally developed — in its completest and most harmonious development in all these directions" (*Prose Works,* I, 28).

This concept of harmonious self-realization may have come from many sources; Schiller is a very likely prospect.[29] It seems to me, however, that a prior and probably more effective influence than any other is that, again, of Vico.

For Vico, the perfected or delivered modern age was one in which men achieved their "compiuta umanità," their complete humanity, and the agent of perfection was, for the contemporary modern age, the Christian religion. Arnold, like Vico, affirmed the definite possibility of delivering modern man by developing his complete humanity, and he saw that deliverance not as the result of the proliferation of Christianity, as did Vico and his own father, but as related somehow to poetic means and poetic effects.

In 1861 Arnold took another significant step away from his early fatalism of the pre-1852 period as he began to direct his prose from criticism per se toward social and political concerns. He became increasingly occupied with society's need for a new "common cultural bond" — what Carlyle would have called a "Social Idea" — for it seemed to him that modern British civilization might be saved from decline if only the right, or, again, the *adequate* social idea could be produced and proliferated. The essay in which Arnold first explored this question is the introduction to his study of public education in France, an essay which he later entitled "Democracy." The essay is, as R. H. Super has observed, the keystone of his political thought (*Prose Works,* II, 330). Like the Inaugural Lecture, it rest⁵ squarely upon his father's interpretation of history. Contemporary England is in a stage of critical transition. Government by "aristocratical parties," closely associated in Arnold's mind with the heroic "grand style" of Homer about which he has just been lecturing at Oxford (*On Translating Homer*), is nearly over as the inevitable laws of history push society forward. Coming in its place is the new democratic age, of which "social freedom" or "equality" is the "characteristic mode." This democratic age is not without its dangers, for the tendency of democracy is ever toward moral and political anarchy; what is wanted to hold things together is an "ideal of high reason and right feeling," which the masses can follow in place of the dying ideal of the aristocracy. Where will that ideal now reside? In the State, says Arnold: "an ideal of high reason and right feeling, representing its [the State's] best self, commanding general respect, and forming a rallying point for the intelligence and for the worthiest instincts of the community which will herein find a true bond of union" (*Prose Works,* II, 19).

Where is the ideal to come from? Arnold is not very clear on this in "Democracy"; but in later political and social writings he is more explicit. The ideal is the creature of the "chosen few" working with the materials supplied them by Europe's intellectual and cultural heritage, the "best that is thought and known." As he writes in the much later essay on "Numbers" (1884), drawing on Plato's *Republic,* the majority are "unsound" and must be saved by the minority of the intelligent, but with the important proviso that the minority do all in its power to educate the majority, to make the ideal prevail, lest they be overrun in the end by the unsound in search of equality.[30] The principal importance of "Democracy" is that it shows Arnold further widening his concept of the individual's power to resist and to control historical process. Society is governed by historical laws, to be sure, he says in "Democracy," but by knowing these laws, one can do something to "adapt" oneself and one's society to them. This is far from being as grandiose and unqualified a concept of human freedom as Carlyle's, but it is enough to provide Arnold with the basis of the social vocation his early poems so thoroughly called into question. He pursues this vocation at first tentatively in the essays and Oxford lectures of the sixties and then with increasing confidence in *Culture and Anarchy* (1867-1869) and the religious writings of the seventies.

So far I have spoken very generally about the actual nature or content of the ideal, the ideal of complete humanity, which Arnold is proposing to make prevail in society. I have been more interested, rather, in his developing attitude toward the individual's relationship to the historical-social process and specifically toward the possibility of the individual's making any difference in that process. In the end, however, the two questions are not easily separable. On the one hand, Arnold as a young man was almost certainly kept back from social commitment not so much by an absolute disbelief in the possibility of breaking the chain of historical destiny—I have spoken of the nagging sense of social responsibility even in his most pessimistic poems—as by the lack of a coherent and positive ideal that he could believe in and, to use his own favorite word, "apply" toward the deliverance of the modern age. In proportion as he was able, with the aid of various poetical and philosophical sources, to formulate this "new spiritual basis," he became ever more confident about the possibility of his doing something to ameliorate the diseased condition of his times. On the other hand, Arnold's initial refusal to meet the age head on in Carlylean warlike stance and his persistent desire for the contemplative life aloof from the common herd (*Prose Works,* III, 290) were instrumental in determining the specific nature of the new spiritual basis he was eventually to offer his countrymen as a "cultural bond." Throughout his life he was deeply influenced by Stoical and, to a lesser extent, Epicurean thought, which meant that he regarded the withdrawal from action not, as Carlyle did, as a nihilistic gesture but as an effort to recover a certain inner harmony of soul. From this basis Arnold articulated, over a space of many years, his own ideal of complete humanity, an ideal which I shall subsequently refer to, after Arnold's own usage, as the ideal of the Best Self.

The "Master-Current" of Modern Thought: Arnold and Spinoza

Late in life, writing of the great "voices in the air" influencing himself and other undergraduates at Oxford in the early forties, Arnold mentioned among others that of Carlyle, "misused since, but then fresh, comparatively sound, and reaching our hearts with true, pathetic eloquence."[31] The influence of Carlyle may be seen in several ways in Arnold's work, but I believe probably the most important and enduring influence was Carlyle's insistence that the one thing needful for society was a new religious mythus. To an extent Dr. Arnold's thought would have supported Carlyle's here; to the extent, that is, that the former considered that religion was essential to social order and that an adjustment of religious belief was necessary if England was to survive the critical transition to the modern epoch.

Dr. Arnold was in one sense more conservative than Carlyle, however. Like the broad church movement with which he has been associated, he envisaged not a new religion altogether but a continuation of Christianity in a form suitably rationalized for the modern world.[32] Carlyle was far readier to see the whole Christian mythus go up in Phoenix flames in order to make room for a new mythus which his readers had every reason to believe would bear no more resemblance to traditional Christianity than did Mohammedism or the religion of Odin. Inasmuch as

Matthew Arnold tended to think that the old religious idea was utterly exhausted and that a radically new one must be constructed on its ashes, it was to Carlyle's rather than his father's voice that he hearkened, as for instance when he speaks, very much in the Carlylean vein, of the need for someone like Goethe who will bring to society an altogether new spiritual basis.

> Dante's task was to set forth the lesson of the world from the point of view of mediaeval Catholicism; the basis of spiritual life was given, Dante had not to make this anew. . . . But when Goethe came, Europe had lost her basis of spiritual life; she had to find it again; Goethe's task was, — the inevitable task for the modern poet henceforth is — . . . not to preach a sublime sermon on a given text . . . but to interpret human life afresh, and to supply a new spiritual basis to it (*Prose Works,* III, 381).

Having said this, one must immediately add that whatever the resemblance of Arnold's thought to Carlyle's on this question of the need for a new spiritual basis, the differences in their ways of conceiving the nature of this idea are so significant as to make the two men's tenets ultimately in- compatible.

Arnold took issue with Carlyle directly or indirectly a number of times in his career (an example of this is the poem "Cromwell"), but the most fundamental parting of the ways came in the 1863 Oxford lecture on Heinrich Heine. Here Arnold begins by acknowledging Carlyle's great contribution in making "England acquainted with German writers" and in particular with Goethe, "the manifest centre of German literature." But, he continues, from Goethe "many rivers [of intellectual influence] flow." Carlyle's failure was that he emphasized the wrong river, the "roman- tic" influence, the influence that is associated, Arnold says, with Tieck, Novalis, and Jean Paul Richter. In this Carlyle, Arnold continues, misconstrued the "master-current," the main movement of mind of the modern epoch. The man he should have picked as Goethe's continuator in his "most important line of activity" was Heinrich Heine (*Prose Works,* III, 107-08). What Arnold almost certainly means by saying that the "romantic" continuation of Goethe's thought is outside the main current of modern thought is that it continued in the manner of traditional religion to look to some form of supernatural Being or spiritual Absolute as the basis of reality; it was not sufficiently critical of the whole concept of an otherworldly Being informing nature and governing the affairs of men. The "most powerful and vital" activity of Goethe's mind was not its otherworldly, Neo-Platonic aspirations, but its "naturalism." "Goethe's profound, imperturbable naturalism is absolutely fatal to all routine thinking; *he puts the standard, once for all, inside every man instead of outside him*" (*Prose Works,* III, 110).

It is precisely this naturalism that Heine, in Arnold's view, continues; this is the "modern spirit" that Heine has applied to literature. Looking elsewhere in Arnold's essays of the early sixties, one finds that the spirit that he is seeking to define here in Goethe and in Heine has still deeper roots. In his next essay but one, "Spinoza and the Bible," he suggests that behind the thought of these two German writers lies that of Spinoza (*Prose Works,* III, 182). In describing the particular nature of Spinoza's influence on Goethe (and presumably Arnold means the point to be extended to Heine,) he vigorously denies Frederick Maurice's contention that Spinoza gave Goethe a Hebrew view of God as an " 'actual being' " which the " 'pagan schools of philosophy could not bring'." No, says Arnold, Spinoza's influence on Goethe had nothing to do with the former's "Hebrew nature" (*Prose*

Works, III, 175-76). On the contrary, Spinoza's influence was a pagan, or more specifically, a Stoical one (Spinoza was, of course, influenced by the Stoics),[33] and it worked in two ways. First, it denied the "exploded" doctrine of final causes, by which Arnold in this context means the notion of a providential God overlooking the affairs of men. Having thus disposed of final causes, Spinoza goes on, according to Arnold, to identify God with natural law. " 'God directs nature, according as the universal laws of nature, but not according as the particular laws of human nature require; and so God has regard, not of the human race only, but of entire nature.' "[34]

The second source of Spinoza's attractiveness for Goethe was the Stoical "moral lesson" drawn from this view of nature, a lesson "not of melancholy quietism, but of joyful activity within the limits of man's true sphere" (*Prose Works,* III, 177). " 'Man's very essence is the effort where-with each man strives to maintain his own being. . . . Man's virtue is this very essence, so far as it is defined by this single effort to maintain his own being. . . . Happiness consists in a man's being able to maintain his own being. . . . Joy is man's passage to a greater perfection. . . . Sorrow is man's passage to a lesser perfection.' "[35] In both these doctrines Spinoza is obviously moving away from traditional theism: God is becoming nature; the chief human happiness lies not in serving God or in a heavenly reward but in the purely naturalistic experience of "being able to maintain [one's] own being." Although Arnold explicitly defends Spinoza from the charge of atheism and speaks warmly of his love of "God," it is clear even at this stage of his career that he is not attaching any supernatural significance to this word "God." Rather, he means, as he takes Spinoza to mean and as he knows the Stoics mean, a *natural law* that is "not ourselves" (to anticipate his famous phrase of *Literature and Dogma*).

Looking forward in Arnold's career, the continuation of his case for the modern spirit of naturalism is easily traced. The 1863 essay on Spinoza is, in fact, an outgrowth of three slightly earlier essays, which Arnold did not republish and which mark his first entrance into the contemporary fray over Biblical criticism.[36] As is well known, the results of nineteenth-century Biblical criticism had begun by the 1860s to have a profound effect on informed Englishmen's view of their religion. In these essays Arnold sought to establish Spinoza's thought as the only proper basis for reinterpreting the nature of Biblical truth in such a way as to answer modern scientific and philosophical criticism while at the same time retaining an essential core of religious meaning. "If the English clergy must err, let them learn from this outcast of Israel to err nobly . . . let it be lawful to cast into the huge caldron, out of which the new world is to be born, the strong thought of Spinoza!" (*Prose Works,* III, 55.) The rather tentative venture into the public dispute over Biblical criticism and the nature of Biblical truth, which is found in these essays of the early 1860s, becomes by the 1870s the center of Arnold's intellectual concerns, resulting in a number of works exclusively on the religious problem. Of these probably the most important is *Literature and Dogma* (1873) and here Arnold offers his famous redefinition of religion as "ethics heightened, enkindled, lit up by feeling; the passage from morality to religion is made when to morality is applied emotion. And the true meaning of religion is thus, not simply *morality,* but *morality touched by emotion*" (*Prose Works,* VI, 176).

As for God, Goethe (in the mainstream of modern thought and Spinoza's continuator, one recalls) warns us against our anthropomorphic tendencies (*Prose Works,* VI, 184); God is not a "Personal First Cause, the moral and intelligent Governor of the universe" (*Prose Works,* VI,

202); he is, rather, *"simply the stream of tendency by which all things seek to fulfill the law of their being"* (*Prose Works*, VI, 189). This last, well-known phrase is, in fact, directly adapted from Spinoza.[37] In short, the extent of Arnold's reliance upon Spinoza for the reinterpretation of religious truth which everywhere informs and ultimately crowns his career as "Victorian sage" cannot be overestimated. As he told T. H. Huxley with regard to his later religious writings, he could have been "drowned" in the morass of contemporary controversy without Spinoza; "to him I owe more than I can say."[38] It would seem that Spinoza performed for Arnold much the same intellectual and spiritual life-preserving function as the German Idealists did for Carlyle.

Returning to my original point of departure, I would emphasize that Arnold, though accepting Carlyle's point that the one thing needful for the spiritually distressed modern age is a new "religious" idea, has at the same time departed radically from Carlyle's understanding of the nature of that idea. As Arnold suggests in the Heine essay, Carlyle was thoroughly implicated in the religious mysticism of men such as Tieck, Novalis, and Jean Paul. Moreover, even when he tended to associate himself closely with the post-Kantian Idealists and what I have called the metaphysics of will, Carlyle's outlook was still, as I have said, essentially transcendentalist and theistical. Much as he talked of the impossibility of Christianity and the need for a new religious mythus, he was not in any sense intending to do away with God or to place man's spiritual deliverance, as Arnold most certainly is doing, ultimately within man himself. The new mythus was simply to be a more convincing vesture for theism or, at worst, Absolute Idealism. Following his seventeenth-century mentor, Arnold goes much farther. He dispenses with God and metaphysical ideals alike and rests his faith, as F. H. Bradley has complained, ultimately on a moral and psychological ideal.[39] Having made this fairly crucial distinction between Carlyle's and Arnold's approach to delivering the age,[40] let us consider more closely what Arnold means when he proposes to make morality inspired by emotion the new spiritual basis of society.

The Ideal of the Best Self

When Carlyle speaks of *Vir-tus* as the hero's great characteristic (*Heroes,* pp. 217-18), he is at great pains to insist that the word means a manly *doing,* an active commitment to moral conduct. Carlyle here is placing a rather limited definition on virtue, for virtue need not mean simply doing moral things, it can also mean *being* something, having a particular type of character. The distinction, an important one, was described by Leslie Stephen in 1882 in these terms: "Morality is internal. The moral law . . . has to be expressed in the form, 'be this,' not in the form, 'do this' . . . the true moral law says 'hate not,' instead of 'kill not . . .' the only mode of stating the moral law must be as a rule of character."[41]

For the internal morality of being, Carlyle had very little use. Thus at a critical moment in *Sartor* he rejects one of the great classical sources of such a morality, the Stoic Epictetus, and turns instead to the one Greek philosopher who more than any other insisted upon the importance of moral *action.* " 'The *Enchiridion of Epictetus* I had ever with me . . . and regret to mention that the nourishment it yielded was trifling.' Thou foolish Teufelsdröckh! . . . Hadst thou not Greek enough to understand thus much: *the end of Man is an Action, and not a Thought, though it were the noblest?*" (*Sartor,* p. 126.)[42] Although Carlyle has picked up Aristotle's often repeated point that the highest good consists not simply in the possession but also in the exercise of virtue, he nowhere shows the least interest in the more "aesthetic" side of Aristotle's moral thought, the side which stresses that moral action presupposes the internal development and harmonization of character. "By human goodness is meant . . . a right condition of the soul, and by happiness a condition of the soul"; "It would be nearer the truth to say that goodness of soul is the beautiful completion of the virtues."[43]

Arnold's concept of virtue, compared with Carlyle's and the earlier Victorian emphasis on moral action, has shifted decisively toward an inward concern with moral *being* or the "right condition of soul." This does not mean that Arnold, no more than Aristotle, denies the need for virtuous action in the world. What does seem to have happened in Arnold's case is that significant questions have been asked from the very outset about the meaningfulness of action; and in the face of what looked like the inability of human will to change the course of history, moral attention has been redirected inward toward the reformation of what is within man's control, his own inner nature.

This moral attitude, which in Arnold's mind was most closely associated, in the end, with Stoicism, he first began to articulate in letters to Clough in the summer and autumn of 1848. Here he speaks of having read with "surprise and profit lately" the *Enchiridion* of Epictetus and quotes from a poem ("To a Friend") he has written in praise of Epictetus (and others), as one who has "propped" his mind in "these bad days" (*Letters to Clough,* p. 90). In later years he went well beyond Epictetus, but the basic position taken by the Greek philosopher, that man's primary business and greatest happiness consist in the perfection of his inner nature and not in active conflict with external circumstances or in mystical union with the Divine, forms the absolute center of Arnold's thought. This belief is the basis of his interpretation of Goethe as one who puts the standard "inside every man instead of outside him," and of Spinoza as one who sees man's "virtue" as "defined by this single effort to maintain his own being." Again, one sees it in his belief that the morality of Marcus Aurelius is superior to dogmatic Christianity in placing the "kingdom of God" within, rather than outside, the self (*Prose Works,* III, 148-49; although Arnold considers that Aurelius' morality falls short of Christianity in other ways).

Arnold's complete expression of the morality of being comes in *Culture and Anarchy,* where he attempts to naturalize the Greek concept of the Best Self to the uncongenial Hebraic world of Victorian England. The English suffer, he writes, from placing their faith in external things; what is wanted is an "idea of perfection as an *inward* condition of mind and spirit," as "the *harmonious* expansion of human nature." The contemporary English attempt to assign to perfection a special or limited character, whether utilitarian or religious, is a sign of what Epictetus calls *aphuia* "that is, of a nature not finely tempered"; "the Greek word *euphuia,* a finely tempered nature, gives exactly the notion of perfection as culture brings us to conceive it: a harmonious perfection, a perfection in which the characters of beauty and intelligence are both present. . . .The *aphues* is the man who tends towards sweetness and light" (*Prose Works,* V, 99). I shall come back to the question of how Arnold conceives of the various virtues or traits that comprise *euphuia,* but first I want to look at the Stoical ideal itself in relation to religion and to my principal theme, historical process.

As my earlier remarks on Arnold's naturalism will have suggested, the Stoical ideal is not easily reconcilable to a religious interpretation of life. Ernst Cassirer describes the difficulty thus:

[The] Stoic theory proved to be one of the strongest
formative powers of ancient culture. But it found itself
suddenly in the presence of a new, and hitherto
unknown force [Christianity]. The conflict with this
new force shook the classical ideal of man to its very
foundations. . . . [T]here always remains one point on
which the antagonism between the Christian and the
Stoic ideals proves irreconcilable. The asserted absolute
independence of man, is turned in the Christian theory
into his fundamental vice and error.[44]

To overcome this antagonism between the Stoical ideal and
the Christian religion may be said to be the object of all
Arnold's writings on religion.

One way out of the conflict is to suppose that the sources
of Christian belief, the Scriptures, do not mean, at least do
not mean *intellectually* or *scientifically,* what they say. If
one is prepared to concede this point, one can then begin, as
Arnold does, to reinterpret the meaning of Scripture in a
way conducive to the Stoical ideal of *euphuia.* Here again
the major influence on Arnold is Spinoza, whose idea of
religion, as I have said, he considered far more Hellenic
than Hebraic. From the *Tractatus Theologico-Politicus*
Arnold appears to have taken the germ of a concept which
became absolutely central for him, the concept of a
fundamental duality in the nature of truth. Spinoza's
discussion of religion in the *Tractatus* rests upon a distinction
between what he alternatively calls scientific, intellectual, or
speculative knowledge and by which he means knowledge
supplied by human reason, and religious knowledge (which
he also calls imaginative and emotional knowledge). Scripture, he believes, "does not aim at imparting scientific
knowledge." "An intellectual knowledge of God, which
takes cognizance of His nature in so far as it actually is, and

which cannot by any manner of living be imitated or followed as an example, has no bearing whatever on true rules of conduct, on faith, or on revealed religion."[45] Knowledge of God, the strictly religious knowledge imparted by Scripture is, rather, for Spinoza, a variety of direct or intuitive knowledge, and the object of this knowledge is "to make men not learned but obedient." "It is not true doctrines which are expressly required by the Bible, so much as doctrines necessary for obedience, and to confirm in our hearts the love of our neighbor, wherein. . .we are in God and God in us."[46]

The point that Spinoza is making here, as throughout the *Tractatus,* is that religious truth does not reveal anything about the nature of reality, but produces in the faithful an *attitude* (obedience) and does this by an immediate, noncognitive appeal to the "heart." "Faith does not demand that dogmas should be true as that they should be pious—that is, such as will stir up the heart to obey."[47] In the 1862-63 essays on religion and Biblical interpretation, Arnold returns again and again to this distinction of Spinoza's between speculative and religious truth and perhaps nowhere more eloquently than in this central passage from "Dr. Stanley's Lectures on the Jewish Church":

> The world of the few—the world of the speculative life—is not the world of the many, the world of the religious life; the thought of the former cannot properly be transferred to the latter, cannot be called true in the latter, except on certain conditions. . . . Religious life resides not in an incessant movement of ideas, *but in a feeling* which attaches to certain fixed objects. . . . In relation to these objects it has adopted certain intellectual ideas; such are, ideas respecting the being of God, the laws of nature, the freedom of human will. . . . But

its essence, the essence of Christian life, consists in the ardour, the love, the self-renouncement, the ineffable aspiration with which it throws itself upon the objects of its attachment themselves in relation to them (*Prose Works,* III, 66-67).

At this point, it is important to bring in one more figure in what Arnold regarded as the mainstream of modern thought and who had a material influence on his formulation of the ideal of the Best Self. I have in mind the German theologian Friedrich Schleiermacher (1768-1834), who was himself an ardent disciple of Spinoza.[48] That Arnold was thoroughly familiar with the general nature of Schleiermacher's thought on religion by at least as early as 1862 may be inferred from two things. First, Schleiermacher was the chief of those reverent or "mediating" German theologians and Biblical critics who formed his father's religious thought; Dr. Arnold's essay "On the Right Interpretation of Scripture" (1831), for instance, rests largely upon Schleiermachian principles.[49] It would seem likely, then, that Matthew Arnold would have been exposed to Schleiermacher's tenets from a fairly early age and strongly predisposed to look to him for guidance on religious questions. More conclusive evidence of Arnold's familiarity with the German theologian, however, comes from his 1862 review of R. Willis' translation of Spinoza's *Tractatus.* Here, as part of his general case against Willis as a translator, he quotes from Willis' "Introduction" an English rendering of Schleiermacher's praise of Spinoza taken from *Reden über die Religion* (1799).[50] The fact that in making his criticism Arnold can supply the original German (Willis neither supplied the original nor did he cite its location) argues a good deal more than a passing knowledge of the *Reden*; it suggests, indeed, that Arnold may well have been lately reading the *Reden* as background for his 1862-63 venture into the fracas over Biblical criticism.

Schleiermacher's object, in general, is to dispense with the "shell" of religion and penetrate to the "kernel." The shell is the "opinions, dogmas, and usages in which every religion is presented," the "ideas and principles" that are "foreign to religion" and "belong to knowledge which is a different department of life from religion."[51] The kernel, the absolute ground for man's experience of religion is *feeling*.

> First of all, let us understand what we are dealing with [in religion]. It is with action as an exercise of feeling, not with any symbolical or significant action meant to represent feeling. We have already seen how those dogmas and opinions that would join themselves more closely to religion than is fitting, are only designations and descriptions of feeling. In short, they are a knowledge about feeling, and in no way an immediate knowledge about the operations of the Universe, that gave rise to the feeling.[52]

Religious "truth," in sum, is not what we "know or believe" about the nature of things. Religion "cannot and will not originate in the impulse to know." What it is, rather, is the *emotional effect* of the nature of things on us: "What we feel and are conscious of in religious emotion is not the nature of things, but their operation upon us."[53] The connection here between what Schleiermacher is saying about religion and Spinoza's concept of the two truths should be evident.

In Schleiermacher, as in Spinoza, Arnold perceived the fine hand of the Hellenic ideal at work. Schleiermacher, he wrote to his mother in 1867, believed "that in the Christianity of us Western nations there was really much more of Plato and Socrates than of Joshua and David."[54] Schleiermacher's account of the nature of religious feeling reveals readily enough the continuity he is trying to achieve with the classical tradition. For Schleiermacher there are essentially two religious feelings, both parallel with what I have called the Stoical ideal and parallel as well, it should be noted, with the two elements of Spinoza's *Ethics* that Arnold focused upon in "Spinoza and the Bible." There is first the feeling of dependence upon and complete harmony with universal laws, and second, the feeling of a perfect inner unity of being. "The whole religious life consists of two elements, that man surrender himself to the Universe and allow himself to be influenced by the side of it that is turned towards him is one part, and that he transplant this contact which is one definite feeling, within, and take it up into the inner unity of his life and being, is the other."[55]

By thus reinterpreting the nature of religious experience as in its essence an inward emotional and moral attitude rather than as a knowledge of the actual nature of things, both Spinoza and Schleiermacher establish a fundamental continuity between the classical ideal of euphoria and the Judeo-Christian religious tradition. To know that Arnold understands religion in essentially the same "Hellenic" fashion as Spinoza and Schleiermacher will be of the greatest importance when one considers what he means by saying, as he eventually does, that religion is replaceable by poetry.

History, Religion, and the Best Self

How does this central Arnoldian concept of the Best Self, with its classical, Spinozan, and Schleiermachian roots, fit into his concept of historical process and the individual's relation to that process? The ideal of all humanity existing in a state of inner perfection is, in Arnold's view, the con-

summation toward which history moves, just as in traditional religious thought all history moves toward the City of
God, the realization of God's Kingdom on Earth.

> And because men are all members of one great whole,
> and the sympathy which is in human nature will not al-
> low one member to be indifferent to the rest or to have
> a perfect welfare independent of the rest, the expansion
> of our humanity, to suit the idea of perfection which
> culture forms, must be a *general* expansion. Perfec-
> tion, as culture conceives it, is not possible while the
> individual remains isolated. The individual is required,
> under pain of being stunted and enfeebled in his own
> development if he disobeys, to carry others along with
> him in his march towards perfection. . . . And here,
> once more, culture lays on us the same obligation as
> religion, which says, as Bishop Wilson has admirably
> put it, that "to promote the kingdom of God is to in-
> crease and hasten one's own happiness" (*Prose Works,*
> V, 95).

Although Arnold thus insists upon the social realization of
his ideal of *euphuia* and although he sees this realization as
something which must necessarily take place in history, the
ideal itself he conceives of, as traditional Christianity conceives of God, as ontologically independent of the socio-his-
torical process.

For Arnold, as for Carlyle before and Pater after him, the
historical process reduces itself ultimately to the development of mind or Spirit, to what he likes to call Zeitgeist.
Zeitgeist is virtually identified by him with the development
of specifically intellectual or philosophical concepts, a development brought about by the "born thinkers," the "speculative few" (*Prose Works,* III, 65-67). This "vast movement of speculation," Arnold appears to be saying, is the

essential *progressive* or *dynamic* element in human experience and hence the basis of history (*Prose Works,* III, 65-68; VI, 92). These intellectual acts cannot and ought not to remain the exclusive property of the elite but must "filter . . . down" to the "scantily-instructed many" (*Prose Works,* III, 44). Ideally this should happen gradually so that the many have time to adjust themselves to new and unsettling ideas, but the process can take place, particularly in the modern world, with dangerous speed causing social convulsion and even bringing on anarchy, as in the case of the French Revolution (*Prose Works,* III, 265-69). It is one of the primary functions of criticism to ensure the "safe," the emotionally and politically acceptable, transition of ideas from the few to the many. But whatever the nature of the transition, the main point is the same: continuously developing intellectual ideas are the prime movers of the historical process. Philosophy and thought says Arnold in *St. Paul and Protestantism* (1870) are the "seat of the developing force" of human culture. "Thought and science follow their own law of development, they are slowly elaborated in the growth and forward pressure of humanity" (*Prose Works,* VI, 92). That is, the growth and forward pressure of humanity express or are the products of the independent development of thought and science. It is very likely that exposure to Hegelian thought had not a little to do with Arnold's concept here of ideas moving history forward. This does not mean that he seriously studied Hegel, for it seems unlikely that he ever did. He had enough secondhand knowledge of him, however, both through the atmosphere of Balliol College, Oxford in the forties (where Jowett succeeded in establishing Hegel as the pre-eminent master of modern thought) and through secondary sources, such as Victor Cousin, François Guizot, Heinrich Heine, Ernest Renan, and David

Strauss, to pick up the notion of developing thought or Reason as the essence and moving power of historical process, as well as the ultimate goal or Absolute toward which history proceeds.[56] Arnold's Hegelianizing is, of course, not carried on on any high metaphysical plane. What he has absorbed, simply, are two fundamental concepts. The first is that Reason or Geist is the motivating force behind historical process. The second is that this Reason develops in a "vast movement" from one intellectual form or *Weltanschauung* to another through time: the "forms in which the human spirit tries to express the inexpressible . . . have or can have, for the follower of perfection, [nothing] necessary or eternal" about them; they are simply phases in "man's total spiritual growth" (*Prose Works,* V, 250-51).

Ultimately, however, whatever Arnold's debt to contemporary Hegelianizing, his attitude toward Zeitgeist and its emanation, history, is radically different from anything in Hegel. Far from making reason and the progress of reason an Absolute, as Hegel does, Arnold characteristically seeks to go beneath the constantly changing forms of Geist to what he takes to be the emotional and instinctual core of human nature. It is there in what he calls the Best Self that he finds his Absolute and not in history. Let us recall his redefinition of religious experience: to discover the enduring kernel of religious experience is, in effect, to dispose of the husk of intellectuality and hence of Hegelian Geist. "Intellectual ideas, which the majority of men take from the age in which they live, are the dominion of [the] Time-Spirit; not moral and spiritual life, which is original in each individual" (*Prose Works,* III, 77).

What one has here is a continuation in the mature Arnold of the extreme misgivings about historical process, and the desire to escape that process, which I have argued permeate the early poetry. The difference is that Arnold now has a much clearer notion than in his early poetry of a positive alternative to the flux of history. That flux, that endless march of mind, for him as for Carlyle, had destroyed the possibility of traditional belief and in doing so threatened the foundations of society. Unlike Carlyle (and Hegel) he was not able to bring the flux under control by idealizing the Geist behind it and postulating a distant goal of Absolute Truth, toward which Geist ever tended. He had instead to get outside history, not as religion does by embracing the otherworldly idea of God that transcends time, but to what I have called the Stoical ideal which rests not in the transcendent beyond but in the psychological and emotional roots of human nature, roots which for Arnold were far more real than any intellectualist Time-Spirit or mystical Absolute.

So far I have discussed the Stoical ideal of the Best Self primarily as a general ontological concept, a concept of absolute value which may be contrasted, on the one hand, to the theist's belief in a supernatural Being and, on the other, to the rationalist's belief in the sovereignty of reason. It remains to say a word about what that Best Self is in itself, to analyze the concept in order to see what qualities in particular Arnold considered ought to make up the finely tempered nature. This analysis, interesting in itself, will be particularly relevant when I discuss the various criteria Arnold applies to the judgment of poetry.

The Principles of Human Nature

Human nature, Arnold says, is a "composite thing" made up of several "instincts" (*Prose Works,* V, 177). These he conceives of both passively as "urgent needs" and more actively as "powers" or "forces." For the sake of convenience I shall refer to them simply as principles.

The greatest sin is to live so that only one side of one's nature receives satisfaction or expression; the greatest happiness is to feel all sides interrelating together in harmonious unity. "The sure truth [is] that the human spirit cannot live aright if it lives at one point only, that it can and ought to live by several points at the same time."[57] Arnold's account of the several principles that must work together in human perfection and how they stand in relation to one another is not always very clear and never systematic. It is, rather, a series of largely experimental efforts in separate essays from the Inaugural Lecture of 1857 down to "Literature and Science" some twenty years later that isolate and explain the principal needs and instincts of basic human nature through the examination of various literary or quasi-literary expressions from all ages, from Greek drama to the latest products of the French theater, from a hymn of St. Francis to a Shiite Muslim passion play. In general, however, Arnold works from a fundamental distinction between the *intellectual* and the *moral* principles in man. This distinction is clearly at work in the Inaugural Lecture where he discusses the modern age as one in need of "intellectual deliverance" as opposed to "moral deliverance." It is still more prominent in the mature Arnold's greatest effort in social criticism, *Culture and Anarchy,* where the predominantly intellectual principle of Hellenism is set against the moral one of Hebraism, and perfection becomes the just combination of the two. Arnold's ultimate source for this duality of human impulses is, as with so much of his thought, almost certainly Greek philosophy. Aristotle in the *Ethics*, a standard text for him from his school days, divides virtue into "two kinds, intellectual and moral," the one largely the result of "teaching," the other the "child of habit."[58] Similarly Plato in the *Protagoras* is preoccupied by the apparent conflict between and ultimate reconciliation of knowledge and virtue, a doctrine which Arnold late in life (1877) refers to as "the old and true Socratic thesis of the interdependence of virtue and knowledge." He then goes on to quote his former tutor Jowett: " 'the moral and intellectual are always dividing, yet they must be reunited, and in the highest conception of them are inseparable' " (*Prose Works,* VIII, 162). Though these two principles do not exhaust Arnold's concept of the composition of the Best Self, they are the ones which clearly dominate his thought.

"An intellectual deliverance," writes Arnold in 1857, "is the peculiar demand of [our age]" (*Prose Works,* I, 18). What he means by intellectual deliverance is not the discovery of any particular truth about the nature of things. It is, rather, the satisfaction of a need, felt instinctively or emotionally, for rational order. A particular world view, for example, the Roman Catholicism of Dante, may offer such an experience, but Arnold holds no brief for any one philosophical or religious interpretation of experience. He is saying simply that human nature needs a sense of order and for this any truth, any coherent "Idea of the World" will do. The present age like every modern age presents a "spectacle of a vast multitude of [confused] facts"; because we cannot connect these facts or rationalize them, we suffer a disconcerting "impatient irritation of mind." To regain our composure we need a "true point of view from which to contemplate this spectacle"; we need "a rational arrangement and appreciation of facts" (*Prose Works,* I, 20, 25). May we not, Arnold questions at one point quoting his much-admired Étienne de Sénancour, assume "that the tendency to order forms an essential part of our propensities, our *instinct,* just like the tendency to self-preservation, or to the reproduction of the species?" (*Prose Works,* V, 297.) Of the several principles of human nature which Arnold discusses, this intellectual principle is, at least until about 1870, the most important for him, the one he wants to emphasize above all others. One sees this in his politics when, for instance, in 1867, the uprooting of the Hyde Park railings drew this comment on the sacredness of the rationally, if somewhat arbitrarily ordered state.

A State in which law is authoritative and sovereign, a firm and settled course of public order, is requisite if man is to bring to maturity anything precious and lasting now, or to found anything precious and lasting for the future.

Thus, in our eyes, the very framework and exterior order of the State, whoever may administer the State, is sacred (*Prose Works,* V, 223).

Not to recognize this principle is to be without "intelligence," without "light." One sees it as well in his frustration with the "hideous anarchy" of English literature in 1862 (*Prose Works,* III, 64) and in his wish that English criticism, on the model of the French Academy, might take up the task of sorting things out according to some natural principle. And one sees it in his poetic theory, in his aesthetic preferences, as I shall show in the next chapter. In sum, before 1870 Arnold everywhere gives priority of place to the mind's demand for an *ordo concatenatioque veri* ("an order and sequence of truth") as he once expressed it in complaining of what he took to be the chaos of Ruskin's thought (*Letters,* I, 58). The reason for this particular emphasis lies primarily in his interpretation of the nature of the modern age as an age in which the complexity of civilization is in danger of overcoming both individual sanity and social integrity; this interpretation in turn comes, as I have indicated, from his father's Viconian doctrine of the nature of the modern.[59]

After 1870 Arnold became increasingly concerned with the moral rather than intellectual needs of society, partly as a result of the collapse of his intellectual models, the French, before the German army in that year, for "want of a serious conception of righteousness" (*Letters,* II, 55). His emphasis accordingly began to shift. In 1867-68, the great force of his rhetoric was still aimed at promoting Hellenism, the Platonic "instinct" for a "firm intelligible law of things" (*Prose Works,* V, 177). By 1870-71 he had begun to talk a good deal more about conduct being three-fourths of life.

The concept of intellectual deliverance is fairly straightforward. Rather more complicated is that of moral deliverance. In 1857 Arnold had simply opposed the moral principle to the intellectual, saying that the former brought a feeling of "consolation" rather than of rational order. In July 1863 having just regretted in an essay on Heine that the German poet's intellectual power was not matched by a balancing moral one, Arnold went on to write an essay on Marcus Aurelius in which he addressed himself specifically to the problem of what is meant by moral deliverance. In large part, the essay is a response to J. S. Mill's discussion of morality, and in particular the relative merits of pagan and Christian morality, in *On Liberty* (1859). Mill had concluded that, all things considered, the pagan moral system though far from perfect was decidedly superior to the Christian. Although Arnold was, of course, exceedingly sympathetic to the pagan moral outlook, Mill's rather unqualified rejection of Christian morality evidently annoyed him and seems to have set him thinking about what, after all, Christianity had added to the concept of morality. Mill's main objection to Christian morality was that it is "essentially a doctrine of passive obedience."[60] Arnold's answer, in effect, is that it is the object of morality in general, Christian or other, to make people obey (recall Spinoza's argument on Biblical "truth" above). Morality must "take possession of human life" and "give it happiness by establishing it in the practice of virtue"; this it does by "prescribing to human life. . .fixed rules of conduct" (*Prose Works,* III, 133). The specific advantage of Christian morality over pagan is that it makes people obey willingly, indeed, joyfully. Obedience to moral rules per se must be for the sage alone.

> The mass of mankind have neither force of intellect enough to apprehend them clearly as ideas, nor force of character enough to follow them as laws. The mass of mankind can be carried along a course full of hardship for the natural man. . .only by the tide of a joyful and bounding emotion. . . . [T]he noblest souls of whatever creed, the pagan Empedocles as well as the Christian Paul, have insisted on the necessity of an inspiration, a joyful emotion, to make moral action perfect (*Prose Works,* III, 134).

The question remains, what is it, after all, that brings this joyful willingness to obedience? Here Arnold finds himself forced back on the concept of religion. In the nature of religious belief there is something which makes morality easier. "The paramount virtue of religion is that it has *lighted up* morality; that it has supplied the emotion and inspiration needful for carrying the sage along the narrow way perfectly, for carrying the ordinary man along it at all" (*Prose Works,* III, 135). What particularly there is about

religion, or as Arnold later prefers, the "religious sentiment," that "lights up" morality and raises it above a merely
passive resignation to external control, Arnold does not
really say in this essay on Aurelius. Just under a year later he
takes up the theme again in "Pagan and Medieval Religious
Sentiment." An obvious objection to Arnold's argument in
"Marcus Aurelius" is that the pagans also had a religion
which presumably could have lighted up their morality just
as the Christian religion lights up its morality. Now in
"Pagan and Medieval Religious Sentiment" he turns to the
problem of describing what specifically there is in the
Christian understanding of religion that carries it beyond
pagan religious sentiment, or at least a particular phase of
that sentiment. Pagan religious sentiment is represented by
Theocritus (b.c. 312 B.C.) and Christian, by St. Francis
(1182-1226). The contrast that Arnold seeks to draw is that
between pagan materialism and sensuousness, in which there
is nothing elevating, and Christian spiritualism, which is
one of the sublimest experiences mankind has known.

> Now the poetry of Theocritus's hymn is poetry treating
> the world according to the demand of the senses; the
> poetry of St. Francis's hymn is poetry treating the de-
> mand of the heart and imagination. The first takes the
> world by its outward, sensible side; the second by its in-
> ward, symbolical side. The first admits as much of the
> world as is pleasure-giving; the second admits the whole
> world . . . painful and pleasure-giving, all alike, but all
> transfigured by the power of spiritual emotion (*Prose
> Works,* III, 225).

St. Francis, says Arnold, is the "beginning of a mighty
stream" that leads to Dante. In an early Oxford lecture on
Dante (which he did not publish), Arnold notes that Dante's
particular characteristic is that "of sacrificing the world to

the spirit, of making the spirit all in all" (*Prose Works,* III, 4). These "spiritual longings" of Dante's and St. Francis', it seems to me, come as close as anything he ever offers to describing what exactly he means by the joy that religion brings to morality. Again, he does not in any way affirm the existence of an otherworldly Being as the object of St. Francis' or Dante's longings any more than in the case of intellectual deliverance he affirms a belief in a particular philosophical synthesis as the object of mankind's longing for rational order. He is talking simply about an emotional condition or need, a need for a sense of complete and mystic transcendence above the material, natural order.

Arnold, then, closely associates morality with religion, which is not especially unusual except that religion here is in a decidedly utilitarian and naturalistic position. Religion seems important to Arnold, not in itself so much as in its capacity to make morality, obedience to fixed rules of conduct, more attractive to the ordinary man. And the particular way it makes this man happy is by giving him, not a conviction about the truth of things but a feeling, a sentiment of spiritual freedom from material necessity; obedience and self-control is, presumably, the price one pays for this joyous feeling of transcendence. Arnold's attempt in these 1863 essays to describe the nature of morality and the bearing of religion on morality is but a preliminary and fragmentary effort that he was later to extend at great length in his specifically religious writings, *St. Paul and Protestantism* (1870), *Literature and Dogma* (1873), *God and the Bible* (1875). Bear in mind that for all the time Arnold spent on defining the moral principle, it was still for him but a part, the Hebraic part, of the harmoniously developed self. The "highest spiritual life" lay, as I have indicated, in the satisfaction of *all* the principles of human nature.

Such a consummation is certainly what Arnold is seeking to suggest when he introduces the concept of *imaginative reason* at the end of "Pagan and Medieval Religious Sentiment." Neither Theocritus nor St. Francis, he writes, represent complete natures. What one wants is a "balance" of the moral or "religious sense" with the "thinking-power" or "reason"; one wants, that is, an ideal of "imaginative reason" by which all "modern epochs" must live (*Prose Works,* III, 230-33).[61] The argument is terribly abbreviated and not entirely consistent with what has gone before, but, recalling *Culture and Anarchy,* one can say that Arnold here is making his first tentative attempt to draw together the two main threads of his account of the principles of human nature, the intellectual and the moral, into an ideal synthesis which will constitute the complete, well-balanced nature. In Arnold's greatest work on the Best Self, *Culture and Anarchy,* this ideal of the imaginative reason simply becomes the ideal of "culture"; the emotional ingredients are essentially the same. The only difference is an increased emphasis in the concept of culture on the *social* dimension of the imaginative reason, on imaginative reason as a spiritual bond, which works like any other social belief to hold the nation together and preserve it from anarchy.

By the time Arnold came to "Literature and Science" in 1882 he had expanded his concept of the powers of human nature to four. There are the old intellectual and moral powers, but in addition there are the powers of beauty and of social life. Actually, these are not new powers so much as articulations of qualities that Arnold had touched upon in earlier discussions. By the power of social life he appears to mean something on the order of the need for a sense of social communion and responsibility as opposed to the sort of individualism and defeatism that one finds, say, in a Lucretius. This is a need which is implicit in his discussion

MATTHEW ARNOLD

of the case for making culture prevail in *Culture and Anarchy*. What he means by the power of beauty is something I must leave for the next chapter.

At the close of his lecture on the "Cultivation of Religion" Schleiermacher writes that "religion and art stand together like kindred beings, whose inner affinity, although mutually unrecognised and unsuspected appears in various ways. Like the opposite poles of two magnets, being mutually attracted, they are violently agitated but cannot overcome their gravity so as to touch and unite."[62] Throughout his efforts to formulate a new spiritual basis for society, Arnold (who almost certainly read these words) is entirely aware of the "inner affinity" between art and religion, so much so that his development of the concept of the Best Self can scarcely be separated from his concept of the nature of poetic excellence.

> I do not for a moment hold [the religious life] cheap; but there is an edification proper to all our stages of development, the highest as well as the lowest and it is for man to press on towards the highest stages of his development, with the certainty that for those stages, too, means of edification will not be found wanting. Now certainly it is a higher state of development when our fineness of perception is keen than when it is blunt. And if, — whereas the Semitic genius placed its highest spiritual life in religious sentiment, and made that the basis of its poetry, — the Indo-European genius places its highest spiritual life in the imaginative reason, and makes that the basis of its poetry, we are none the better for wanting the perception to discern a natural law, which is, after all, like every natural law, irresistible (*Prose Works,* III, 368-69).

From what Arnold says here, it would seem that his view of the affinity between the "highest spiritual life" of the "imaginative reason" — his substitute for conventional religion — and art was one of cause and effect: the ideal of imaginative reason is the *basis* of poetic excellence. It is also true that, in an important sense, Arnold's concept of aesthetic excellence lies at the basis of his ideal of imaginative reason. What I have called his fear of history, his melancholic preoccupation with the decline of civilization before the relentless march of Zeitgeist, drove him inward upon the self in search of a constant spiritual-cum-emotional condition beyond the power of the vicissitudes of developing speculative culture (Geist) to disrupt. That condition he found philosophically in the work of Epictetus, Spinoza, and Schleiermacher, but more immediately he seems to have found it in the experience of art. It is not just Epictetus, he writes in that early sonnet already noticed, but Homer and Sophocles who "prop" his soul. In the end, Arnold's criteria for poetry and for the highest spiritual life are the same, which is another way of saying that what Arnold was engaged in was, pace Schleiermacher, an attempt to bring the affinity of religion and art into an identity. On the surface of it, this is not too different from what Carlyle was doing except in Arnold's case the basis of the identity is not, as with Carlyle, an idealist, or as I. A. Richards would say, a revelationist one. It was a thoroughly naturalistic, or perhaps better, psychologistic one, and this essential difference made for quite a new approach to poetics on Arnold's part.

4

A REFORMER IN
POETICAL MATTERS

Arnold, H. W. Garrod once remarked, has had the "ill-luck to be best remembered by a travesty of his views on the relation between poetry and moral ideas."[1] This was true when Garrod first said it in 1929—only a year before in the Preface to the latest edition of *The Sacred Wood* Eliot had written, if not exactly a travesty, certainly a significant distortion of Arnold's position on the relation between poetry and morality:

> [It] will not do . . . to call [poetry] a "criticism of life," than which no phrase can sound more frigid to anyone who has felt the full surprise and elevation of a new experience of poetry. And certainly poetry is not the inculcation of morals, or the direction of politics; and no more is it religion or an equivalent of religion, except by some monstrous abuse of words.[2]

I think it safe to say that Garrod's point continues by and large to be true today. What Wimsatt and Brooks write in their *Literary Criticism* (1957) seems to me to express something like the standard mid-twentieth century attitude toward Arnold as critic of literature, an attitude which sees his work blending in comfortably with the dominant didacticism and moralism of the Victorian period: "Very simply, very characteristically, and very repetitiously, Arnold spent his career in hammering the thesis that poetry is a 'criticism of life.' This led to a spectacular involvement in some of the difficulties that have always appeared for didactic theory."[3]

There is no question that the issue of poetry's relation to moral and religious ideas is one of the most important critical problems Arnold deals with. It is an oversimplification of Arnold's position, however, to act as if he had no serious concerns beyond didactic ones and to fail to give him due credit for his reaction against a criticism and a poetic practice that does not take sufficient account of the formal aspects of poetry. In another essay Eliot complains of Arnold that he is too "little concerned [in his criticism] with poetry from the maker's point of view."[4] I would have said, on the contrary, that in the context of Victorian poetics, Arnold stands as the leading representative of a classicist and formalist reaction against Romantic expressionism and as one of the greatest advocates of his time of the proposition that poetry is very much a matter of craftsmanship. It is worth quoting in this context a letter of 1849 to his sister "K" in which he shows a characteristic sense of being in combat with the inadequate critical standards of his day:

> I feel rather as a reformer *in poetical matters*. . . . If I have health and opportunity to go on, I will shake the *present methods* until they go down. . . . More and more I feel bent against the modern English habit (too much encouraged by Wordsworth) of using poetry as a channel for thinking aloud, instead of making anything.[5]

Looking at the contemporary reaction to Arnold as poet and critic, one finds that his sense of his own position "as a reformer in poetical matters" was largely shared, although not always approved, by the literary world around him. Henry James, whom Wimsatt and Brooks single out among later nineteenth-century critics as having produced an "aesthetically acceptable" statement of "a moral perspective upon literature," was a great admirer of Arnold's criticism.[6] In 1865 James found Arnold's position remarkable among contemporary English critical performances for its "exclusively literary character."[7] James's judgment is not an isolated one. J. A. Froude, W. C. Roscoe, W. E. Aytoun, J. C. Shairp, C. Patmore, all see Arnold as the voice of the "classical school." Though they all regret what they take to be his exaggerated devotion to the Greeks, all are to some degree prepared to recognize and appreciate the attempt he is making to bring a new self-consciousness about "beauty of form" to English poetics.[8] Roscoe, for instance, congratulates Arnold for recognizing that "in the study of Greek literature a poet may learn much of the beauty that lies in form" and that "what our modern literature most wants is a sense of the value of completeness and finish in this respect."[9]

To be sure, there are not many examples in Arnold's criticism of the close technical discussion of poetry that Eliot and, following him, modern critics in general, have called for. Arnold's formalist precepts are not matched with a significant body of practical criticism; he was always, as Eliot complains, inclined to go "for game outside of the literary preserve altogether."[10] But I do not believe this need alter the fact that Arnold's criticism by precept, if not practice, did a great deal more than that of any other critic of his generation to awaken his countrymen to their responsibility to the formal side of the poetical. This, it seems to me, must be the proper point of departure for a consideration of Arnold as critic: the recognition that however moralistic and didactic he may seem by twentieth-century standards, in the

1850s and early sixties his was a rather lonely English voice urging upon critics and poets alike the distinctly *aesthetical,* "literary character" of poetry.

"Neotato Classicism"[11]: *Arnold's Formalism*

Arnold, as I have suggested, was entirely self-conscious about his classicist and formalist mission to England, the "stronghold of the romantic school" (*Prose Works,* I, 39). I think it important to ask why he undertook it in the first place, why he should have felt it necessary to urge upon his countrymen the importance of the "immortal beauty of consummate form." Alba Warren in his discussion of Arnold in *English Poetic Theory* has suggested that the whole classical enterprise was a "desperate — and romantic — escape from the unresolved problems of his personality and his art."[12] What exactly these problems were and more importantly why an "escape" to a formalist aesthetic should help, I am not sure from Warren's account. In any event, it seems to me that less sensational explanations are available besides those that depend upon postulating deep inner conflicts in Arnold, who seems, after all, to have been a man of almost philistinic self-possession.

Arnold virtually identified the beauty of consummate form with the aesthetic accomplishments of the ancients and, in particular, of fifth-century Greece. The son of Dr. Arnold was, of course, bound to have had a strong predisposition in favor of the classics. The great works of Greek and Roman literature, Thomas Arnold would tell his Rugby boys, show us the workings of a mind that is not only "in all the essential points of its composition our own," "but our own mind developed to an extraordinary degree of perfection."[13] Behind these remarks is the Viconian concept of historical cycles which the last chapter emphasized. When Matthew Arnold started to urge the imitation of the ancients upon his contemporaries in 1853, he was convinced, like his father, that history in the process of repeating its fundamental cycles had brought the English round to a point of civilization where their advanced intellectual self-consciousness and the complexity of social arrangements demanded a classical literary expression parallel to that found in the great Greek poets of that magical period of the fifth century B.C. The revolution in favor of formalism which Matthew Arnold was promoting, then, has at its base not psychological problems or even, as contemporary critics were inclined to suggest, a blind Rugbean/Oxonian devotion to the ancients but a theory of historical process, imbibed from his father no doubt at a very early age, according to which the modern era was intellectually ripe for a classical revival. This is the first and fundamental connection between Arnold's critical concerns and his view of history. As we shall see, the connection becomes increasingly more complex, but before going into these complexities I want to clarify exactly what constitutes Arnold's formalism or "neotato classicism."

There are two main themes to the formalist side of Arnold's criticism: "architectonics" and "grand style." Although both were in his view absolutely essential to the highest poetic excellence, it is probably architectonics which was just slightly more important for him.

The need for an architecturally ordered poem, the poem with all its parts reasonably "grouped" into a symmetrical whole, is one that Arnold never tired of pressing on his readers from the earliest letters to the last essays. To Clough in 1848, he wrote of the "atmosphere of modern feeling" with its "multitude of new thoughts and feelings." He mentioned that he, as poet, was straining to "unite matter" rather than express it in all its uncontrolled variety (*Letters to Clough,*

p. 65). Again in 1852, reacting against Keats' profusion of sensuous imagery and elaborate diction he tells Clough that "the language style and general proceeding of a poetry which has such an immense task to perform [as that of the modern age], must be very plain, direct and severe: it must not loose itself in parts and episodes and ornamental work, but must press forwards to the whole (*Letters to Clough,* p. 124).

Very much the same point is made a few months later in the 1853 Preface. This essay is often taken to be primarily about the subject matter of poetry,[14] but the question of subject matter, though important to Arnold here, is not quite central. He wants the poet to imitate "some noble and severe action" outside himself, an action which has to a large degree been formed by tradition (the "old mythic story"), rather than to follow the Romantic and Spasmodic practice of writing a " 'true allegory of the state of one's own mind' " (*Prose Works,* I, 8). Most important to him is what the poet does with that subject matter, how he *shapes* or *structures* it. The "radical difference between [Greek] poetical theory and ours" is that

> with us attention is fixed mainly on the value of separate thoughts and images which occur in the treatment of an action. They regarded the whole; we regard the parts. . . .

and that

> what distinguishes the artist from the more amateur, says Goethe, is *Architectonicè* in the highest sense; that power of execution, which creates, forms, and constitutes: not the profoundness of single thoughts, not the richness of imagery, not the abundance of illustration (*Prose Works,* I, 5, 9).[15]

The focus on architectonics as the primary formal condition of poetic excellence continues throughout Arnold's work. In the Inaugural Lecture it is associated not only with the "regulative laws" of aesthetics but with the cultural condition of "intellectual deliverance" in the age of Pericles (*Prose Works,* I, 35-36). Since this lecture has already been discussed at some length, the only point I want to add here is that the lecture makes it quite clear that by architectonics Arnold means the "intellectual instinct" at work in poetics; the architecturally ordered poem is analogous to the well-ordered state, and so on, as an expression of man's desire for an *ordo concatenatioque veri.*

In 1858 Arnold wrote a Preface to his poem *Merope,* itself a self-conscious attempt to re-create the effect of Sophoclean "beauty of form" for a Romantic age (*Prose Works,* I, 39). The essay is an extended and extremely competent defense of classicism and, in particular, the value of the "peculiar distinctness and symmetry which constitutes the vital force of Greek tragic forms" (*Prose Works,* I, 62). Later, as Arnold moved out of his predominantly classical phase (about 1861-62), he still retained a fundamental bias in favor of the principle of architectonics. The penultimate Oxford lecture on "The Literary Influence of Academies" (June 1864) provides as good an example of this as any. Here he pays just so much deference to the Romantic tradition as to concede that in poetry genius "is the first thing" (*Prose Works,* III, 238). He then goes on to say, however, that it is not genius, that is, originality and energy of creativity, that English poetry needs — this it has plenty of — but *intellect.* By intellect he means that principle in an artist which is responsible for producing the "form, the method of evolution, the precision, the proportions, the relation of the parts to the whole" (*Prose Works,* III, 238). As the lecture unfolds, Arnold

characteristically associates the qualities of energy and originality that make up genius with their excesses, "crudeness,
provincialism, eccentricity, violence, blundering" (*Prose
Works,* III, 241). He concludes that though genius can
bring the literature of a society up to a particular stage of
culture, what is needed is a further advance onto a cultural
"platform where alone the best and highest intellectual work
can be said fairly to begin": "Work done after men have
reached this platform is *classical;* and that is the only work
which, in the long run, can stand" (*Prose Works,* III, 245).

Moving on in Arnold's career to the late essay on Keats
(1880), the criterion of architectonics still remains very
much at the center of things. Whereas Keats in 1853 had
been presented as a prime example of Romantic violation of
the principle of wholeness (*Prose Works,* I, 10), by 1880 Arnold has discovered a new Keats, one who showed clear signs
of developing an intellectual, as against merely sensuous,
tendency before he died. The truth that Keats discovered,
writes Arnold in the later essay, is that the "beautiful" is not
the sensuous; rather, it "is an intellectual and spiritual passion." It is " 'connected and made one,' as Keats declares
. . . 'with the ambition of the intellect.' "[16] Keats recognized
this theoretically, but did not, unfortunately, live to realize
it poetically: "For the architectonics of poetry, the faculty
which presides at the evolution of works like the *Agamemnon* or *Lear,* he was not ripe" (*Essays II,* p. 120). In this essay on Keats, Arnold comes very close indeed to identifying
beauty with architectonics, which, again, is the same as
identifying it with the intellectual principle in poetry. Although he does not, in fact, go quite so far as this, the near
approach is a sufficient indicator of his aesthetic priorities.
Beauty is pre-eminently not a thing of genius, or self expression, or sensuousness; it is the manifestly self-conscious intel-

lectual "grouping" of experience toward a "total impression."

Closely related to architectonics is Arnold's rather better known criterion of the *grand style*. Arnold characteristically finds both qualities in the poets he considers truly great, Sophocles, Dante, Shakespeare, Milton, Goethe, and Wordsworth, and it is not always easy to disengage the one from the other; still there does appear to be a real distinction between the two in Arnold's mind. By grand style he means not the overall structure of the poem but the "movement and manner" of individual lines. The famous "touchstone" method of criticism, first used by Arnold in the Homer lectures of 1860-61 and later (1880) offered as the key to the "study of poetry," is not a method of judging poetic wholes but of evaluating the quality of the poet's local expression. The distinction here recalls that of J. C. Ransom between structure and texture in a poem, although Ransom, of course, does not mean by texture what Arnold means by grand style. Moreover, Arnold does seem to consider that it is possible for a poet to achieve the grand style without achieving the higher excellence of architectonics. Homer, who is the greatest master of grand style, but whom Arnold never commends for architectonics, is the most important example of this. Conversely, perfection of overall structure is possible without achieving grand style, as one sees in Voltaire's classically ordered but shallow art (*Prose Works,* I, 50-51). The greatest poets, however, are those who exhibit both these formal qualities in full measure.

Arnold was always reluctant to define the grand style. He wanted the concept to retain a certain flexibility, even to have an air of mystery about it. It is like faith, he writes at one point, either you have it or you do not, and those who do not must be content "to die in their sins" (*Prose Works,* I,

188). Still, he has by direct explanation and example provided enough information to make clear generally what he means. An essential element of grand style is simplicity or severity of speech (*Prose Works*, I, 188). This is not a question simply of diction; Arnold is thinking of the far more complex problem of the total movement and quality of the line, which includes besides diction, questions of syntax and meter. Syntax, he says, expresses the poet's "evolution of thought," and the nature of the syntax depends upon the level of intellectual sophistication in the poet. Homer is a poet of "unrivalled clearness and straightforwardness [in] his thinking; in the way in which he keeps to one thought at a time, and puts that thought forth in its complete natural plainness" (*Prose Works,* I, 114).

Opposed to the clearness and straightforwardness of thought and language in Homer there are, Arnold appears to be saying, two forms of artistically unacceptable stylistic complexity, a sophisticated and an unsophisticated one. In his translation of the *Iliad,* Pope has produced a "literary and intellectualized" Homer: "One feels that Homer's thought has passed through a literary and rhetorical crucible, and come out highly intellectualized" (*Prose Works,* I, 114). It does not follow from this that Homer's thought and language are, as many of Arnold's contemporaries were inclined to believe, "primitive."[17] For Arnold, Homer's thought and language are early modern, not so advanced as Sophocles', but far more so than the thought and language of the European Middle Ages. In George Chapman's sixteenth-century translation of the *Iliad* there are still the "grotesqueness . . . conceits . . . irrationality" of the Middle Ages, which are not truly Homeric: "Homer expresses himself like a man of adult reason, Chapman like a man whose reason has not cleared itself" (*Prose Works,* I, 113).

So far Arnold is expressing essentially the same desire for intellectual precision and clarity, the distaste for the elaborate, the complex, the overcrowded, that underlies the concept of architectonics. But the grand style goes beyond simplicity and intelligibility; it has as well the absolutely indispensable quality of *nobleness* (*Prose Works,* I, 121). It is this nobility of manner that, in the end, most distinguishes the grand style from everything else; to the basic ingredient of simplicity is added something which elevates and inspires. It is at this point that Arnold begins most closely to reflect the writer who is the probable source of his concept of grand style in the first place, Longinus. The grand style, says Longinus, uplifts our souls to the true sublime: we are "elevated and exalted" and "filled with joy and pride." The basis of grand style is the poet's greatness or nobility of soul, which is at once an innate moral quality and the result of "impregnating" the mind with "noble thoughts."[18] Arnold takes up both these themes. Grand style proceeds from a "noble or powerful nature" (*Prose Works,* I, 189), and it implies the "noble and profound application of ideas to life," ideas " 'On God, on Nature, and on human life' " (*Prose Works,* I, 210-11). It is this latter quality that distinguishes Homer from the primitives with whom he is often associated and places him in a position roughly analogous to that of Milton (*Prose Works,* I, 210).[19]

Arnold's examples or "touchstones"[20] of the grand style reveal the kind of character and thought he is associating with nobility. One recurring attitude is especially prominent: the expression of dignified, but pitiful human endurance in the face of great suffering.

etlen d' oi ou po tis epichthonios Brotos allos
andros paidophonio poti stoma cheir oregesthai

> (And I have endured—the like whereof no soul upon
> the earth hath yet endured—to carry to my lips the
> hand of him who slew my child.)[21]
>
> . . . . .
>
> Io non piangeva; sì dentro impietrai.
> Piangevan elli . . .
>
> (I did not weep; I was so turned to stone inside.
> They wept . . .)[22]
>
> . . . . .
>
> And courage never to submit or yield
> And what is else not to be overcome . . .
>
> (*Essays II,* p. 19)[23]

It is difficult to know from Arnold's account how the grand
style, in the form of the poetry itself, as opposed to its cognitive moral content, produces the effect of nobility. In the
case of simplicity and severity one can talk intelligibly, as
Arnold does do, of the abstract, noncognitive feeling of a
line. With nobility, however, this is rather more difficult.
Still, it does seem clear that in this concept of grand style
Arnold is with the aid of Longinus at least attempting, and I
think to some extent succeeding, to give to certain standard
Victorian assumptions about the moral functions of poetry,
assumptions regarding the expression of character, manliness, strength, and piety, a specifically aesthetic or formal
reference. This simply had not been attempted in any important way by any of his Victorian predecessors.

Finally, it will be apparent that just as architectonics is for
Arnold the formal expression of the intellectual principle in
human nature, so style, grand or otherwise, is the formal
expression of the moral principle. The luxuriant
Elizabethan style of Keats, the closely related "natural magic" of Maurice de Guérin, the "painted shell" of Tennyson's

poetry, all these expressions in poetic style of what amounts to the "pagan" fullness of sensuous life, Arnold shows a marked tendency to associate with moral enervation, with an absence of the *"virtus verusque labor* so necessary for every kind of greatness, and for the great artist, too" (*Essays II,* p. 101). On the other hand the simplicity, severity, and nobility of the grand style provide for Arnold the guarantee of adequate moral character, of the self-discipline and the inner strength necessary to confront the manifold miseries of life.

I noted in the last chapter that Arnold considered that the concept of poetic excellence was rooted in the concept of imaginative reason or the harmoniously developed Best Self. At this point one begins to see more clearly what Arnold meant by this. His principal poetic or formalistic criteria, architectonics and grand style do not exist, as it were, in a formalistic vacuum, but are intimately linked in his mind with specific elements in his concept of the Best Self. What I want to consider now are some of the larger implications of this connection between poetic criteria and the concept of the Best Self. In particular I shall be concerned, first, with the way in which the connection serves Arnold's desire to establish a permanent or "real," that is, nonhistorical, nonrelative, standard for critical judgment, and, second, with the way in which it influences his response to that problem which I have maintained is centrally characteristic of Victorian criticism, the problem of the relation between poetry and public belief.

Historicism and the Problem of Poetic Value

During the 1850s one of the most frequent charges made against Arnold was that of anachronism and artificiality. He was attempting, wrote one reviewer after another, to foist classical forms upon a modern age to which they bore no real relevance, no organic relationship. Thus Arnold's friend and fellow student at Rugby, J. C. Shairp: "We agree with [Arnold's] more hostile critics that no strength of imagination can turn back the world's sympathies to the shores of Greece, and the poet who tries to do so while his own land and all Christendom lies fresh around him is wasting himself on an unprofitable task."[24]

Arnold in effect answered such charges in the Inaugural Lecture when he drew on his father's Viconian theory of history to argue that the classics had a peculiar spiritual relevance to contemporary England. At the same time, he was not insensitive to these complaints of artificiality. One has a good sense of this from a letter of 1858 on *Merope,* a poem which must surely rank as the most painfully artificial of his efforts to imitate the ancients. The letter is to his sister Fanny, to whom he complains of the public's failure to appreciate what he was doing in *Merope.* "What I meant them was to see in it a specimen of the world created by the Greek imagination. This imagination was different from our own . . . but it had a peculiar . . . grandeur. . . . But the British public prefer, like all obstinate multitudes, to "die in their sins," and I have no intention to keep preaching in the wilderness" (*Letters,* I, 68-69).

Arnold was, in fact, the last man to believe that genuine poetic excellence could be achieved by the simple imitation of aesthetic forms of an earlier age, no matter how superior those forms might appear to present practice. Thus he repeatedly told Clough that stylistic accomplishment was something that might be learned but that the best poetry must in the end grow from the "inward poetic life," or, put another way, the form must flow organically from the artist's spiritual content. This is a constant theme of Arnold's and one perhaps best expressed in the late essay on "The Study of Poetry."

> The superior character of truth and seriousness in the matter and substance of the best poetry, is inseparable from the superiority of diction and movement marking its style and manner. The two superiorities are closely related and are in steadfast proportion one to the other" (*Essays II*, p. 22).[25]

This spiritual substance which Arnold argues is inseparable from formal qualities is to a large degree inborn and individual in the artist, but at least as important, as Arnold sees it, is the spirit of the age, and here we return to something very like Carlyle's point in "Characteristics." Without an adequate cultural condition the poet is hard put to produce his best. Thomas Gray, for instance,

> with the qualities of mind and soul of a genuine poet, was isolated in his century. Maintaining and fortifying them by lofty studies, he yet could not fully educe and enjoy them; the want of a genial atmosphere, the failure of sympathy in his contemporaries were too great (*Essays II*, p. 92).

What Arnold says here of Gray applies directly to his view of his own situation. "People do not understand," he laments to his sister "K" in 1858,

> what a temptation there is, if you cannot bear anything not *very good*, to transfer your operations to a region where form is everything. Perfection of a certain kind may there be attained . . . but to attain or approach perfection in the region of thought and feeling, and to unite this with perfection of form, demands not merely an effort and a labour but an actual tearing of oneself to pieces. . . . It is only in the best poetical epochs that

you can descend into yourself and produce the best of your thought and feeling naturally, and without an overwhelming and in some degree morbid effort; for then all the people around you are more or less doing the same thing. *It is natural, it is the bent of the time to do it;* its being the bent of the time, indeed, is what makes the time a *poetical one* (*Letters,* I, 84-85; my italics in last sentence).

The feeling of frustration expressed here becomes a major critical principle six years later.

The grand work of literary genius is a work of synthesis and exposition, not of analysis and discovery; its gift lies in the faculty of being happily inspired by a *certain order of ideas.* . . . But it must have the atmosphere, it must find itself amidst the order of ideas. . . . [For] the creation of a masterwork of literature two powers must concur, the power of the man and the power of the moment (*Prose Works* III, 261).

These remarks occur in the context of defining and justifying the "function of criticism." Arnold's point is that in "these bad days" it is criticism's highest business to help supply the necessary spiritual "atmosphere" for the creative writer.

One sees the difficulty of arguing, as some have, that Arnold in his classicism held aloof from the historicizing spirit of his age.[26] He can talk about the possibilities open to individual talent and about the enduring value of ancient aesthetic models, but, in the end, like Carlyle and, as I have maintained, the great majority of his Victorian contemporaries, he comes to recognize that the highest art does in certain crucial ways depend upon the spirit of the age. Dropped is the Romantic notion implicit in the Inaugural Lecture that the poet himself can somehow deliver the age. In its place is a far more realistic concept of the relation between poetry and history: there is, according to Arnold, a recurring spiritual condition of maturity in society, which may perhaps best be described as the Viconian modern epoch, intellectually and morally delivered. The agent of that deliverance is not the poet but the man of ideas. This man of ideas, however, is not the philosopher whose mind works on a plane far above the majority's comprehension. He is, rather, a man of letters, an interpreter to the public at large of the best that is thought and known; he is a rhetorician with the mythopoetic aspirations of a Romantic poet, but he is, after all, like so many rhetoricians, a poet manqué. In short he is, in Arnold's special understanding of the word, a *critic*.

One must not, however, conclude from this that Arnold's poetic has been swallowed up by the historicist spirit. To make the possibility of producing the highest poetry contingent upon a particular cultural situation is to recognize what seemed to the Victorians an inescapable reality, but it is not, as Arnold sees it, tantamount to subordinating aesthetic value to history. There is, rather, in his criticism as in his thought in general, a characteristic attempt to give the historicist spirit its due while at the same time keeping back a certain vital area of experience that is to remain free from historical determinism.

Arnold is, in fact, at once thoroughly alive to the historicist problem in criticism and far more subtle in dealing with it than any of his major contemporaries with the possible exception of Pater. Probably the best-known example of his resistance to the historicization of aesthetic value is found in the contrast between the historical estimate and the real estimate made in "The Study of Poetry." The historical estimate occurs, he maintains, when the critic pays more attention to the historical conditions underlying the production of the poetry than to the "real" intrinsic, ahistorical value of the poem. In its extreme form what Arnold calls the historical estimate identifies aesthetic value with poetry's success in expressing the supposed intellectual and social conditions of its age.

When Arnold wrote against this kind of estimate, he almost certainly was familiar with the work of its foremost contemporary advocate, Hippolyte Taine.[27] Taine's position amounts to a thoroughgoing and entirely unapologetic capitulation to the century's historicist tendencies. "The final explanation" of works of art, he says, lies in "the general state of mind and manners in the period to which they belonged." That is, artists' standards are set by the intellectual and social conditions of their time, and a work of art is "good" only insofar as it is in accord with these conditions.[28] As the example of Taine suggests, the historical estimate tends either to reduce the study of literature to a study of origins, or, inasmuch as it retains the concept of value at all, to make conformity to a particular historical condition the basis of value. In this case, value is always historically determined or relative, never absolute. Much as they were disposed to assume the proper historical condition or spirit of the age was necessary to the highest art, Victorian critics were in general ill-prepared to acquiesce in what for Taine was so logical an outcome of the historicist spirit, that is, the ultimate relativity of all aesthetic value. Instead, these two apparently contradictory strains of thought, historicist and normative or aesthetic, were held at one and the same time with little serious awareness of the difficulties they presented for one another or, if there was awareness, of how to overcome these difficulties. Carlyle's position is characteristic of this unresolved tension between historicist concerns and aesthetic ones. What differentiates

Arnold from Carlyle and his Victorian contemporaries in general is that he introduced a reasonable and very interesting aesthetic way out of Taine's historicist logic. Important as historical conditions are in creating a background or "atmosphere" conducive to great art, it is not, according to him, in these conditions themselves that aesthetic value lies, but in something else.

What is this something else? With what I have called Arnold's formalistic bias in mind, it might be argued that for him "real" value lies in the creation or reproduction of certain fixed poetic forms associated with ancient Greece. To an extent, this is certainly true, but it is only half the story, and the less important half at that. As I have already indicated, Arnold does not consider poetic form as existing in a vacuum. On the contrary, he closely associates the forms that are most important to him with the enduring principles of human nature, that is, the intellectual and moral principles, of which form is the aesthetic expression. In other words, whatever enduring value Arnold attributes to certain poetic forms cannot be dissociated from these forms' relation to the basic principles of human nature.

The nature of this relation may be considered from two standpoints. First, one may say, as I have interpreted Arnold above as saying, that a developed intellectual principle and a developed moral principle are necessary in the poet if he is to produce the desired formal values. To put this in a historicist context, one may add, following the implications of Arnold's letter to "K" and his remarks on Gray, that certain historical or cultural conditions make easier and more natural the balanced exercise by the poet of these principles of human nature.

On the other hand, one can view the relation between poetic form and the principles of human nature from another quite different stance and consider that the poetic forms themselves, the specifically aesthetic expressions of the harmoniously developed human nature, produce in the reader of poetry a similarly salutary state of psychic repose or balance. Poetic forms become the means of transmitting certain valuable inner qualities, the qualities of *euphuia,* from poet to reader — and this transmission occurs, incidentally, regardless of the historical situation the reader finds himself in. The point may as readily be extended to Arnold's notion of poetic content. Heine is admired for the importance of the *ideas* in his poetry: he is a noble soldier in the "liberating War of humanity" (compare Carlyle's praise of Schiller's poetry for being in the "vanguard" of the "march of Mind"). But Heine at the same time is criticized by Arnold for failing to transmute these new ideas into emotionally acceptable form; the German poet neither consoles nor rejoices the reader (*Prose Works,* III, 131-32). The instance of Arnold's reaction to Heine is not untypical. As one looks at his attitude toward the place of ideas in poetry in general, one finds a marked tendency to reduce those ideas to an undifferentiated Zeitgeist, a Zeitgeist that insofar as its intellectual content is concerned is ultimately as irrelevant to Arnold's concept of poetic value as it is to Spinoza's and Schleiermacher's view of religious experience.[29]

What this comes to is that what Arnold finds valuable in poetry, whether in its form or its content, rests on what modern aestheticians would call its *affectivist* powers or what Arnold in his less technical vocabulary calls its power to "inspirit and rejoice" (*Letters to Clough,* p. 100), to "compose and elevate" (*Prose Works,* I, 2), in its direct appeal to the "permanent affections," "to the great primary human affections: to those elementary feelings which subsist permanently in the race, and which are independent of time" (*Prose Works,* I, 4). Thus in defining the nature of the real estimate as distinct from the historical (and the personal) in "The Study of Poetry," he suggests that the "best poetry," the poetry we judge to be really excellent, we judge so because of the way it satisfies our basic psychic needs. "The best poetry will be found to have power of forming, sustaining, and delighting us, as nothing else can" (*Essays II,* p. 5). In sum, to make the true estimate, the critic must have the "tact" to know what is going on within himself when he experiences a poem.

The principle of poetic value which Arnold assumes, then, is an affectivist one, is, in essence, the same as that worked out far more systematically some twenty years later by the philosopher and critic George Santayana. Let us turn to Santayana for the elucidation of what Arnold has in mind.

> Value springs [writes Santayana] from the immediate and inexplicable reaction of vital impulse, and from the irrational part of our nature. The rational part is by its essence relative; it leads us from data to conclusions, or from parts to wholes; it never furnishes the data with which it works.
>
> . . . . .
>
> Beauty is an ultimate good, something that gives satisfaction to natural function, to some fundamental need or capacity of our minds.[30]

For Santayana as for Arnold the value of art (or of anything else, for that matter) has nothing to do with the art object's expression of cognitive truth but resides solely in the reader's immediate or intuitive emotional and moral response to that object. The correspondence between the two men's basic position on value is not, I think, simply coincidental. Santayana, like Arnold, was an admirer of Spinoza and is almost certainly drawing for his distinction between the rational and the valuable on Spinoza's distinction between intellectual and religious knowledge.[31] The great significance of this mutual dependence upon Spinoza will become apparent when I come to distinguish the particular kind of affectivism that Arnold and Santayana represent from the empiricist version of the affectivist aesthetic that exercised Carlyle's indignation.

In addition to Santayana there is another very prominent and very influential critic of the early twentieth century, I. A. Richards, who has produced a systematic elaboration of Arnold's fundamental position. Richards begins with a distinction between scientific and emotional truth that apart from its strongly linguistic bias relates closely to the distinction Arnold and Santayana make. For Richards a scientific statement is one made by the logical, discursive intellect, whereas a poetic statement is a "pseudo-statement" which appeals not to the intelligence but to the emotions or impulses. "A pseudo-statement is a form of words which is justified entirely by its effect in releasing or organising our impulses and attitudes . . . a [scientific] statement, on the other hand, is justified by its truth, i.e., its correspondence, "in a highly technical sense, with the fact to which it points."[32] The connection between Richards' poetic and Arnold's is one which Richards himself invites by using Arnold's introductory remarks to "The Study of Poetry" as the epigraph to his own *Science and Poetry* — although he is not, I believe, entirely conscious of the degree to which Arnold had anticipated not accidentally but entirely self-consciously his own point of critical departure.[33]

In making these connections between Arnold, on the one hand, and Santayana and Richards, on the other, I do not intend in any way to suggest that Arnold has approached these later theorists in sophistication of philosophical, psychological, and critical analysis. As in the case of his desire to reintroduce formalistic concerns into criticism, there is more a signal change of attitude toward the function of criticism and the nature of poetic value than a thoroughgoing theoretical development of that attitude. What I am seeking to indicate is that in the development of Arnold's thought may be seen not only the beginning of an important tradition in modern critical discourse but, more importantly, the probable reasons behind the development of that tradition.

In emphasizing the originality of Arnold's affectivist approach and its relation to the critical thought of Santayana and Richards, it is necessary to distinguish what Arnold as well as his twentieth-century continuators are doing from the psychologistic pleasure-pain approach characteristic of the empiricist strain of eighteenth-century criticism and found, for example, in Hume, Burke, Kames Gerard, and Carlyle's old nemesis, Archibald Alison.[34] From one standpoint, Arnold is, to be sure, reviving this empiricist tradition insofar as he is reasserting its essential point that aesthetic value lies not so much in the aesthetic object itself as in the onlooker's response to that object. In discussing the nature of taste (and admittedly exaggerating the tendency of the empiricist aesthetic), Hume remarks that "beauty is no quality in things themselves: it exists merely in the mind which contemplates them."[35] In Arnold's—as in Santayana's and Richards'—case the concept of aesthetic response has been vastly enlarged and deepened; it becomes something far more emotionally and morally complex than the essentially hedonistic, pleasure-pain formulae characteristic of the empiricist tradition.

Arnold's desire to focus critical attention on the inner

response to the work of art does not derive, as does the empiricist aesthetic, from skepticism over the existence of any reality outside the perceiving self. It derives, rather, from another kind of skepticism which I prefer to call historicist. This is a skepticism about the reality of objective, value-giving concepts, religious or metaphysical, that will be true for all time. His affectivist approach seeks to place value in the emotional and moral experience of the perceiver rather than in the object itself because he has ceased to believe that the truths of religion or metaphysics are anything but relative and has come instead to believe that the only truths one can be sure of are deep emotional reactions within oneself. What I am saying is that Arnold's position on the value of art is inseparable from his efforts, described in the last chapter, to redefine religious experience. The kind of response he is seeking from poetry is so thoroughly implicated with traditional moral, religious, and social values, with cultural values rather than simply sensuous and emotional experiences, that words such as "feeling" or "emotion" or "psychological effect," are not adequate to express the sort of experience that he is talking about, and it is necessary to continue to use the rather larger, value-evocative terms such as "moral" and "religious" and "Best Self" to convey Arnold's meaning.

This conflation of the psychological with the religious and moral which is evident in Arnold's poetic is present also in Santayana and Richards. When these men describe the affectivist basis of beauty it is apparent that they are describing a variety of religious and moral experience and not simply "feeling." For them the aesthetic experience is a complete harmonization of impulses that brings a transcendent calm and elevates one from the cares and concerns of the workaday world. Thus Santayana:

MATTHEW ARNOLD

Now, it is the essential privilege of beauty to so synthesize and bring to a focus the various impulses of the self,
so to suspend them to a single image, that a great peace
falls upon that perturbed kingdom. In the experience
of these momentary harmonies we have the basis of the
enjoyment of beauty, and of all its mystical meanings.
. . . [The experience of beauty] raises us above [the
world].[36]

Arnold does not make the effort that Santayana and
Richards do to analyze the nature of aesthetic experience.
Yet he shares with them the general notion that the highest
poetic experience is that in which the various "powers" or
"impulses" of human nature are brought into harmonious
unity by the perception of the art object and, as Santayana
puts it, the individual is raised above the world. There are,
moreover, times when he can be very specific and subtle indeed about the nature of the "right" poetic effect. For
example, the passage which follows seems to me to compare
favorably with anything Santayana or Richards has written
on the aesthetic "organization" of "impulses"; in it Arnold is
attempting to describe the precise effect of what for him is
the highest form of poetry. Greek tragic forms

satisfy, in the most perfect manner, some of the most
urgent demands of the human spirit. If, on the one
hand, the human spirit demands variety and the widest
possible range, it equally demands, on the other hand,
depth and concentration in its impressions. Powerful
thought and emotion, flowing in strongly marked
channels, make a stronger impression. . . . This sense of
emphatic distinctness in our impressions rises, as the
thought and emotion swell higher and higher without
overflowing their boundaries, to a lofty sense of the
mastery of the human spirit over its own stormiest
agitations; and this, again, conducts us to a state of

feeling which it is the highest aim of tragedy to produce, to a *sentiment of sublime acquiescence in the
course of fate, and in the dispensation of human life*
(*Prose Works,* I, 58-59).

Beside Santayana's and Richards' account of the experience
of beauty, Arnold's description of the effect of tragedy may
well be judged a description of emotional "unity by exclusion" rather than "inclusion."[37] Arnold characteristically,
whether as poet or critic, yearns after an inner repose of con-
tainment in which experience is straitly ordered and the
desire for emotional variety kept in its "true place," subor-
dinate to the need for "strongly marked channels." Still it is
clear that in the passage quoted above one has a pretty fully
developed anticipation of the approach Santayana and
Richards were later to take in their efforts to describe the
consummate psychic unity that they identify with the
beautiful.

Poetry and Belief

One of the great advantages of the affectivist theory of
poetic value is that it resolves the conflict between belief and
poetic enjoyment discussed in Chapter Two. By the affectivist account, poetic enjoyment does not depend upon the
literal truth of what the poem says, only upon the psychological effect of what it is saying and how it is saying it. Mill,
who was to an extent an affectivist in poetics but whose
affectivism unlike Arnold's derives directly from the English
empiricist tradition, makes this point: the peculiar nature of
poetry and what distinguishes it from science is that it is a
"representation of feeling."

[Science] addresses itself to the belief, [poetry] to the
feelings. The one does its work by convincing or per-

suading, the other by moving. The one acts by presenting a proposition to the understanding, the other by offering interesting objects of contemplation to the sensibilities.[38]

For Arnold this question of the relation between poetry and belief centers on the status of those moral and intellectual ideas which he believes essential to poetic excellence. The scientific truth of these ideas is something Arnold is never prepared to affirm. That scientific truth is undermined to begin with by Arnold's participation in the historicist tendency of the age: all moral and intellectual ideas are subject to change and correction in time; therefore, the actual truth of any one idea is subject to serious question — "there is not a creed that is not shaken, not an accredited dogma which is not shown to be questionable" (*Essays II,* p. 1). Arnold's object is to avoid the relativist implications of this outlook. To do this he has shifted the nature of truth or belief from the scientific to the emotional realm. Ideas, if not true scientifically, may be true emotionally, and it is this emotional truth that one experiences when ideas are expressed in poetry. In other words, the ideas in poetry are for Arnold beliefs that cannot be "scientifically" affirmed but which are to be valued nonetheless because they produce certain emotional effects: they console, they elevate, they rejoice. They are virtually the same experiences Richards calls "objectless beliefs," which, though they may have lost their "truth" as far as science is concerned, still have important emotional value and accordingly account for some of the "most important and valuable effects which the arts produce."[39]

Contrasting what Arnold is saying about poetry and belief with Mill's position, one discovers a significant difference. When Mill says that poetry addresses the feeling, he is speaking in a strictly empirical sense of what Carlyle despised as the pleasure principle. What he means is simply that poetry evokes simple sensations and simple emotions which the reader finds pleasurable. He is not in any way saying that the condition of feeling produced by poetry can rise to a point of complexity and inner resolution at which it may be substituted for belief. Like his mentor Bentham, whose views on poetry and truth I earlier cited, Mill maintains a strict separation between these two categories of feeling and belief. For Mill there are no conditions under which a belief could have value apart from its ability to express "scientific" truth about the nature of things. Not so for Arnold; Arnold has enlarged and sophisticated the concept of aesthetic feeling from the simple empiricist condition Mill is talking about into something that might more properly be called a moral or spiritual condition or, perhaps better, a pseudobelief. At the same time, a rationalist such as Mill is bound strenuously to object that Arnold has impoverished the concept of belief and reduced it from a scientific or rational state to an emotional one.

Again, what Arnold is saying about ideas in poetry he is saying about ideas in life as well. Hence the famous substitution of poetry for religion: "More and more mankind will discover that we have to turn to poetry to interpret life for us, to console us, to sustain us. Without poetry, our science will appear incomplete; and most of what now passes with us for religion and philosophy will be replaced by poetry" (*Essays II,* pp. 2-3). One may say, as William Madden has done, that this merging of poetry and religion relates Arnold back to the Romantic tradition in which art first began to set itself up as a substitute for religion.[40] In a more important sense, which Madden overlooks, the connection with Romanticism is misleading, for Arnold's concept of religion and of belief bears no resemblance to the various Neo-Platonic, Pantheistic, and Idealist creeds that were held by the Romantics, and, as I have argued, by Carlyle. Accordingly, what Arnold means by the identity of poetry and religious belief is not at all what they mean. They have tended to substitute poetry for orthodox religion, in the sense that they have made poetry the embodiment of the Divinity or the Absolute that Church and dogma once embodied. In this they have, as it were, brought poetry up to religion. Arnold, on the other hand, takes quite the opposite course. He has said, in effect, that religion is like poetry inasmuch as its value resides in an *emotional attitude*. He has *aestheticized* religion or brought it down to poetry. The difference is an extremely important one. For criticism it is auspicious, for it has caused attention to be redirected from what poetry is saying about truth, to how it is affecting the reader. For religion it is no doubt unfortunate.

Toward this position Arnold has been moved by nothing so much as the desire to achieve a spiritual basis, a ground for belief, that will be independent of the vicissitudes of the Zeitgeist. He has achieved his end, but only by a rather radical revaluation of the concept of belief. Perhaps the revaluation is a dubious undertaking, one likely to lead, in the end, to complete skepticism about the independent intellectual, as against poetical, truth of any concept moral, philosophical, or religious. Nonetheless it is important to note that Arnold, like Carlyle before him, is still making the effort, that he obviously continues to believe in the possibility of achieving a new formula of belief that will deliver society from the abyss of historical relativism. In Walter Pater, as we shall see, this great hope of establishing a new basis for belief has virtually disappeared.

WALTER PATER

Just as modern truth has gradually freed itself from the chains of Greek and then medieval transcendence, the modern theory of logic has withdrawn philosophy from heaven or from the peak on which it practiced its sterile contemplation of the Ideas. It has invited and constrained it to descend towards the earth, while, in the same act, it has withdrawn history from its lowly function as a collector of anecdotes, a chronicler of what happens, and has raised it towards Heaven . . . making it meet philosophy half way, embrace it and mingle with it into a new spiritual personality.

—*Croce*

5

HISTORICISM AS
WELTANSCHAUUNG

Reviewing *Marius the Epicurean* in 1885, Mrs. Humphrey Ward approved generally but had serious reservations about its author's "lack of respect for truth."[1] What disturbed her was that Pater's hero had gone through life experimenting with one intellectual or religious system and another without ever committing himself to belief in any. What Pater seemed to be saying quite clearly in this book was that any such commitment to belief was somehow wrong. "There were days when [Marius] could suspect . . . that that early, much cherished religion [of his childhood] might come to count with him as but one form of poetic beauty, or of the ideal in things; as but one voice, in a world where there were many voices it would be a moral weakness not to listen to."[2]

In making her criticism of *Marius,* Mrs. Ward was reflecting nothing so much as the moral and intellectual earnestness of that earlier generation of honest Oxford doubters to whom she was so close by family ties and friendship. I refer to men such as her father, Thomas Arnold the young-er, Arther Clough, J. A. Froude, and even her uncle Mat-thew, all of whom had had their crises of faith in accus-tomed beliefs, like Marius above, but all of whom had gone on to seek out some form of spiritual deliverance rather than abandon the possibility of belief itself. Some three years later, Pater had his chance to answer Mrs. Ward's criticism when he reviewed her popular *Robert Elsmere,* a book about just such a man as her father or Clough or Froude. In his review Pater gently suggests that Mrs. Ward's faith in the power of human reason to decide on the truth or falsity of any belief is naïve, that perhaps the whole strenuous effort of men, such as Elsmere, to deny one belief and affirm another is misguided. Pater speaks, instead, of another sort of mind, a mind which has learned to acquiesce in a stage of "philosophic uncertainty" (*Guardian,* p. 68). The point is not elaborated in this short review, but from Pater's work in general one knows that he is describing a mind that no longer finds it possible to affirm belief or disbelief in any particular system or even to fall back on the comforting notion that the sure progress of Geist, the March of Mind, will eventually bring some final and absolute revelation.

In implying, as he does, that Mrs. Ward's intellectual outlook belongs to an earlier, less philosophically sophisti-cated generation, Pater is showing a fair sensitivity to the spirit of the times. From the mid sixties onward the intellec-tual bias of the most advanced thinkers in England had be-gun to show a swing toward the condition of philosophical skepticism, or to put it more positively, toward a recognition of the many-sidedness of truth. Henry Sidgwick took cogni-zance of it in 1869:

We are growing . . . more sceptical in the proper sense of the word: we suspend our judgment much more than our predecessors, and much more contentedly: we see that there are many sides to many questions: the opinions that we do hold we hold if not more loosely, at least more at arm's length: we can imagine how they appear to others, and can conceive ourselves not holding them. . . . We are gaining in impartiality and comprehensiveness of sympathy.[3]

Sidgwick is talking, of course, not simply about reserving belief as to the truths of Christianity—although this was certainly the most important expression of contemporary skepticism—but reserving belief as to the final truth of any philosophical or religious interpretation of life. It would be difficult to find a more appropriate rendering than this of Sidgwick's of the general intellectual background behind Pater's work and, at the same time, of the distance separating his thought from that of Carlyle and of Matthew Arnold.[4] To be sure, few Victorians in the period Sidgwick is talking about went so far as Pater toward total "suspension of belief." Still, by the seventies the skeptical outlook had risen to such prominence—primarily through the offices of various adherents of the positivist outlook, Mill, Lewes, H. Spencer, George Eliot, T. H. Huxley—as to make it look as if the efforts of men such as Carlyle and Arnold (not to mention Ruskin, Newman, Maurice, and many others) to retain the possibility of some positive social belief had been but so many Teufelsdrockhian ventures in Unreality.

The Empiricist Outlook

It is important to be as specific as possible about the intellectual basis and particular character of Pater's skepticism, for these things have much to do with defining the nature of his critical outlook. When the positivist John Morley reviewed *Renaissance* in 1873, he made a distinction which still seems self-evident to many readers of Pater. He said Pater belonged to the contemporary "aesthetic movement" of Ruskin, the Pre-Raphaelites, Swinburne, Morris, and others, and that this movement was, among other things, in reaction against the commanding position J. S. Mill's *Logic* was beginning to take in the intellectual life of the nation.[5] However much these other aesthetes many have been opposed to Mill's outlook, that opposition cannot, in fact, be extended to Pater. It appears likely that Pater's intellectual tone was set at least as much by Mill and the positivist thought of the day as by those other more obviously aesthetic and antipositivist sources such as Winckelmann, Goethe, Hegel, Heine, Ruskin, and T. Gautier. By the time Pater came up to Oxford in 1858 and in the ensuing years when he was an undergraduate and young Fellow, Mill's thought and the empiricist outlook in general had begun to penetrate University intellectual life, and even the curriculum, to an unprecedented extent.[6] Pater was far from behindhand in participating in this new concern with empiricism.[7] Evidence of this is apparent throughout his work, from the earliest essays onward. One may see it as well in his warm tribute to Mill shortly after the latter's death as "one who had meditated very profoundly on the true relation of means to ends in life, and on the distinction between what is desirable in itself and what is desirable only as machinery (*Appreciations,* p. 62). Given that this is the sole instance in Pater of unequivocal praise for a contemporary English thinker, I believe it a reasonable assumption that Mill was a very important "voice in the air" for him as an undergraduate.

It was not so much Mill's *Logic,* however, that seems to have impressed Pater as the later *An Examination of Sir*

William Hamilton's Philosophy (1865).[8] This book was a key document in what was certainly the most important philosophical debate being carried on by the nation's intellectual leaders during the period 1860-1870, when Pater as an undergraduate and Fellow was orienting himself philosophically.[9] At the heart of the debate was the question of the "relativity of human knowledge." The concern was not with the tendency of knowledge and belief to change from one generation to the next (although this was implied) but with the more fundamental epistemological question of the human mind's capacity to achieve objective, that is, real or nonrelative, knowledge of things and ideas outside its own subjective existence. Mill's own lucid discussion of the relativity of knowledge in *Hamilton* outlines the principal issues involved. The doctrine of the relativity of knowledge, he remarks, is the keystone of the specifically empiricist outlook and is to be opposed to all "philosophies of the Absolute" in its primary assumption that the mind can know nothing of external reality "in itself"; it can only know its own sensations and perceptions of that external reality or "Non-Ego." An object is "to us nothing else than that which affects our senses in a certain manner," and the same is true of imaginary or ideal objects which we construct in our minds, "so that our knowledge of objects, and even our fancies about objects, consist of nothing but the sensations which they excite, or which we imagine them exciting in ourselves."

Here is the doctrine of the relativity of knowledge in its simplest form. Of this doctrine there are two subspecies. The first and more extreme holds that there is no reality other than the sensations that occur in the mind and that the whole concept of a substratum of objective reality is but a mental fiction. Those who hold this view are called "Idealists"[10] or "Sceptics" and include the followers of

175

Berkeley and Hume. Most, however, hold the doctrine of the relativity of knowledge in its second more moderate form. They believe that there actually exists behind the "phenomenon" of sensation and, independently of mind, the "noumenon" of reality, the "thing in itself." They do not, it must be borne in mind, believe that human consciousness can know anything of this objective reality but what the senses tell it: "We know it not and can assert nothing of it with a meaning. Of these ultimate Realities we know the existence and nothing more." Now this second form of the doctrine of relativity can be further subdivided. On the one hand, are those who, accepting that we cannot know things in themselves, nonetheless argue that we know more than what our senses tell us; we know as well certain things which "are added by the mind itself" to our perceptions and conceptions of the external world; these additions, for example, the ideas of space and time, "result from the nature and structure of the Mind itself." This is the position of Kant (and of Hamilton). Beside this, one must place the "older interpretation of relativity" held by what amounts to the mainstream of the British empiricist tradition from John Locke and David Hartley through Jeremy Bentham and James Mill, down, of course, to J. S. Mill himself. According to this interpretation, the relative knowledge received from the noumenon is still essentially the *passive* knowledge of sensations and association.[11]

At different points in his career Pater manages to adopt each of the various understandings of the doctrine of relativity that Mill enumerates. What is important to note at the moment, however, is that he unquestionably shares with Mill the general position that all knowledge is relative to the knowing mind and that no absolute knowledge whatsoever is possible with regard to the noumena or things in themselves.

One of his earliest and most impressive statements of this position is found in what eventually became the famous Conclusion to *Renaissance.* It was originally part of a review of William Morris' poetry where he was evidently offering it as a summary of the tendency of contemporary thought, his own version, as it were, of the Arnoldian "main current." Here Pater expresses something like the extreme Humean interpretation of the relativity of human knowledge. The grounds of knowledge, he writes, are reducible to the "narrow chamber of the individual mind" where objects exist simply as "impressions, unstable, flickering, inconsistent" and where "what is real in our life fines itself down" to the "passage and dissolution of impressions, images, sensations" and even our very self, our supposed identity, is a "continual vanishing away" (*Renaissance,* pp. 235-36).[12] In the later, more philosophically self-conscious *Marius,* Pater presents this relativist outlook as the necessary first step in his hero's attempt "sich im Denken zu orientiren" ("to orient himself intellectually").

Those external doubts as to the *criteria* of truth reduced themselves to a scepticism almost drily practical, a scepticism which developed the opposition between things as they are and our impressions and thoughts concerning them — the possibility, if an outward world does really exist, of some faultiness in our apprehension of it — the doctrine in short, of what is termed "the subjectivity of knowledge." That is a consideration, indeed, which lies as an element of weakness, like some admitted fault or flaw, at the very foundation of every philosophical account of the universe; which confronts all philosophies at their starting, but with which none have really dealt conclusively, some perhaps not quite sincerely; which those who are not philosophers dissipate by "common," but unphilosophical, sense, or by religious faith. The peculiar strength of Marius was, to have apprehended this weakness on the threshold of human knowledge, in the whole range of its consequences (*Marius,* II, 37-38).

In a still later essay he places the doctrine of relativity in a more contemporary historical perspective. It is, he says, the central doctrine of modern thought, and he traces its origins in this case to Kant.

After Kant's criticism of the mind, its pretensions to pass beyond the limits of individual experience seemed as dead as those of old French royalty. And Kant did but furnish its innermost theoretic force to a more general criticism, which had withdrawn from every department of action, underlying principles once thought eternal. A time of disillusion followed (*Miscellaneous Studies,* p. 11).

In Pater's persistent refusal to overlook the fundamental "fault" in human knowledge, the relativism or subjectivity that must necessarily qualify all experience there is, it seems to me, an essential intellectual affinity with Mill and the contemporary empiricist movement at whose head Mill stood, an affinity which must not be obscured by any easy opposition between aesthetic and positivistic, art and science. This is not to say that Pater, in the end, thought about life or about art in the same manner as Mill or Spencer or Leslie Stephen—far from it. What I want to insist upon, rather, is that this notorious aesthete in all his thought throughout his career demonstrates that he has found it impossible intellectually to deny the validity of what Mill and the positivists are saying about the relativity of human knowledge. To put the point somewhat more graphically if perhaps too simply: if an elemental distinction is to be drawn along the lines suggested by Mill near the outset of the Victorian era between the Coleridgean school of idealists and the Benthamite school of empiricists, Pater must, in his commitment to the doctrine of relativity and in his denial of all Absolutism, fall with Mill into the camp of the Benthamites.[13]

A corollary of Pater's empiricist orientation, as one would expect, is a thoroughgoing skepticism about the claims of the contemporary metaphysical idealism emanating from Germany, which Coleridge and Carlyle earlier in the century had done so much to introduce to England and which certain of Pater's own contemporaries at Oxford were in the seventies and eighties busily establishing as a significant movement in English philosophy (notably his one-time tutor Jowett, as well as T. H. Green, William Wallace, Richard Nettleship, and, slightly later, F. H. Bradley). I make a point of Pater's inability to embrace this philosophical tradition precisely because he was closely associated with the Hegelian idealist set at Oxford[14] and because this association has caused certain modern scholars to reach what seems to me the untenable conclusion that he was, in fact, a part of that tradition, a proper intellectual descendant of Coleridge and Carlyle and a companion in arms of Jowett, Green, and so on. Pater's sympathy with the Oxford idealist tradition and with the Hegelian aspect of it in particular is extremely important to his intellectual make-up. As I shall show, it deeply colored the character of his fundamentally empirical or skeptical way of thinking. But sympathy with the idealist tradition, deep as it may have been, as in the parallel instance of his lifelong sympathy with the religious outlook, did not in Pater's case ever make a true believer. As he once said of the Idealist quest for a metaphysical absolute, it is

> a quest (vain quest it may prove to be) after a kind of knowledge perhaps not properly attainable. Hereafter, in every age, some will be found to start afresh quixotically, through what wastes of words! in search of that true Substance, the One, the Absolute, which to the majority of acute people is after all but zero, and a mere algebraic symbol for nothingness (*Plato,* p. 40).

Confronted with such an attitude as this, it must be conceded that Pater shared with contemporary positivism, if not its tendency to scorn outright the German metaphysical idealism that had meant so much to Carlyle, at least its conviction that that idealism was flawed at its very base.

Having argued that there is an essential affinity between Pater's thought and contemporary empiricism, I want to return to Morley's sense, the sense anyone must have, that there is still something very different in Pater's outlook from that seen in Mill and others. The difference is not fundamental, as is that between metaphysical idealism and empiricism, absolutism and relativism, but it is nonetheless significant. What one is dealing with are, in fact, two quite distinct varieties of empiricism and of relativism; one of these, Mill's, I shall call for convenience sake "positivistic," the other, Pater's, "Epicurean" or "aesthetic."

Faced with the impossibility of both theism and metaphysics Pater does what a good empiricist ought to do: he calls for a retreat to the "primary data" of experience. "How reassuring, after so long a debate about the rival *criteria* of truth, to fall back upon direct sensation, to limit one's aspirations after knowledge to that!" (*Marius,* I, 139.) This is orthodox enough. But, Pater's notion of the sort of satisfaction to be obtained from the primary data reveals the first of two major partings of the way with contemporary positivism. Thrown back upon the "deep original materialism or earthiness of human nature," he comments, let man "make the most of what [is] 'here and now' " (*Marius,* I, 146). Let him devote himself to what the ancient Cyrenaics[15] called "culture," the

> expansion and refinement of the power of reception; of those powers above all, which are immediately relative to fleeting phenomena, the powers of emotion and sense (*Marius,* I, 147).

Let him be sure

> that [he] miss no detail of this life of realised consciousness in the present! Here at least is a vision . . . which reposes on no basis of univerified hypothesis (*Marius,* I, 147-48).

Or in the somewhat less restrained words of the Conclusion, let him recognize that

> every moment some form grows perfect in hand or face; some tone on the hills or sea is choicer than the rest; some mood of passion or insight or intellectual excitement is irresistibly real and attractive to us. . . . Not the fruit of experience, but experience itself is the end (*Renaissance,* p. 236).

This is the "vision" which Pater eventually calls the " 'aesthetic' philosophy" (*Marius,* I, 149).

For the positivist, such a "philosophy" would be anathema. For him experience is never an end in itself, to dwell upon luxuriously for the sheer pleasure of it. Nor is there in the positivist's return to the certainty of the senses that aloof, tired fatalism that everywhere pervades Pater's relationship with the physical—"the desire of physical beauty mingled [with] . . . the fear of death—the fear of death intensified by the desire of beauty" (*Miscellaneous Studies,* pp. 189-90). The positivist, rather, conducts his minute exploration of experience as a means to ends beyond immediate experience, as a means to abstract knowledge and the advancement of society; the primary data in themselves are neutral. He proceeds, moreover, in a spirit of the utmost confidence in things to come, confidence in his power ultimately to comprehend the universe, confidence that he will some day bring nature and society under rational control. As George Eliot once put it,

> The great conception of universal regular sequence — the conception which is the most important force at work in the modification of our faith and of the practical form given to our sentiments — could only grow out of that patient watching of external fact, and that silencing of pre-conceived notions which are urged upon the mind by physical science.[16]

Where the inspiration for Pater's aesthetic philosophy is coming from ultimately is, in fact, not the nineteenth-century empiricist tradition at all but the more ancient empiricist tradition of Aristippus, Epicurus, and Lucretius (*Marius,* I, 123-137). It is a tradition which had not yet learned the modern faith in endless intellectual and material progress, and which, having for all practical purposes dispensed with the spiritual realm, turned to what might be called a metaphysics of pleasure. Epicurus finds that "the mind, having attained a reasoned understanding of the ultimate good of the flesh and its limits and having dissipated the fears concerning the time to come, supplies us with the complete life."[17]

Closely related to the Epicurean tendency of Pater's empiricism is a second major divergence from contemporary positivism, his willingness to push the doctrine of the relativity of knowledge to its solipsistic extreme. Given that what we know we only know through the relative means of our senses, may it not follow, argues Pater, that nothing exists except the ego, all else being simply an image thrown up by the subjective mind.

> [Marius] was ready . . . to concede, somewhat more easily than others . . . that the individual is to himself the measure of all things, and to rely on the exclusive certainty to himself of his own impressions. To move afterwards in that outer world of other people, as though taking it at their estimate, would be possible henceforth only as a kind of irony (*Marius,* I, 133).[18]

The source of Pater's thought here, at least as far as the ancients are concerned, is still the Epicurean tradition, inasmuch as Epicurus counsels withdrawal into the self. Still more important would be Protagoras, whose best-known dictum, "man is the measure of all things,"[19] Pater appears to be quoting above. Worth mentioning as well is Heraclitus, whose thought if not actually solipsistic does call into question the substantiality of the external world.[20] Mill and the positivists of the nineteenth century, on the other hand, take great pains to counter the solipsistic implications of their doctrine of relativity. "The world of Possible Sensations succeeding one another according to laws, [writes Mill] is as much in other beings as in me; it is an External World."[21]

The difference between Pater's approach to the doctrine of the relativity of knowledge and the approach of contemporary positivism is that Pater pushed the positivists' position to extremes which they would have rejected as morally unwholesome and intellectually debilitating. What he called his aesthetic philosophy is not something radically opposed to contemporary positivism or empiricism. On the contrary, it rests on the same essential epistemological basis. It moves from this basis, however, to conclusions entirely unacceptable to the positivist spirit, conclusions that would, on the one hand, give the simple receptivity of phenomenal experience something like a transcendent value and, on the other, drive the individual into a profound sense of irremediable isolation from the world without.

This, then, is the particular nature of Pater's involvement in the empiricist tradition; it is his interpretation of the consequences of the spirit of his age increasingly dominated — and for Pater irrefutably so — by the skepticism and phenomenalism of Mill and, behind Mill, Hume and Kant. The tendency toward hedonism, the retreat to the narrow chamber of the individual mind are, of course, what one immediately thinks of when one thinks of Pater. These are his great hallmarks and, for some readers, his principal claim to intellectual importance. Marius, explains Harold Bloom, for example, is, like Pater, committed to the "universe of death," a believer in the "noble and hopeless doctrine of the Conclusion." Marius expresses

> the burden of modern lyric, from Wordsworth to Stevens, the near solipsism of the isolated sensibility, the naked aesthetic consciousness deprived of everything save its wavering self and the flickering of an evanescent beauty in the world of natural objects, which is part of the universe of death.[22]

As in the case of Kermode's Arnold, Pater is most attractive for the way he anticipates modern anxieties. But to leave Pater at this point is to leave out a good deal of interest. In particular it leaves out a lifetime's effort to find some philosophically acceptable way of transcending the "primary data" of the "mystic now" and the isolation of the self: "To create, to live, perhaps, a little while beyond the allotted hours . . . it was thus that his longing defined itself for something to hold by amid the 'perpetual flux' " (*Marius,* I, 154). I have already shown how the enduringly empiricist basis of Pater's thought precluded a theistical and a metaphysical solution to the kind of "longing" he describes here. I want now to consider another sort of solution altogether and one which has received virtually no serious attention from Paterian scholars. I shall be arguing that Pater, in the manner of certain contemporary Continental thinkers, notably Wilhelm Dilthey (whose work he almost certainly did not know) and in anticipation of certain early twentieth-century thinkers such as Meinecke, Croce, and Collingwood, came gradually to look to history itself and its philosophical significance as the "something to hold by" amidst the chaos of experience. This Pater could do, as did the others I have just named, without in any way denying empiricism's doctrine of the relativity of human knowledge or its insistence upon suspension of belief.

Pater's Complete Historicism

"Scepticism," wrote Leslie Stephen in 1877, "in the absolute sense of the word—a rejection of belief as belief— is, if not a rigidly unthinkable at least a practically impossible state of mind."[23] Pater in his fascination with the solipsistic implications of empiricism came closer than any other Victorian of note to what Stephen calls here skepticism in its "absolute sense." The belief that the individual is the measure of all things is, in fact, the rejection of any form of public belief, the rejection of common feeling and common experience, as Pater explains:

Of other people [says Marius in his most skeptical phase] we cannot truly know even the feelings, nor how far they would indicate the same modifications, each one of a personality really unique, in using the same terms as ourselves; that "common experience," which is sometimes proposed as a satisfactory basis of certainty, being after all only a fixity of language (*Marius,* I, 138).[24]

This, it seems to me, may be fairly taken as an expression of the principal intellectual problem Pater is confronting in *Marius,* the problem of whether there is such a thing as a "common experience" that will somehow free the individual from the prison of self and enable him to overcome that "impossible state of mind," absolute skepticism.

At times Pater's thought may seem to resemble Bergson's in its preoccupation with the radically discontinuous nature of experience. The difference between the two is that Pater, unlike Bergson, does finally accept that the mind is capable of rising above the mere reception of phenomena to the construction of concepts or "intellectual formulae" for life. Even at his most skeptical, as, for instance, in the Conclusion to *Renaissance,* he makes it clear that not simply exquisite sensations but ideas of the world, or "speculative culture," make up the experience that one is to enjoy for its own sake (*Renaissance,* pp. 236-37). Although it is hardly apparent from the impressionistic or aesthetic treatment of ideas in the Conclusion, this ability of mind to formulate concepts and systems of belief is for Pater the fundamental means of escape from the Protagorean isolation of the self. In a late essay on "Plato's Doctrine," probably drawing directly on Mill's *Hamilton,* he distinguishes between realism, which supposes a conceptual idea (for example, Justice) to be "a thing in itself, independent . . . of the particular mind which entertains it"; nominalism, which believes such concepts are "mere names" with nothing beyond linguistic existence; and conceptualism which is the belief that conceptual ideas have no existence or reality independent of the subjective mind.[25] He then goes on to describe his own position.

> Taking our own stand as to this matter somewhere between the realist and the conceptualist: — See! we might say, *there is a general consciousness, a permanent common sense, independent indeed of each of us, but with which we are, each one of us, in communication.* It is in that, those common or general ideas really reside. And we might add . . . that those abstract or common notions come to the individual mind through language, through common or general names . . . into which one's individual experience, little by little, drop by drop, conveys their full meaning or content; and *by the instrumentality of such terms and notions, thus locating the particular, between our individual experience and the common experience of our kind, we come to understand each other, and to assist each other's thoughts,* as in a common mental atmosphere, an "intellectual world", as Plato calls it (*Plato,* pp. 151-52; my italics).

The answer to Marius' search for a common bond among men, a bond with which to overcome the skeptic's isolation, lies in the realm of general ideas or concepts created by and embodied in language. The question of how the mind forms these ideas and this "intellectual world" in the first place is a problem with which Pater is really not concerned. He characteristically takes the ideas and beliefs thrown up by speculative culture as given and devotes himself primarily to understanding them and to placing them in relation to one another in what Mill frequently calls the "thread of [human] consciousness" that runs through time. In other words, his interest in ideas is essentially a historical interest. The speculative culture, which represents the basis of communion between "individual experience and common experience" is for him, as it was, after all, for Carlyle and Arnold, a Zeitgeist of ever-changing ideas of the world or belief systems that can best be understood from the historical point of view.

That Pater both as critic and imaginative writer is, in the end, a good deal more concerned with tracing the historical development of speculative culture or the general consciousness of mankind than he is with burning with a hard gemlike flame is a point that needs more recognition than it has generally received from modern writers. Those who have found *Marius* pre-eminently interesting for its expression of the aesthetic philosophy and the alienated self have chosen not to notice that upon reaching manhood Pater's hero finds the "perpetual flux" and the "pleasure of the ideal present" intellectually unsatisfying and, in "a desire, after all, to retain 'what was so transitive' " (*Marius,* I 154-55), turns to a very sober and thoroughly Victorian vocation.

> To understand the various forms of ancient art and thought, the various forms of actual human feeling . . . to satisfy with a kind of scrupulous equity the claims of these concrete and actual objects on his sympathy, his intelligence, his senses — to "pluck out the heart of their mystery," and in turn to become an interpreter of them to others: this had now defined itself for Marius as a very narrowly practical design: it determined his choice of a vocation to live by (*Marius,* I, 152).

What is said here of Marius applies equally to Pater, for Pater as much as anyone in his historicizing age, was engaged in unraveling and interpreting the "mystery" of the mind of the past. Indeed, he was in one sense more ambitious here than most of his contemporaries, for at various points in his career he attempted to resuscitate the mind of past cultures from ancient Greece through Imperial Rome, the late Middle Ages, and the Renaissance down to the Romantic movement of the late eighteenth and early nineteenth centuries. The type of history he was interested in was the relatively new *Kulturgeschichte* being developed in his period in various forms notably by men such as Jacob Burckhardt on the Continent, by W. E. Lecky and J. A. Symonds in his own country.[26] Within the general field of Kulturgeschichte what interested him in particular was the expression of the historical mind in art. As he once put it, his principal object was to record the various "chapters" in the "history of the human imagination" (*Greek Studies,* p. 81), chapters, that is, in mankind's developing modes of aesthetic expression. In adopting this bent Pater was no doubt influenced by many factors, but two pioneer works in the field were of crucial importance in forming his thought. The first was Winckelmann's *Geschichte der Kunst des Altertums* (1764). Friedrich Meinecke has aptly described Winckelmann's distinctive achievement as a whole-hearted devotion "to the historical world of artistic creations, [an] intense desire to grasp its meaning, the steady activity of all his intellectual and spiritual powers alongside of the critical and more specifically optical and artistic faculties";[27] the second was a work greatly influenced by Winckelmann's *Geschichte,* Hegel's *Ästhetik.*

Pater's claim to the status of historian has often been disputed. Mrs. Mark Pattison, reviewing his *Studies in the History of the Renaissance* in 1873, complained that the title of the book was misleading because it was precisely the "historical element" that was wanting, by which she meant the "true scientific method" of researching and organizing materials from the past.[28] More recently Paul More has objected along similar lines that for Pater "history was only an extension of his own Ego, and he saw himself everywhere he turned his eyes."[29] I want to spend some time responding to this kind of criticism because it seems to me that it is centrally related to the distinctive way Pater had of conceiving of history, which in turn relates back to the fundamentally skeptical tendency of his mind.

As Mrs. Pattison's and More's remarks suggest, the case against Pater as a historian turns essentially on his failure to maintain a suitably "scientific," or objective view of the past, his tendency, that is, to project his own ego onto the historical mind that he is describing. But the scientific approach to history that dominated nineteenth-century historiography and against which Mrs. Pattison and More are judging Pater, the desire, in Leopold von Ranke's memorable phrase, to know the past "as in itself it really was," no longer seems quite the obvious way for a historian to proceed that it once did.[30] Significant philosophical objections to the possibility of achieving the ideal of historical objectivity have been raised, and these have frequently been accompanied by an emphasis on the necessity of the historian's penetrating the past precisely through the medium of what More disapprovingly calls his own Ego.[31] Thus R. G. Collingwood, for a notable example, argues that the historian can know the past only by "re-thinking" it in his own mind and that this rethinking process necessarily involves an abandonment of the scientific model and a self-conscious projection of the historian's own Ego into the past:

> The historian himself, together with the here-and-now which forms the total body of evidence available to him, is a part of the process he is studying, has his own place in that process, and can see it only from the point

of view which at this present moment he occupies within it.

. . . . .

We shall never know how the flowers smelt in the garden of Epicurus . . . we cannot relive . . . the bitterness of Marius; but the evidence of what these men thought is in our hands; and in re-creating these thoughts in our own minds by interpretation of the evidence we can know, so far as there is any knowledge, that the thoughts we create were theirs.[32]

The position of the historical relativist that Collingwood outlines here amounts essentially to the application of what I have described as the doctrine of the relativity of knowledge, the conviction that one cannot know objects in themselves but only one's subjective impressions of them, to the study of the past. Collingwood's own position, in fact, grows out of an attitude toward the study of history that first became an important consideration near the end of the nineteenth century when, as I earlier suggested, philosophy in general under the influence of a new empiricism was showing an increased self-consciousness about the relativity of knowledge. Pater's near contemporary at Oxford, F. H. Bradley, Benedetto Croce in Italy, and in Germany Wilhelm Dilthey were all to become deeply concerned with this problem of how one can know the past.[33]

I am not, of course, arguing that Pater's approach to the problem of historical knowledge ranks with any of these in philosophical importance. What I am saying, however, is that in the light of late nineteenth- and early twentieth-century developments in the philosophy of history, Pater's unscientific subjectivism in historical writing is perhaps a good deal more intellectually interesting than it is usually given credit for being. He was sufficiently sophisticated philosophically, sufficiently wrapped up in the contemporary concern with the relativity of knowledge to have come to some of the same fundamental conclusions about the interpretation of the past as these rather more impressive thinkers. To further elucidate these very important points about Pater's distinctive position in nineteenth-century intellectual history, I propose to place his historical thought in a rather unusual context: beside the thought of Dilthey, almost exactly his contemporary and easily the most significant nineteenth-century philosopher of history after Hegel.

One of Dilthey's most important concerns as philosopher of history is with the problem I have just been discussing, the epistemological problem of how to know the past. For Dilthey, as for Hegel, what we call history is the "externalization in manifold structural systems" of human consciousness; it is the "manifestation of the mind in the world of the senses — from the fleeting expression to the century-long rule of a constitution."[34] In this objective mind or common consciousness of mankind which realizes itself in various political, social, and religious structures through time, each individual consciousness necessarily participates: "We live in this atmosphere, it surrounds us constantly. . . . We are at home everywhere in this historical . . . world . . .; we ourselves are woven into this common sphere."[35]

At this point, Dilthey with his primarily epistemological concerns begins to diverge significantly from Hegel's more metaphysical bias as philosopher of history. Because we are ourselves an integral part of the common consciousness that is the essence of history, says Dilthey, it is within our power empathetically to rethink in our own consciousness, to *understand* (a key word for Dilthey), the meaning of the past. In general, the way we understand any action outside ourselves is "to become aware of our own mental content," and this in turn enables us "to interpret that of others."[36] In the particular case of historical action, "the historian stands in the midst of the . . . remnants of things past, the expressions of minds in deeds, words, sounds, and pictures," and then on the basis of "connections which [he] has experienced within himself he transfers his knowledge of customs, habits, political circumstances and religious process to these remnants."[37] In sum, history is the concrete expression of developing human consciousness and it is best understood or interpreted by an imaginative transposition of the historian's understanding of his own mental operations onto the mind-products which he confronts as the remnants of the past. This conception of the historian as "living in his object or rather making his object live in him," says Collingwood, marks a tremendous advance over anything previously achieved by the nineteenth century in the field of historical hermeneutics.[38]

Turning now to Pater, one finds that, like Hegel and Dilthey, he assumes that history is the concrete emanation of a general developing consciousness or mind in which each individual participates. There is, he writes in that rather remarkable passage from *Plato and Platonism* quoted earlier, "a general consciousness . . . independent indeed of each of us, but with which we are, each one of us, in communication." In emphasizing the intimacy and inevitability of the individual's relationship to the development of general consciousness, he comes close, in fact, to Dilthey's weaving or clothes-making metaphor:[39]

We come into the world, each one of us, "not in nakedness," but . . . clothed . . . in a vesture of the past . . . in the language which is more than half of our thoughts; in the moral and mental habits, the customs, the literature . . . which we did not make for ourselves; in the vesture of a past, which is . . . of the race, the species: that Zeit-geist, or abstract secular process (*Plato,* p. 72).

Holding these assumptions about the historical process and the individual mind's relation to it, Pater can then approach the problem of historical interpretation in much the same spirit as Dilthey does. We understand the past, Pater says, by understanding ourselves in the past. We can never come "face to face" with the past;[40] still, there are "threads" of the mind of the past that run through time and recur in minds in the present. The secret of Winckelmann's "divinatory power over the Hellenic world," for instance, is owing to the "subtler threads of temperament" "interwoven" into his consciousness that bear a close affinity with that past time (*Renaissance,* p. 184). In *Greek Studies* (mainly written 1875-1880), one of his most remarkable efforts at resuscitating the mind of the past, he sets himself among what Dilthey has called the "ruins and remnants of things past" and seeks to "conjure up" the ancient, pre-Hellenic mind they objectify. In doing this he objects specifically to the "cynicism" of that "over-positive temper, which is so jealous of our catching any resemblance in the earlier world to the *thoughts that really occupy our own minds"(Greek Studies,* p. 111; my italics). Instead, he urges his own "imaginative method": "We *feel our way backwards* to that engaging picture of the poet-people" (*Greek Studies,* p. 112; my italics); we discern the past "through a multitude of stray hints in art and poetry and religious custom . . . *through traits and touches in our own actual states of mind, which may seem sympathetic with those tendencies* (*Greek Studies,* p. 53; my italics).

Finally, turning to *Marius,* one finds Pater's most ambitious effort at reviving the past through a process of almost mystic self-projection into that past. The book exists, as it were, at the intersection of history and autobiography, for Marius is two things at once. He is a mind (he scarcely has any existence other than as mind) in the past, a mind which Pater has made something of a conduit for what he takes to be the Zeitgeist or common consciousness of Antonine Rome. On another level Marius is not a mind in the past at all but Pater's own mind, a projection of his own intellectual development. One may, of course, dismiss what Pater is doing here as the merest fantasy with no serious historical pretensions, but that would be to overlook a more serious undertaking. Pater is attempting in this book imaginatively to embody his firm belief that there is no essential discontinuity between our consciousness in the present and the mind of the past. Accordingly, the study of the past is, in an important sense, a process of intense introspection, a process, as Marius puts it at one point, of "retracing in [one's] individual mental pilgrimage the historic order of human thought" (*Marius,* I, 134). Or, in Dilthean terms, Marius with his dual existence, historical and autobiographical, seems, however unphilosophically and imperfectly, to be making the point that it is "our own lives and the energy with which we reflect upon them that are the foundation of historical vision."[41]

In the late nineteenth century the focus of philosophical thinking about history began to shift, as the example of Dilthey and others shows, toward its present epistemological concern with the nature of historical knowledge and away from its traditional metaphysical concern with the *meaning* of historical process itself.[42] Still, these late nineteenth-century philosophers of history and philosophical historians retained a strong predisposition to talk, as their predecessors had persistently talked, of the overall meaning of history. Pater whose historical thought, as I have argued, participated in the late-century epistemological concerns, was no exception here. He too, like Carlyle and Arnold before him, was deeply concerned with deciphering the overall metaphysical significance of historical process.

Traditional philosophy of history has essentially two ways of treating the meaning of history, what may be called an intrinsic and an extrinsic way. The first asks whether the events of history form a pattern and if so, what sort of pattern; the second asks what the meaning of history is for life in general, what it says about the nature of the universe and the destiny of mankind. As for the first question, there appears to have been in the later Victorian period no significant diminution in the assumption I have already noticed in the case of Carlyle and the Arnolds that history has an intrinsic meaning or pattern. If anything, there was an intensification of that assumption under the pressure of the contemporary triumph of positive science that assumed that there must be discoverable laws everywhere.[43] Robert Flint, a contemporary expert on the subject, spoke for most when he maintained in 1874 "that the reign of law somehow extends over human affairs—that history has not been abandoned to caprice and chance, is not mere anarchy and chaos, but embraced within a system of order, more or less perfect."[44]

In Pater's historical writing one sees no such overriding confidence in the "reign of law" in history. Rather there is a greater tendency than is ordinarily found in the nineteenth century to treat history as if it were but a collection of "clauses of experience," each interesting in itself as a particular moment of past life quite apart from its relation to any larger philosophical or scientific scheme.

> We cannot love or live upon *genus* and *species* . . . but
> for our minds as for our bodies, need an orchard or a
> garden, with fruit and roses. Take a seed. . . . What
> interest it has for us all lies in our sense of potential dif-
> ferentiation, to come: the leaves, leaf upon leaf, the
> flowers. . . . It is so with . . . humanity, individually or
> as a whole, its expansion into a detailed, ever-chang-
> ing, parti-coloured history of particular facts and per-
> sons (*Plato,* p. 155).

In other words, Pater is showing a positive pleasure in the
concrete and discrete moment of historical experience and a
reluctance to speculate on larger interconnections or patterns in history. Here, again, is the characteristic movement
of Pater's skeptical mind away from intellectual abstractions
back toward the "primary data" of experience.

If one looks to the late nineteenth- and early twentieth-
century developments in philosophy of history with which I
have been seeking to associate Pater's thought, one finds
very much the same retreat from the metaphysical and positivistic patterning back to the empirical experience of history. Dilthey repeatedly condemns "the intervention of
speculation into the empirical sphere of the historian."[45]
And Croce, who in most essential points follows Dilthey, has
no use for those who impose a "logicalness" of design on history and thus shun the "excitements of passions and interests" found in the empirical reality of history.[46]

Although Pater is skeptical of finding a grand *Weltplan*
or a system of laws in history, he is not prepared, in the end,
any more than are the Continental philosophers, to say that
historical process is totally without logic, loose and elusive as
that logic may be. In the very flux even Heraclitus seemed to
see some "intelligible relationships."

   In this "perpetual flux" of things and of souls, there

was, as Heraclitus conceived, a continuance, if not of their material or spiritual elements, yet of orderly intelligible relationships, like the harmony of musical notes, wrought out on and through the series of their mutations (*Marius,* I, 131).

Pater characteristically writes as if history were not simply an eclectic jumble of events but expressive of some principle of development, not a principle superimposed upon it from without, but a principle inherent in it. Thus he describes the movement of ideas from one age to the next.

Nature, which by one law of development evolves ideas, hypotheses, modes of inward life, and represses them in turn, has in this way provided that the earlier growth should propel its fibres into the later, and so transmit the whole of its forces in an unbroken continuity of life (*Appreciations,* p. 65).[47]

Pater never explicitly develops his thought on the "logic" of history, the "unbroken continuity of life," but I believe a fair idea of his attitude toward the particular kind of intelligibility exhibited in historical process is evident in the following account of his favorite "dialectical" logic. Such a logic involves

repeated acts of qualification and correction; many readjustments to experiences; expansion by larger lights from it.

It is

a process . . . a movement of thought, which is the very converse of mathematical or demonstrative reasoning, and incapable therefore of conventional or scholastic form of "exactness" . . . which proceeds to truth, not by the analysis and application of an axiom, but by a gradual suppression of error (*Plato,* pp. 178-180).

Such a process aptly describes the journey of the mind portrayed in *Marius* and *Gaston Latour,* and it is not too great an inference to say it also describes Pater's notion of the movement of the "general consciousness" of mankind through history. Here again Pater's position compares closely with Dilthey's for whom, though there is no overall design or teleology to history, there is nonetheless a discernible "development" a "system" of complicated inner connections —

> Every age refers back to the preceding one, for the forces that developed in the latter continue to be active in it; at the same time it already contains the strivings and creative activities which prepare for the succeeding age. [Cf. Pater's "unbroken continuity" and interconnecting "fibres" from one age penetrating to the next.][48]

— and with Croce for whom "there is a logic in history" but not, again, a logicalness. Historiography should conceive history

> as the history of the mind in development, or of the spirit, and . . . should re-make the story of events no longer according to external rhythms . . . but according to the internal rhythm of spiritual life.[49]

Pater's refusal to place a design on history in the manner of traditional nineteenth-century philosophy of history, his belief that the logic of history was of its own empirical, internal making, is important in its own right; for my present purposes, it is still more important because it leads directly into his views on what I have called the *extrinsic* meaning of history, the meaning of history, that is, for life in general. The patterns and strictly determined directions that nineteenth-century philosophy of history imposed upon history were almost inevitably attached to some extrahistorical ideal. As Maurice Mandelbaum sees it, "Every philosophy of history becomes a form of apologetics based upon a belief in the omnipotence and omnipresence of the forces of Providence or Progress."[50] It was possible to see — or suppose that one saw — the movement and direction of history so clearly, precisely because that movement and direction were decided for it by quite unhistorical criteria, criteria that had to do with religious and metaphysical beliefs, on the one hand, natural laws, on the other.

Skeptical to begin with about the metaphysical and positivistic beliefs behind contemporary philosophies of history, Pater necessarily becomes skeptical about the patterns themselves. But the same skepticism that works against the logical patterning and teleological explanations of history works at the same time toward reversing the subordination of history to extrahistorical interpretations of experience, to metaphysics, religion, natural law, and so on. For Pater history becomes the intellectual realm in which the skeptical mind is freest to roam, moving from one form of belief to another, participating in the warmth and immediacy of each but remaining aloof from commitment to any. With this outlook it becomes possible, ultimately, for him to turn to the study of history not as an illustration of some other transcendent belief but as an *alternative* to such beliefs.

Much of what I have already said about Pater's concept of the general consciousness and his desire to escape from aesthetic isolation into the continuity of the historically developing mind will have served to suggest that he is indeed thinking in terms of history as ultimate knowledge and ultimate value. But I think the point is most conclusively illustrated by the intellectual resolution which in my view, pace Mrs. Humphrey Ward and a number of modern critics, he does manage to achieve in *Marius,* his most ambitious and mature attempt to give some kind of syncretic expression to his beliefs. At the beginning of the third book Pater describes Marius as having achieved a "narrow perfection," a perfection which is, in fact, twofold, involving, on the one hand, the *aesthetic* capacity of exquisite sensuous receptivity, and, on the other, a perfection of the *moral* capacity of "imaginative sympathy." At this point he is prepared at last to bring his hero outside his perfected individuality to a wider philosophical and social vision, a vision which is the direct outgrowth of Marius' historical vocation. It is a vision which has been implicit throughout Pater's earlier work but which now for the first time receives full expression.

There is a venerable system of sentiment and idea, widely extended in time and place, in a kind of impregnable possession of human life — a system, which, like some other great products of the conjoint efforts of human mind through many generations, is rich in the world's experience; so that, in attaching oneself to it, one lets in a great tide of that experience, and makes, as it were with a single step, a great experience of one's own, and with great consequent increase to one's sense of colour, variety, and relief, in the spectacle of men and things. The mere sense that one belongs to a system — an imperial system or organisation — has, in itself, the expanding power of a great experience; as some have felt who have been admitted from narrower sects into the communion of the catholic church; or as the old Roman citizen felt. It is, we might fancy, what the coming into possession of a very widely spoken language might be, with a great literature, which is also the speech of the people we have to live among.

A wonderful order, actually in possession of human life! — grown inextricably through and through it;

penetrating into its laws, its very language, its mere habits of decorum, in a thousand half-conscious ways; yet still felt to be, in part, an unfulfilled ideal; and as such, awakening hope, an aim, identical with the one only consistent aspiration of mankind (*Marius,* II, 26-27).

In the unity of culture described here, moving through time as a "system," a "wonderful order," Marius finds his grounds for hope, his belief in the possibility of transcendence beyond the Protagorean isolation of self to the "great experience" of the continuously developing mind of the race. That this, in fact, is intended by Pater to be Marius' ultimate vision of life and not simply another stop "along the way," is, it seems to me, quite clear from his climactic reiteration of the historicist vision as Marius' dying experience of revelation.

Revelation, vision, the discovery of vision, the *seeing* of a perfect humanity, in a perfect world — through all his alternatives of mind, by some dominant instinct, determined by the original necessities of his own nature and character, he had always set that above the *having,* or even the *doing,* of anything. . . . And how goodly had the vision been! — one long unfolding of beauty and energy in things, upon the closing of which he might gratefully utter his "Vixi"! (*Marius,* II, 218.)

Again, the direction of Pater's thought here in *Marius* as throughout his career seems to me to become most intelligible when placed in the light of the major conclusion toward which the Continental philosophers of history and the Englishman Collingwood were moving in the quarter of a century or so following Pater's death: all other philosophical and religious presuppositions are being disposed of in favor of a knowledge simply of the development of mind in history. As Dilthey remarks, there are no transcendent, un-conditioned beliefs; there are only the "processes of posit-ing" these beliefs, and it is to these processes alone that mankind's highest philosophical attention must be directed.

> History itself is the productive force for the creation of valuations, ideals, and purposes.
>
> The historical consciousness of the finitude of every historical phenomenon, of every human or social condition and of the relativity of every kind of faith, is the last step towards the liberation of man. With it man achieves the sovereignty to enjoy every experience to the full and surrender himself to it unencumbered, as if there were no system of philosophy or faith to tie him down. . . . Everything beautiful, everything holy, every sacrifice relived and interpreted, opens perspectives which disclose some part of reality. . . . And in contrast to relativity, the continuity of creative forces asserts it-self as the central historical fact.
>
> We are open to the possibility that meaning and sig-nificance arise only in man and in his history.[51]

As Dilthey's editor H. P. Rickman has pointed out, one has, with such a view as this, crossed a major intellectual threshold.[52] Historicism has changed from being what it had been for the first three-quarters of the century. It has ceased to be the single most important ancillary to philoso-phy and usurped the position of philosophy itself; it has assumed the belief that no value or knowledge exists outside the process of history, outside mankind's constant positing or creation of cultural systems. Or in Croce's more poetic rendering, history has become "its own mystic Dionysus, its own suffering Christ, redeemer of sins."[53]

Pater, it seems to me, has very definitely passed this par-ticular intellectual threshold, and in this he is virtually unique among his fellow mid and late Victorians. He has been propelled toward his conclusions by essentially three intellectual forces, the same forces which, in fact, are at work in Dilthey, Croce, and Collingwood. There is, first of all, a fundamental skepticism over the validity of traditional metaphysical idealism, a skepticism induced at once by the critical side of Kant's thought and the revitalization of the empiricist concern with the relativity of knowledge. Second, there is a resistance, as much temperamental as intellectual, to the comprehensive claims of the scientific method and a desire to insist upon the distinctly human, subjective imagination as a primary means of knowing. Finally, there is the belief, the logical outcome of the century's preoccupation with history, that the human mind finds its highest expression in the weaving of a vast and continuous system of human culture through time and that the meaning of man in the present can be no more or less than as a participant in that historical culture.

As I earlier noted, Pater's efforts to trace the mind of the past focused on art. Art in all its forms was for him the most interesting expression of that "inexhaustible activity and creativeness of the human mind itself" (*Renaissance,* p. 34) in which, ultimately, he placed his faith. It is, of course, as a critic and not as a philosopher of history that Pater is known. But the latter vocation, the one which I have emphasized here, bears closely on the former. The desire to see in historical process the ground of all knowledge and all belief is certainly not unrelated to the kind of aestheticization of life for which Pater as critic is famous. As Meinecke has suggested, the apotheosis of man's culture-weaving powers can very easily lead to the apotheosis of art or "what is called culture in the highest sense," those glorious "breakthroughs and revelations of the spiritual within the causal complex of nature."[54] Beyond this, and probably more important, the attitude adopted by the complete historicist toward what traditionally have been the most serious of man's cultural productions, his religious and philosophical systems, the attitude, that is, of conscientious aloofness from commitment to belief or to any fixed system of valuation is essentially an *aesthetic* attitude. One does not *believe* in ideas and values; one *admires* them as remarkable exertions of the human spirit. In other words, what I am suggesting, through the example of Pater, is a special kind of conjunction in intellectual history — a conjunction which may also be observed to an extent not only in Dilthey, but in Meinecke, Croce, and Collingwood — between, on the one hand, the tendency toward a complete historicism, which is but the logical outcome of the century's preoccupation with the meaning of history, and, on the other, the rise of a predominantly aesthetic interpretation of life, which stands at the threshold of and points toward distinctly modernist concerns.

6

HISTORICISM AND THE
HELLENIC IDEAL

In 1876 W. J. Courthope, in the context of a vigorous attack on what he called the "Romantic" tradition in English criticism, singled out Pater for special reproach as one of the foremost contemporary exponents of that tradition. The doctrine of the Conclusion to *Renaissance,* he complained, was sensual, mindless, unmanly, and antisocial.[1] Courthope's reaction to Pater, insensitive as it may seem to modern eyes, is interesting from two standpoints, first, for its association of Pater with the Romantic tradition and second, for what it says about mid-Victorian attitudes toward that tradition.

The New Hedonism: Pater and the Romantic Tradition

Pater's thought on poetry and art ultimately stands apart from Romantic theory of the early nineteenth century as something quite distinct, something which could only have come after the mid century, after the rise of philosophical skepticism and the triumph of physical science. Still there are elements in his thought that do definitely represent a continuation of the Romantic tradition.[2] Most significant is that side of his aesthetic which was obviously most disturbing Courthope, namely, its "unmanly" call for a return to primary emotional and sensuous experience. That such a call was, as Courthope suggests, characteristic of Romanticism needs no undue emphasis. As Robert Langbaum and others have noted, Romanticism was, after all, in one of its aspects a continuation of eighteenth-century empiricism in its emphasis on the supreme validity of concrete experience.

> Post-Enlightenment romanticism is historically unique just to the extent that it uses for its reconstructive purpose the same scientific or empirical method which is itself unique to the modern world. Like the scientist's hypothesis, the romanticist's formulation is evolved out of experience and is continually tested against experience. . . . Romanticism is in this sense not so much a reaction against eighteenth-century empiricism as a reaction within it, a corrected empiricism.[3]

Or as Santayana describes it, "The great merit of the romantic attitude in poetry . . . is that [it puts] us back at the beginning of our experience," back, that is, "to immediate perception and primordial will."[4] This tendency to move with empiricism rather than against it may be seen, for a notable instance, in Wordsworth's insistence in the 1800 Preface that poetry's purpose is to impart pleasure by appealing to the "primary laws of our nature," the "simple," "unelaborated," "essential" passions, and that the poet is one who possesses a more than usual "organic sensibility" to sensations and feelings.[5] It appears again in Coleridge's view that the "peculiar business" of poetry is to impart pleasure, by which he means emotional and sensuous pleasure: "A poem is that species of composition, which is opposed to a work of science by proposing for its *immediate* object pleasure, not truth.''[6] As Coleridge's emphasis on "immediate" suggests, the Romanticist is far from seeing poetry's final end as the expression of and appeal to the feelings, but he is, nonetheless, inclined to see that expression and that appeal as the *distinctive* quality of poetry.

Victorian critics, it hardly needs saying, were far less easy with the sensuous and emotional in poetry (as Courthope's review suggests). This is not to say they denied them absolutely; it is just that they were characteristically extremely wary of allowing them any real freedom of scope. This is as true of the better, more enlightened critical minds as it is of the lesser ones. Mill, for example, writing on Tennyson in 1835 recognizes that "fine senses" and "nervous susceptibility" are "distinctive" characteristics of the "poetic temperament." The object of his essay is, however, to congratulate Tennyson on having made an effort to control that "poetic temperament" with philosophy: "The achievements of any poet in his art will be in proportion to the growth and perfection of his thinking faculty."[7] Arnold, just under thirty years later, finds in de Guérin's "natural interpretation," his Keatsian susceptibility to feeling and lack of moral and intellectual faculties, the basis of his "poetic" power. This essay, however, like the later one on Keats himself, is far more about the dangers of such a susceptibility than its advantages: "The temperament is *devouring;* it uses vital power too hard and too fast"; it must be counterbalanced by "the inward world of man's moral and spiritual nature" (*Prose Works,* III, 33). Examples might be multiplied, but it seems to me the general Victorian attitude toward this question is fairly summarized by Robert Buchanan's 1871 remarks against the "fleshly school" (he had in mind writers such as D. G. Rossetti, Morris, Swinburne). Sensuous and passionate qualities are all very well in poetry, he notes, but they become unwholesome when "they [have] no moral or intellectual quality to temper or control them."[8] For the Victorians the sensuous and the passionate had become, far more than they ever were for the Romantics, morally ambiguous qualities, qualities whose value is but doubtfully allowed and then only with the qualification that certain saving intellectual and spiritual controls be firmly placed upon them by the artist.

Viewed from one standpoint, Pater's criticism represents one of the most important efforts of the time to vindicate the "sensuous wisdom" of the artist and thus to return, as it were, over the heads of the great mid-century critics Carlyle, Mill, Ruskin, Lewes, Arnold, to the Romantics. For Pater that which is "essentially artistic" is the "sensuous element" (*Renaissance*, p. 130). "Sooner or later," he remarks, "art returns to the simple passions and what corresponds to them, the sensuous world."[9] Corresponding to this understanding of the essential nature of art is Pater's injunction upon the critic to refine his receptivity to pleasure, to learn "to distinguish . . . that special impression of beauty or pleasure" in art (*Renaissance*, pp. ix-x). And, of course, informing the whole critical position is the Aristippean doctrine of sensuous wisdom discussed in the preceding chapter.

Behind Pater's aesthetic was, to be sure, a native affinity for the sensuous and the emotional.[10] At least as important was his reading in what has been called the German Hellenist movement, a movement closely associated with the rise of Romanticism in Germany.[11] Particularly influential here would have been Winckelmann, his great disciple in Hellensim, Goethe, and then Schiller, Heine, and, above all, Hegel. This was very much the same movement in aesthetics that had attracted Carlyle's attention (Hegel and Heine excepted) much earlier in the century. However, Pater has what Carlyle lacks, a proper appreciation of that aesthetic's effort to vindicate the sensuous and instinctual wisdom of art. What these German Hellenists meant to Pater in general is best indicated by Heine's remarks in *Zur Geschichte der Religion und Philosophie in Deutschland* (1834). The thing of most importance at the moment, says Heine, is to restore faith in the sensations and the emotions. "[T]he immediate aim of all our modern institutions is the rehabilitation of matter, its restoration to former dignity, its moral recognition, its religious sanctification, its reconciliation with the spirit."[12] What they meant to his aesthetical outlook in particular is epitomized by Schiller's or Hegel's insistence that art is above all the "sinnliches Scheinen der Idee" ("the sensuous appearance of the idea").[13]

This then is the essential nature of Pater's affinity with Romantic theory. At this point it is clear that Pater's concern to re-emphasize the role of the sensuous and the emotional in art differed — and necessarily differed owing to developments in contemporary science and philosophy — from the Romantic tradition. When his Romantic predecessors, English or German, urged a return in art to the primary data of experience, they did not, after all, do so in a purely empirical spirit. In Langbaum's phrase, theirs was a "corrected" empiricism. They expected, in short, that they would find in sensuous nature and unelaborated feelings evidence of the One Life or Absolute Spirit that knit all experience together into a Divine Whole. This is as true of Schiller, Goethe, and Hegel as it is of Blake, Wordsworth, and Coleridge. The Romanticist might define the nature of the One Life behind empirical phenomena in a number of ways, but the point is that in general those phenomena were corrected or sanctified by some variety of metaphysical or religious idealism. Like Coleridge the Romanticist characteristically gazed on nature until the necessary spiritual transformation took place:

> . . . until all doth seem
> Less gross than bodily; and of such hues
> As veil the Almighty Spirit.
> ("This Lime Tree Bower my Prison")

With the advance of the geological and biological sciences after 1830 this kind of faith became ever less tenable and the return to the empirical data ever more threatening. This is not the place to describe in detail this development in the history of ideas, but one may sketch the general outlines. Physical nature ceased to demonstrate evidence of spiritual immanence, and man's emotional aspect was seen as the one in which he most closely resembled the lower forms of animal life. An altogether new sort of continuity between spirit and matter became current, a descendental rather than transcendental one, which talked no longer of the One Life, within us and abroad, but of the "Physical Basis of Life."[14] As the *Westminster Review* put it in 1865, reviewing Spencer's *Principles of Biology,* there can be no doubt about the tendency of modern science.

> The identification of the two regions [of matter and spirit] can hardly . . . yet be said to be accomplished, but so far as their general aspects are concerned, it seems to be approaching.

The reviewer goes on to discuss what amounted to one of the most important doctrines of contemporary science, the law of the conservation of force throughout all nature, organic and inorganic:

> Let us think [of Life as] . . . an *eddy* in a stream. All around it runs a large continuous current, from which it is marked off — individualised. . . . Yet it consists of the very same elements, material and dynamic, as the

stream around. . . . That stream represents the great stream of force; that eddy the living organism. . . . The eddy presents to us opposite motions, down and up, united and mutually dependent. The force-liberating downward motion produces the force-absorbing upward, and they dwell together in one definite shape — definite yet transient.[15]

This "great stream of force," a purely physical or natural force with no metaphysical pretentions whatsoever, was what mid-century science was offering by way of an underlying principle unifying nature and mind. The prospect of everything's being thus reduced to matter and physical force, in T. H. Huxley's words, weighed "like a nightmare . . . upon many of the best minds of these days," threatening to drown the soul in an "advancing tide of matter."[16] Huxley himself, of course, did not feel particularly threatened by the materialistic flood, but the nightmare he describes was real enough for the great majority of his contemporaries.

Pater was entirely aware of what contemporary science had done to the Romanticist vision of empirical experience. The Conclusion, to *Renaissance* which, again, in its original 1868 context claimed to be an account of the truths of the modern age, envisages the reduction of life to matter and force and reflects the same materialistic principle of the conservation of force that the *Westminster* reviewer outlined in the passage quoted above.

Like the elements of which we are composed, the action of these forces extends beyond us: it rusts iron and ripens corn. Far out on every side of us those elements are broadcast, driven in many currents; and birth and gesture and death and the springing of violets from the grave are but a few out of ten thousand resulting combinations. . . . This at least of the flamelike our life has, that it is the concurrence, renewed from moment to moment, of forces parting sooner or later on their ways (*Renaissance,* p. 234).

When Pater enjoins his readers to burn with a "hard gem-like flame" and "to be present always at the focus where the greatest number of forces unite," then, he is not being simply "aesthetic"; he is showing himself aware of the latest scientific interpretation of experience and of mind. More important, however, is Pater's emotional attitude toward the new materialism. Clearly he regrets the vanished splendor in the grass:

> Experience, which has gradually saddened the earth's colours for us, stiffened its motions, withdrawn from it some blithe and debonair presence, has quite changed the character of the science of nature [from what it was at the beginning of the century] (*Appreciations,* p. 76).

Beyond this simple nostalgia for the Romantic vision are far more painful emotions. Thus he considers that Dionysus is his symbolic "Romantic." With Dionysus as the god of that joyous life in flowing, sensuous things, that "glory of nature," he is in deepest sympathy. But Dionysus has a double nature; besides the joy of sensuous wisdom, are darker possibilities:

> Like Persephone, [Dionysus] belongs to two worlds, and has much in common with her, and a full share of those dark possibilities which, even apart from the story of the rape, belong to her. . . . [L]ike Hades himself, he is hollow and devouring, an eater of man's flesh (*Greek Studies,* p. 44).

This other, darker Dionysus inevitably overshadows all Pater's arguments for the rehabilitation in art of man's sensuous and emotional nature. Everywhere for him there is that materialist nightmare that Huxley speaks of, that "vague fear of evil" (*Marius,* I, 22) that intertwines with

Marius' inherently sensuous nature and which finds expression in his deep aversion for the bestiality of the arena and the sexuality of Faustina, and in such passages as this description of a boyhood encounter with breeding snakes:

> One fierce day in early summer, as he walked along a narrow road, he had seen the snakes breeding, and ever afterwards avoided that place and its ugly associations, for there was something in the incident which made food distasteful and his sleep uneasy for many days afterwards (*Marius*, I, 23).

This painful consciousness of the "dark possibilities" and "ugly associations" of natural experience impart to Pater's desire for sensuous and emotional wisdom an altogether different quality from what one finds in the earlier Romantics. Absent is Wordsworth's "cheerful faith that all which we behold is full of blessings." In its place is a sense of an underlying horror in both nature and the inner instinctual or passionate self. The return to the beginnings of experience becomes from one standpoint a sort of decay or dying into mere matter, from another a sort of animalism. Above all, one is not approaching the primary data with anything like pure pleasure or joy but with a distinct air of fatalism, with a sort of desperation, pushed there by the force of the contemporary scientific and philosophical Zeitgeist. One falls back to the primary data, says Pater at one point, with a "sense of *ennui*" brought about by the recognition that man's spiritual and metaphysical powers have, after all, committed a "sort of suicide" (*Marius,* I, 141).

Against this background what is one to make of Pater's "Romantic" call for a return in art to "the simple passions and what corresponds to them, the sensuous world"? Several have responded by treating his aesthetic as "decadent," that is, as part of the late-century tendency among English poets to see it as precisely the business of art to express the darker Dionysus.[17] Pater's friend and contemporary Swinburne, for instance, issued his own resounding call for a return to the sensuous and the passionate.[18] He did this with the understanding that this meant a need for the artist to express, as he put it in his tribute to Baudelaire, all the cruelty and suffering in nature, "the sides on which nature looks unnatural," even the "loathsomest bodily putrescence and decay."[19] In this call Swinburne was followed by such "decadents" of the next generation as George Moore, Lionel Johnson, and Ernest Dowson. For all that modern students of Pater are inclined to associate him with the Decadent movement — and there is no question but that there is some justice in the association — there are still very significant aspects of Pater's thought that are not contained under the designation "decadent." Purple passages such as the too-well-known description of the "Mona Lisa" in *Renaissance* notwithstanding, Pater, in the end, lacks that fascination with the horrible and the grotesque to be found in Swinburne and Baudelaire, and, more to the point, he seems to entertain a positive objection to its expression in art. Thus he refuses to review a book by George Moore on the grounds that it contains "violent incidents" and "abnormal states of mind" which are inappropriate to art.[20] In "Winckelmann" what is attractive about Greek sensuousness is precisely that it "does not fever the consciousness: it is shameless and childlike" (*Renaissance,* pp. 221-22). Summing up Pater's position on this point, one may quote from the same essay his concept of the function of art as "the putting of a happy world of [the artist's] own creation in place of our common days" (*Renaissance,* p. 213). In all this there is a quite different, a far more ascetic sensibility from what one finds in Swinburne or Baudelaire or any of the nineteenth-century seekers after "strange beauty."

The question remains: How does Pater reconcile his thoroughly Victorian anxieties over the fleshly and the bestial with his desire that art should deal, above all, with the sensuous and the passionate? What does he mean by "Greek sensuousness," and how does he imagine it can be recaptured in the modern age? When he states that art is a "sort of cloistral refuge from a certain vulgarity in the actual world" (*Appreciations,* p. 18), there is an inclination to imagine that he is advocating a sort of monkish self-censorship according to which artists will screen out of their sensuous and passionate representations all "ugly associations." But what Pater means, in the end, is something rather more complex than this. He is not talking about *what* the artist ought to present so much as the particular *way* or *form* in which he ought to present it.

To begin with, Pater's entire attitude toward aesthetic representation is profoundly unnaturalistic. He is not in search of the full-bodied, realistic depiction of physical nature and emotion characteristic of earlier nineteenth-century poetry and art.[21] Rather, he constantly urges that in art the materials of nature must be exquisitely "modelled" by the "Asiatic" hand of the consummate craftsman until they achieve the condition of a minute and curious loveliness, which, at the same time, is a virtually *denatured* loveliness. Everything is to be rendered delicate and light, and not a little cold, by the endlessly refining hand. The warmth and vitality of immediate sensuous and emotional experience is to be reduced to strictly formal, rhythmical qualities that by being free of body, as it were, become free as well of corruption. What is sought, in short, is the "thaumaturgic" effect of a sensuous presentation such as Ronsard's.

Here was a poetry which boldly assumed the dress . . .
of contemporary life and turned [it] into gold. . . .

Things were become at once more deeply sensuous and more deeply ideal. As at the touch of a wizard, something more came to the rose than its own natural blush. Occupied so closely with the visible, this new poetry had so profound an intuition of what can only be felt. . . . And still that was no dubious or generalised form it gave to flower or bird, but the exact pressure of the jay at the window. . . . [T]he visible was more visible than ever before, just because soul had come to its surface (*Gaston,* pp. 54-55).

Described here is a sensibility that is neither Romantic nor Decadent, a sensibility that demands a sensuousness and a passion that is experienced not so much on the senses and in the blood as *in the mind;* experienced not as a reality or as an imitation of reality but as a form. This is part of what Pater means in the passage above when he speaks of bringing the soul to the surface of the natural world. What else he means has to do with more specifically historicist concerns. Let us now look more closely at these two ways of transmuting and, as it were, sanctifying the sensuous and passionate in art.

The Spiritual Principle in Art

In his comments on Baudelaire, Swinburne shows little appreciation for that side of the French poet's aesthetic on which he requires the presence of a spiritual principle to offset what Swinburne sees as his fascination with the luxuries of pleasure and pain, the putrescence of the flesh. Characteristic is Baudelaire's 1852 attack on Heine, whose Hellenistic call for a renovation of the flesh I have already noticed. Heine, he complains, has led art into a dangerous preoccupation with merely sensuous beauty and instinctual passion. In this new "paganism" he omits those "notions du juste et du vrai," which are necessary to social as well as personal well-being. "Literature must revitalize its forces in a better atmosphere. The time is not far when people will understand that any literature that refuses to march hand-in-hand with science and philosophy is a literature both homicidal and suicidal."[22] Such remarks as these nicely illustrate Michael Hamburger's point that Baudelaire as critic had more in common with his Victorian contemporary Matthew Arnold "than with his acknowledged master Poe or his acknowledged disciple Mallarmé."[23] Like Arnold he was still of a generation and a disposition that required that high ideas, moral, intellectual, and religious, be somehow incorporated into poetry. It was for a later generation to revise this outlook radically and to hold with Mallarmé the more strictly aesthetic position that "you don't write sonnets with ideas . . . but with words."[24]

Toward this later more properly aesthetic outlook Pater's thought was definitely tending. With Arnold and Baudelaire he recognized the importance of a spiritual principle or what he called "soul" in art, a principle that would in some way redeem the vulgarity of natural experience; unlike his mid-century predecessors he did not think of this principle in terms of *ideas* to be put into or contained by art. Rather, he tended to see the spiritual principle in art as a result of a way of perceiving experience. Beginning as he always did from the relativist position, from the fundamental flaw at the basis of all knowledge, he assumed a gap between the artist's perception of reality and reality itself. The artist imitates, he writes in "Style," not actual fact but "soul fact," that is, his "peculiar intuition of the world . . . changed somewhat from the actual world."

[I]n proportion as the writer's aim, consciously or unconsciously, comes to be the transcribing, not of the

world, not of mere fact, but of his sense of it, he becomes an artist, his work *fine* art; and good art. . . .
[A]ll beauty is in the long run only *finesse* of truth, or
what we call expression, the finer accommodation of
truth to the vision within.

. . . . .

Literary art, that is, like all art which is in any way
imitative or reproductive of fact — form, or colour, or
incident — is the representation of such fact as connected with soul, of a specific personality, in its preferences, its volition and power (*Appreciations,* pp. 8-10).

In this understanding of how mind or spirit is joined to
matter in art, there is, it seems to me, something quite new
in English criticism. Pater is not saying, as his Romantic
predecessors were, that the idea in art is a metaphysical
entity inherent in the external world, which the artist imitates. Nor is he saying with Carlyle and several other of his
Victorian predecessors that the idea is culturally created
and somehow applied to or bodied forth in art, in which
case the idea would still be conceived of as an objective spiritual entity that one is bringing to the art object. Like Mallarmé Pater is working against all metaphysical and intellectualist approaches to the spiritual principle in art. Ideas as
such have no place in art except as conditions of the artist's
perception: "Art . . . is . . . always striving to be independent of the mere intelligence, to become a matter of pure
perception" (*Renaissance,* p. 138). By thus conceiving of the
spiritual principle *as a condition of the artist's perception,*
Pater is, in effect, seeking to explain how in the highest art
one has the impression of consummate union between matter and spirit, form and content:

. . . the ideal examples of poetry and painting being
those in which the constituent elements . . . are so
welded together, that the . . . subject no longer strikes

the intellect only; nor the form, the eye or the ear only; but form and matter, in their union or identity, present one single effect (*Renaissance,* p. 138).

Something of the importance of Pater's relativist way of conceiving the idea in poetry has been suggested by G. N. G. Orsini, who, commenting on Croce's aesthetic, observes that Pater's essay "Style" contains a "remarkable anticipation" of Croce's concept of art as the expression of the artist's immediate intuition of experience.[25] The connection that Orsini is making is an extremely interesting one, for it suggests that Pater, who in his aesthetic thought was to a significant degree working, like Croce, from a Kantian base, has introduced something of a "Copernican revolution" into English criticism. The effect of this revolution was, in Pater's case, ultimately to push art away from its mid-century metaphysical and intellectualist preoccupations toward a more direct concern with sensuous and formal presentation.

Pater tends to treat what he calls the artist's "ideational" impression of reality in two different ways. First, as with Croce, it is an immediate, unreflective intuition of the external world, an intuition produced by the innate make-up of the perceiving mind. Second, it is something far more complex and, as it were, cultural; it is an idea of the world supplied to the artist by the Zeitgeist into which he is born. In the finest art both these ideational impressions are present, transmuted into a sensuous representation.

In my last chapter I noticed the distinction Mill makes in *Hamilton* between two approaches to the doctrine of the relativity of knowledge. On the one hand, there is Mill's own tradition of British empiricism, which argues that the basis of all knowledge lies in the mind's passive perception of the *sensa* or phenomena of the external world; on the other, there is Kant who agrees that the basis of knowledge is the perception of phenomena but who differs from the empiricists in believing that knowledge is in part the result of the active mental formation of the external world of appearances in the very act of perceiving. In dealing with the "soul fact" that is art, Pater seems to have adopted the Kantian approach to the relativity of knowledge, to have taken the position that the artist's mind in the act of perception to an important degree forms, or perhaps better, formalizes, reality.

My license for making this connection between Pater's concept of "soul fact" or artistic intuition and Kant's version of the doctrine of the relativity of knowledge comes from Pater himself. Shortly after defining art as the expression of the artist's sense of fact in "Style," Pater refers to a book of "fascinating precision" on the "technical laws of logic" by H. L. Mansel, one of the foremost mid-Victorian explicators of Kant.[26] Pater says he has learned from Mansel that "all depends upon the original unity, the vital wholeness and identity, of the initiatory apprehension or view." This, he continues, applies directly to art, where "such logical coherency may be evidenced not merely in the lines of composition as a whole, but in the choice of a single word" (*Appreciations,* p. 22). Somewhat later he describes what he takes to be the nature of the artistic intuition of experience.

> Into the mind sensitive to "form," a flood of random sounds, colours, incidents, is ever penetrating from the world without, to become, by sympathetic selection a part of its very structure, and in turn, the visible vesture and expression of that other world it sees so steadily within (*Appreciations,* p. 31).

In view of the earlier reference to the Kantian Mansel with his concept of the a priori wholeness of one's "initiatory apprehension" of the world, it would seem likely that behind this description lies something very close to the Kantian concept of the "transcendental aesthetic," to the belief that the human mind has an a priori, "category" through which it perceives the random data of the phenomenal or sensuous world as if they had a regular shape and order:

> That which in the *phenomenon* corresponds to the sensation, I term *matter;* but that which effects that the content of the phenomenon can be arranged under certain relations, I call its *form.* . . . It is . . . the matter of all phenomena that is given to us *a posteriori;* the form must lie ready *a priori* for them in the mind. . . . And accordingly we find existing in the mind, *a priori,* the pure form of sensuous intuitions in general, in which all the manifold content of the phenomenal world is arranged and viewed under certain relations. . . . [All these ordered relations] belong to pure intuition, which exists *a priori* in the mind as a mere form of sensibility.[27]

It would not do to push Pater's Kantianism too far. Still, it is reasonable to say that Pater has drawn from Kant to make the point that the idealization of reality which takes place in art begins with an intuitive formal perception, that is, an active and automatic ordering of experience by the mind, such as Kant is talking about in his concept of the transcendental aesthetic.

How does this active perception make itself felt in the art object itself? Pater seems to be saying in "Style" that the artist's formal intuition of experience is what lies behind both the structured "lines of composition as a whole" (Arnold's architectonics) and the intricacies of local style (what Pater elsewhere calls "tectonics" [*Greek Studies,* p. 192]). Of these two formal qualities in art Pater, as opposed to Arnold, is primarily concerned with the latter, the endlessly hesitating search for the "last finish" of style, the "blowing away of the last particle of invisible dust" from the gem (*Appreciations,* p. 19). This he also refers to as that "Asiatic *poikilia,* that spirit of minute and curious loveliness" (*Greek Studies,* p. 222) which lies behind all fine craftsmanship and is the necessary basis, although not the totality, of artistic expression.

Let us return to what is certainly Pater's most distinctive aesthetic criterion:

> *All art constantly aspires towards the condition of music.* For a while in all other kinds of art it is possible to distinguish the matter from the form, and the understanding can always make this distinction, yet it is the constant effort of art to obliterate it. . . . [T]hat the mere matter of a picture, the actual circumstances without the form, the spirit, of the handling, that this form, this mode of handling, should become an end in itself, should penetrate every part of the matter: this is what all art constantly strives after, and achieves in different degrees (*Renaissance,* p. 135).[28]

When Pater argues, as he does here, that it is the peculiar nature of art to strive to obliterate the distinction between matter and form, he is by no means continuing, as Ruth Child has suggested he is, the Romantic tradition that sees art as the consummate, metaphysical union of the separate ontological realms of matter and spirit.[29] He is saying something quite different; he is saying that art strives to express in as pure a way possible that inherent formalizing tendency of mind, to exhibit nakedly the structure by which the mind in the act of perception holds the manifold of phenomena together.

This difference between Pater's conception of the artist's ideation of primary experience and that of the Romantics, it seems to me, is intimately implicated in the difference I have already noted in their presentation of sensuous and emotional data. When the Idea is conceived as immanent and objective, as in Romantic art, one has a corresponding naturalism of presentation, for the real world is in itself holy. When the power of ideation retreats as it has in Pater, to the relative, perceiving consciousness, the presentation becomes "Byzantian" as the artist self-consciously seeks to make a now unholy nature conform to the supposed forms of the mind, which are, as with Kant, the key to any hope man may have of spiritual transcendence over the phenomenal world. At the extreme, one approaches a new kind of mysticism in which the mere matter of "real" life fades away, leaving not the pure white light of the Absolute but the equally cold, world-weary whiteness of pure categorical form. As Pater's student and continuator Oscar Wilde concluded:

> As civilisation progresses and we become more highly organised, the elect spirits of each age . . . will grow less and less interested in actual life, and will seek to gain their impressions almost entirely from what Art has touched. For life is terribly deficient in form.[30]

Responding to the formalistic preoccupations of American new criticism, Lionel Trilling has observed that

> there inheres in a work of art of the past a certain quality, an element of its aesthetic existence, which we can identify as its pastness. Side by side with the formal elements of the work, and modifying these elements, there is the element of history, which in any complete aesthetic analysis, must be taken into account.[31]

Pater's Kantian concept of the artist's formal intuition of experience and its analogue in the art object, Asiatic *poi-*

kilia, are, like Arnold's Best Self and its aesthetic analogues, outside history. They are the product of a native condition of human perception and as such stand beyond the vicissitudes of Zeitgeist. As the example of Wilde suggests, it is to this side of his critical thought that Pater owes his reputation as the founder of English Aestheticism, the intellectual fountainhead from whom flowed the almost religious formalism of "art-for-art." But it would be very surprising, given the historicist concerns in Pater, if he did not seek "side by side with the formal elements" that "element of history" Trilling discusses. As I have said, Pater tended to think in terms of two sorts of ideation in art. To the unconscious categorical intuition of form must now be added the expression in art of man's intellectual, reflective knowledge of himself. Thus Pater talking of the artist's impressions of reality in "Style" distinguishes between "mind" and "soul" in art. "By mind the literary artist reaches us, through static and objective indications of design in his work." By soul, however, he reaches us through our sympathy with "widely different and largely diffused phases of religious feeling in operation . . . in style" (*Appreciations,* pp. 24-25). This kind of distinction goes back to the very beginning of Pater's career. In "Winckelmann," discussing the spiritual background behind Greek art, he distinguishes between the permanent "unprogressive ritual element" common to all religious experience and the particular myth, which is superimposed upon this element and which is the "unfixed element," developing "with the freedom and mobility of things of the intellect (*Renaissance,* pp. 201-203). In "Coleridge," with a slight variation on the theme, he distinguishes the two functions of criticism as (1) the classification of the "imitative moments" of "strange excitement" which are presumably timeless and (2) the "study" of the artistic product" in connection with the intellectual and spiritual condition of the age."[32]

Behind this second phase of Pater's concept of ideation in art (and correlatively of critical method) is the general historicizing tendency of his period. More specifically, and more importantly, there is the influence of Hegel's *Ästhetik*. Though Pater, as I have said, had little use for Hegel's metaphysical absolutism, he clearly found in the *Ästhetik* an indispensable guide to the interpretation of art, for its influence may be seen everywhere in his critical work. Indeed, it may be argued that one of Pater's most important claims to serious consideration as a critic resides in the fact that he was the first English critic to make understanding use of Hegel. Lewes had preceded him in introducing the *Ästhetik* to the English reading public,[33] but Lewes never really appreciated what Hegel was saying about the specific nature of the aesthetic as opposed to the philosophical and the moral. After Pater, came three other great Hegelianizing critics and aestheticians, J. A. Symonds, A. C. Bradley, and Bernard Bosanquet, all from Oxford and descended, like himself, from Jowett and T. H. Green. It is ultimately to Pater that credit must go, however, for first introducing Hegel's insights on the relation between history and art into English criticism.

That Pater from very early on in his career knew at least the lengthy theoretical introduction to the *Ästhetik* is evident from "Winckelmann."[34] Recognizing this, a number of commentators have spoken generally of a Hegelian influence in Pater's criticism.[35] I shall briefly discuss here what I take to be the essence of that influence, emphasizing particular points of connection, especially with regard to the historical interpretation of art, which seem to me not to have been adequately noted by others.

According to Hegel, art is, in general, the mediator between spirit and matter.

> From the wealth of its own resources [the mind] brings into being the works of fine art as the primary bond of mediation between that which is exclusively external, sensuous and transitory, and the medium of pure thought, between Nature and its finite reality, and the infinite freedom of a reason which comprehends.[36]

From this fundamental position derive two points that are extremely important to Pater's critical outlook, but which still fall short of being specifically historicist concerns. Insofar as Hegel emphasizes that art is specifically the *sensuous* expression of the spiritual —

> the peculiar distinction . . . of art [is] that its presentation of the most exalted subject-matter is in sensuous form, thereby bringing [that spiritual subject matter] . . . closer to our sensitive and emotional life[37]

— Pater would have found support for his own conviction, already noticed, that "sooner or later art returns to the simple passions and what corresponds to them, the sensuous world." Insofar as Hegel, in self-conscious opposition to the tendency of Romantic theorists to treat aesthetic creation as analogous to *natural* process,[38] emphasizes the role of the radically "unnatural" human intelligence in the making of art —

> the real and indeed sole point to maintain as essential is the thesis that although artistic talent and genius essentially implies an element of natural power, yet it is equally indispensable that it should be thoughtfully cultivated. . . . The fact is that an important aspect of the creating process is merely facility in the use of a

medium; [that is] a work of art possesses a purely technical side, which extends to the border of mere handicraft[39]

—Pater would have found support for his own criticism of Romanticism's analogy between natural and aesthetic process, his own conviction that art was very much the product of the self-conscious intellect. Coleridge, following Schelling, he complains, has made the artist a "mechanical agent."

> The work of art is likened to a living organism. That expresses the sense of a self-delighting, independent life which the finished work of art gives us: it hardly figures the process by which such work was produced. . . . By exquisite analysis the artist attains clearness of idea; then, through many stages of refining, clearness of expression. He moves slowly over his work, calculating the tenderest tone, and restraining the subtlest curve (*Appreciations,* p. 81).[40]

For Hegel the spiritual principle or Idea that art expresses is, of course, the Idea of the age, the Zeitgeist, or man's concept of himself and his universe as that concept develops through time. "It is in works of art that nations have deposited the richest intuition and ideas they possess"; art is the expression of "the definite and comprehensive views of the world in their series of gradations."[41] That Pater adopted this fundamental Hegelian principle is evident throughout his work and nowhere more explicitly than in these remarks from "Winckelmann": we must ask of a work of art, he writes in virtual paraphrase of Hegel, "Did it at the age in which it was produced express in terms of sense . . . man's knowledge of himself?"[42] Whether he is talking about Greek sculpture of the fifth century B.C., Renaissance painting, Reformation architecture, or Romantic poetry, art is always for Pater, as for Hegel, the sensuous expression of a "particular stage of self-reflexion" (*Renaissance,* p. 206) in the ongoing development of the "general consciousness."

If Pater departs at all from Hegel's aesthetic on this point, it is in his greater willingness to allow scope to the role of individual talent and personality in the creation of art than Hegel does. At the same time it would be a serious mistake to press this individualistic tendency of Pater's too far, as Ruth Child certainly does when she argues that Pater gives the individual talent precedence over the age in the creation of the work of art and that he is accordingly the English parallel to Eugène Véron (the French aesthetician who reasserted the primacy of individual talent in explicit opposition to the Hegelian aesthetician Taine).[43] Even when Pater approvingly quotes Blake, the arch-Romantic prophet of genius, to the effect that "genius is always above the age," he makes it quite clear in the same passage that his own definition of genius is one who is the "receptacle," the "refinement" and the "elevation" of the "sentiment of the age" (*Renaissance,* p. x).

The view that art embodies the spirit of the age was, as I have indicated, one of the most distinctive features of Victorian criticism, and so Pater would hardly have been proposing anything very startling when, on the model of Hegel, he set it out as the business of criticism to study art as an expression of the "spiritual condition of the age." But against the background of contemporary historicist criticism, Pater's approach does stand out as having accomplished something quite new. Implicit in Trilling's remarks above is the assumption that the historical element sought in art beside the formal element comes across not as history or Zeitgeist per se but as a distinctly aesthetic experience. It is not simply the direct expression in art of past ideas, beliefs, sociological conditions, and so on that he has in mind, but something in the actual make of the art, in its "aesthetic existence," that is there and can only be there by virtue of its having been made at a particular time. It is this element of pastness in the mode of aesthetic presentation, in the style itself, which appeals. Pater's difference from his Victorian contemporaries lies precisely in his ability to trace the transmutation of the spirit of the age into an aesthetic or formal condition rather than treating it, in A. O. Lovejoy's phrase, as so many "philosophical ideas in dilution." For this specifically aesthetic development of the historicist approach Pater, it seems to me, again owes a significant debt to Hegel.

The most distinctive feature of Hegel's aesthetic as seen against the intellectualist and/or sociological tendencies of most nineteenth-century spirit-of-the-age criticism is the emphasis he places on the transmutation of the Idea of the age into a sensuous "presentment." This is not a question simply of fitting philosophical and religious ideas out in appealing sensuous dress. Rather, it has to do, Hegel is saying, with a way of grasping experience and of thinking, which in turn is the result of a particular level of self-consciousness in the artist. What made the ancient Greek sculptors so superior was that they did not think and perceive as modern men do. With them the Idea was not "wholly explicit" in a cognitive or philosophical sense, but manifested itself "without defect under an immediate and *sensuous* mode. The Greek god is the object of naïve intuition and sensuous imagination."[44] Pater has followed Hegel closely here in his admiration for the "sensuous imagination" of the Hellenes. Thus Plato is admired (no doubt to Jowett's chagrin) as one whose intelligence was essentially "aesthetic" because he "supposed a kind of visible loveliness about ideas" (*Miscellaneous Studies,* p. 57); while Winckelmann, who fascinates Pater precisely because he is a throwback to the Greek mind, "has gradually sunk his intellectual and spiritual ideas in sensuous form"; he is one "[whose] soul . . . becomes more and more immersed in sense, until nothing which lacks the appeal of sense has any interest for him" (*Renaissance,* p. 221).

Moving beyond this general definition of the artistic consciousness and its historical association with the ancient Greeks, Hegel goes on to do something which had not been done before in any significant way. He explains and illustrates in the greatest detail the ways in which an Idea, as a distinct historical stage of consciousness, causes or demands an equally distinct sensuous expression or "form." We must not imagine, he writes, that Ideas in art accept just any plastic configuration. The nature of the Idea determines the configuration, and since the nature of the Idea in turn is determined by history, particular types of artistic configuration correspond to particular historical-spiritual conditions.

> We must quit ourselves of the idea that it is a matter of mere accident that an actual phenomenon of the object world is accepted as the mode in which to embody such a form coalescent with truth. Art does not lay hold of this form either because it is simply there or because there is no other. The concrete content [a particular Idea of the world] itself implies the presence of . . . the sensuous appearance.
>
> . . . . .
>
> [Mind] is constrained to traverse a series of stages . . . and to this course of stages which it unfolds to itself, corresponds a coalescent series . . . of the plastic types of art.[45]

He then delineates three general types of aesthetic expression, the symbolical, the classical, and the romantic, corresponding to what he takes to be the three major phases in the progress of Geist toward total self-consciousness. This extremely important principle of a causal relation between historical Idea and aesthetic form is picked up by Pater, who, in fact, reproduces Hegel's triad of symbolic, classical, and romantic art types in "Winckelmann."

> Different attitudes of the imagination have a native affinity with different types of sensuous form. . . . The arts may thus be ranged in a series, which corresponds to a series of developments in the human mind itself (*Renaissance,* p. 210).[46]

Throughout his subsequent criticism Pater, often following Hegel, often embarking upon his own interpretations, characteristically treats form in art as something determined by the historical phasis of the Idea, and in particular that Idea's religious expression, through which the artist is passing. One may illustrate the point chronologically. The "Dorian" religious belief developed by the Greeks as they became increasingly self-conscious and conceptual in their thought did not, as Pater sees it, have any place for the sense of shame or sin. Consequently the Greek artist perceived the sensuous world innocently. "To the Greek this immersion in the sensuous was, religiously . . . indifferent." The result in terms of aesthetic expression is the *Heiterkeit* of Greek sculpture, was its "repose" and "serenity" (*Renaissance,* pp. 221-22). This innocence of apprehension of the sensuous was not, however, available to the more advanced, religious consciousness of Christianity. The whole religion of the Middle Ages, Pater says in "Morris," was a "disorder of the senses," with the effect, again, that the artist created according to the spirit he was "of": a "passion of which the outlets are sealed begets a tension of nerve, in which the sensible world comes to one with a reinforced brilliance and relief." "Hence a wild, convulsed sensuousness in the poetry of the middle age, in which the things of nature begin to play a strange delirious part."[47]

Moving on to the Renaissance, Pater describes Botticelli as one who, developing a "meditative subtlety," has moved beyond the simple religion of his "Gothic" predecessors and found his own artistic vision peculiarly affected by this new spiritual condition: "The genius of which Botticelli is the type usurps the data before it as the exponent of ideas, moods, visions of its own; in this interest it plays fast and loose with those data" (*Renaissance,* p. 53). The effects of this awakening of the intellect in Botticelli and in other Renaissance artists is to impart to the naïve naturalism of predecessors such as Giotto or Masaccio a sense of mind or spirit seeking to escape its limitations. The "weight of meaning" is put into "outward things, light, colour, every-day gesture" (*Renaissance,* p. 52). Everywhere in *Renaissance* Pater seeks to describe the effect of this awakening intelligence on the plastic configurations of art. Certain figures which he (mistakenly) attributes to Leonardo, show "all those finer conditions wherein material things rise to that subtlety of operation which constitutes them spiritual. . . . It is as if in certain significant examples we actually saw those forces at their work on human flesh" (*Renaissance,* p. 116).

The difference between Michelangelo's sculpture and that of Hellenic Greece is that in Michelangelo one has a "genius spiritualized" by the human race's accumulated experience of Medieval Christianity, a genius "penetrated by [a Christian] spirit of inwardness and introspection, living not a mere outward life like the Greek but a life full of intimate experiences."[48] For such a genius a sculptural "system" (the Greek) "which sacrificed so much of what was inward and unseen could not satisfy him" (*Renaissance,* p. 67). Acordingly, to render his Idea with all its inwardness, Michelangelo leaves his statues unfinished: "That incompleteness is Michelangelo's equivalent for colour in sculpture; it is his way of relieving its stiff realism, and communicating to it breath, pulsation, the effect of life" (*Renaissance,* p. 68).

For a final example I cite Pater's interpretation of the years following the Renaissance, the years of the Reformation, in which a spirit of doubt and disorientation begins to make itself felt. Diversities and particularities become ultimate, "the priceless pearl of truth lying if anywhere, not in large theoretic apprehension of the general, but in minute vision of the particular" (*Gaston,* p. 93), and this vision of life, according to Pater, produces its own special artistic expression. In the absence of a synthetic Idea of the World the artist becomes preoccupied with detail for its own sake, with the finesse of "that last so desirable touch" and the "grace" of "reiterated refinements" that brings with it an "exquisite faintness," a "certain tenuity and caducity" (*Renaissance,* pp. 160-166). Such a movement of the Zeitgeist and with it the artistic imagination toward decadence Pater seems to be offering in "Joachim du Bellay" and again in *Gaston Latour* as the evening farewell of Renaissance "inwardness."

In bringing this particular Hegelian approach to English criticism, Pater succeeded as no other critic of his time had in constructing an organic, genuinely aesthetic connection between the all-important concept of a developing religious and philosophical Zeitgeist and its expression in art. He did not, as Arnold did, push the Zeitgeist aside altogether in favor of a recurring and, for all practical purposes, a historically undifferentiated aesthetic condition. Nor did he, in the manner of others of his contemporaries, treat the Zeitgeist as something art merely talks about, as it were. To see the difference here, simply contrast Pater's approach to a characteristically Victorian interpretation of art as the index of the spirit of the age, to that, for instance, of his contemporary Leslie Stephen. Writing in 1875 on the spirit of the late eighteenth century as reflected in the poetry of Cowper, Stephen observes that

> what [Sainte-Beuve], as a purely literary critic, passed over as comparatively uninteresting, gives the exposition of Cowper's intellectual position. The poem [the *Task*] is in fact a political, moral, and religious disquisition interspersed with charming vignettes, which . . . illustrate the general thesis. . . . To understand Cowper's mind . . . we must take the now obsolete meditation with the permanently attractive pictures.[49]

For Stephen there is the world of "meditation" and the world of "permanently attractive pictures," and in his critical intelligence never do the two meet.[50] Through the aid of Hegel, Pater has brought together what the "purely literary critic" such as Sainte-Beuve wants (and, one might add, what Sainte-Beuve's great English disciple, Matthew Arnold wants) and what the student of intellectual history such as Stephen wants.

Returning to my earlier point about Pater's view of art as being not the imitation of reality but the expression of "soul fact," it is possible to see still more clearly why Pater was able to make organic connections between the spirit of the age and aesthetic presentation. From the essay on "Style," as throughout his work, it is clear that Pater believed that to a very important degree an artist's actual perception of reality, his "soul fact," is conditioned not only by the innate categories of his mind but by the peculiar religious or philosophical spirit he is "of." Holding this *subjectivist* view of artistic process, Pater was able, in fact, to move even beyond Hegel in organicism. He has taken what for Hegel is a metaphysical point about the nature of spirit in art and transposed it into an epistemological point. The stage of Zeitgeist into which one is born, the particular beliefs one inherits are necessary conditions upon one's perception of the sensible world. They produce a distinctive, historical way of seeing, and that way of seeing, inevitably and organically finds its way into the artist's formation of reality.

The Problem of Aesthetic Value

Pater's characteristically Victorian assumption that it is criticism's business to treat art as an expression of the spirit of its age leads again, as it did with Carlyle and Arnold, to the question of how such historicist approach affects the normative function of criticism. As I have indicated in the previous chapter, Pater's adoption of something like a complete historicism in the manner of Dilthey or Croce led him to the kind of cultural ecumenicalism that is bound to frustrate the critic's attempt to determine what Arnold called "real" value, that is, historically transcendent value in art. Dilthey's remarks on value are symptomatic of the difficulty. There are, he suggests, "no values which are valid for all nations. . . . History itself is the productive force for the creation of valuations."[51] Much the same spirit is implicit in Pater's own dictum that "nothing which has ever interested living men and women can wholly lose its vitality" (*Renaissance*, p. 49). Pater's general receptivity to a wide variety of aesthetic experiences and his reluctance to censor any has led to the belief that he was, after all, pretty much of a relativist in critical matters,[52] that he was as constitutionally unable to take a position on the value of a work of art as he was to commit himself to belief in a particular philosophy or religion. To some degree this is true of Pater, but it would be a mistake to treat him as one would Taine, for instance, as a critic for whom the whole question of value is irrelevant. On the contrary, it is clear throughout Pater's work and especially in essays such as "Winckelmann," "Giorgione," and "Style" that he does consider it meaningful to talk of the nature of aesthetic value and to try to formulate some criterion for evaluation. Pater's efforts in this direction take essentially two forms. On the one hand, he brings together his historicist and normative concerns and writes as if the value of art depended significantly on its expression of the "wonderful order" of developing human culture or Zeitgeist. On the other, he takes a more strictly aesthetic approach and talks of what he calls a "Hellenic ideal" in art, which, although not actually independent of historical concerns, does, in an important sense, rise above them.

In considering the relation between Pater's two concepts of ideation in art, the formalist and the historicist, it is important to recognize that he definitely regards the latter as imparting a higher interest and a higher value to art than it would have as a merely sensuous and emotional or as an abstract, geometrical expression of formal intuition such as one might find, say, in a Persian carpet or a Japanese print. Thus in *Greek Studies* he quite carefully distinguishes between the Asiatic impulse, with its "pure skill of hand," "unelevated by the divination of the spirit of man" (*Greek Studies,* pp. 187, 222), and what he calls, again, the true *Hellenic* mode. The latter reveals the effects on art of larger religious and philosophical conceptions, conceptions of the "informing reasonable soul," which implies the "development of the thoughts of man concerning humanity, the growing revelation of the mind to itself." Nowhere in the world of "Asiatic tectonics," the "exquisite world of design," "is there as yet any adequate sense of man himself, nowhere is there an insight into or power over human form as the *expression of human soul*" (*Greek Studies,* pp. 220-223; my italics). This development of "soul" in artistic expression does not cancel out the beauty of pure form but adds to it a warmth and vitality that it would otherwise lack.[53] The point is still more explicit in the distinction Pater makes in "Style" between "good art," which is formally excellent, and "great art," which besides formal excellence expresses some high philosophical or religious idea. Great art is that which is devoted

> to the increase of men's happiness . . . to the enlargement of our sympathies with each other, or to the presentment of new or old truth about ourselves and our relation to the world as may ennoble and fortify us in our sojourn here. . . . [Great art] has something of the soul of humanity in it, and finds its logical, its architectural place, in the great structure of human life (*Appreciations,* p. 38).

It seems fairly clear in passages such as these that Pater is resting value in art upon the historicist Weltanschauung that I discussed in the last chapter. The "architectural" "structure" of humanity that he talks of above is no more than Marius' vision of the "venerable system in impregnable possession of human life." In other words, the historicist ideal is doing for Pater much the same thing as the metaphysics of will was doing for Carlyle, the ideal of the Best Self, for Arnold: it is providing the essential spiritual basis for determining aesthetic value.

In Pater's case, more than in that of either Carlyle or Arnold, a great deal of trouble is taken to treat this spiritual basis only in its specifically aesthetic presentation. Still it must be observed that Pater here is, to a significant degree, bringing concerns to bear on critical evaluation which are not strictly aesthetical, but are moral and philosophical. He himself would scarcely have denied this. His reputation as a founder of the English art-for-art movement aside, he shared with his Victorian contemporaries the view that art must have a moral function.[54] The duty of modern art to society, he says in "Winckelmann," is "so to rearrange the details of modern life . . . that it may satisfy the spirit." The way it satisfies the spirit is to give it a "sense of Freedom" from the "universality of natural law, even in the moral order," freedom from the "web" of mechanical forces that is "woven through and through us" (*Renaissance,* p. 231). When Pater speaks thus of art's giving us a sense of freedom from natural law and when he talks in the passage from "Style" of its bringing happiness and enlarging our sympathies, he is talking about essentially the same moral effect that Marius experiences in the face of Cornelius' Christianity. "There had been a permanent protest established in the world, a plea, a perpetual after-thought, which humanity henceforth would possess in reserve, against any wholly mechanical and disheartening theory of itself and its conditions" (*Marius,* II, 221). It is not that Marius believes in Christianity, it is simply that Christianity, like any great spiritual construct from the worship of Demeter to Hegel's philosophy of mind at once testifies to mankind's capacity to transcend the mechanical world of natural law and to his need to make sympathetic contact with others through the means of common belief. Both these moral needs, for spiritual transcendence and sympathetic fellowship, the greatest art satisfies quite apart from what it does to its audience's aesthetic sense.

The notion that great art ought to express the developing "soul of humanity" establishes a criterion beyond that of mere skill of hand or craftsmanship, but it does not help one distinguish the value of one expression of man's "informing reasonable soul" from another. According to this criterion as it stands, there is no reason why one should value *The Divine Comedy* any differently from *Paradise Lost* or *Paradise Lost* any differently from *The Prelude*. All are equally expressions of soul in the sense that Pater is discussing above. To meet this difficulty and to satisfy his normative impulse, Pater very early on developed the concept of the Hellenic ideal in art, a concept which he seems to have derived from Hegel but at the same time significantly modified. According to this concept, it is the intimacy of the relation between soul and artistic expression that determines value in art.

Value in art, Hegel believes, is the result of the complete organic fusion of content, which is the Idea, and form, which is the aesthetic handling of that idea, the shaping of the sensuous into conformity with Mind.

> The value and intrinsic worth of . . . [aesthetic] presentment consists in the correspondence and unity of the two aspects, that is the Idea and its sensuous shape, the supreme level and excellence of art and the reality, which is truly consonant with its notion will depend upon the degree of intimacy and union with which Idea and configuration appear together in elaborated fusion.[55]

Put aside Hegel's emphasis on the self-consciousness of the shaping or aesthetic process, and one has here essentially another expression of the Romanticist concept of beauty as a reconciliation of spirit and matter, subject and object, such as Hegel would have found in Schiller or Schelling or, had he cared to look, Coleridge. The great difference, however, is that Hegel, unlike his Romantic predecessors, does not consider that such a perfect fusion of idea and matter can be produced at any time by individual genius, but that it is dependent upon history, that is, upon the stage of development at which the Idea finds itself when it is embodied in art. His concept of beauty is no less metaphysical than theirs, but it is thoroughly impregnated, as theirs is not, by historicism.

The consummate aesthetic union of Idea and sensuous form happened, according to Hegel, at one particular historical phase of mind, the classical, and in one type of sensuous representation, sculpture. The classical art-type was "the perfected coherence of spiritual and sensuous existence": "the free and adequate embodiment of the Idea in the shape which, according to its notional concept, is uniquely appropriate to the Idea itself."[56] As Mind developed in sophistication, became, that is, increasingly self-conscious, subjective, and "inward," it destroyed this classical balance of beauty, and art became romantic. "The romantic type of art annuls the completed union of the Idea and its reality, and [returns] if on a higher plane, to the . . . opposition of [Idea and reality] which remained unovercome in symbolic art."[57] In other words, the Idea in its classical representation, although it had reached an aesthetic ideal, was not expressed in its true or highest form; it was still limited by the sensuous, and it is the nature of Mind to want to achieve complete freedom from the sensuous.[58] The freedom toward which Mind strives is the freedom of Absolute, self-conscious Spirit, and this is the freedom expressed in philosophy, not art. So Hegel is, in effect, saying that beauty in its highest sense is no longer possible in the modern world.

241

As Croce points out, "The Aesthetic of Hegel is . . . a funeral oration: he passes in review the successive forms of art, shows the progressive steps of internal consumption and lays the whole in its grave, leaving Philosophy to write its epitaph."[59]

Pater appears to have accepted Hegel's basic point that the classical art-type is the standard of aesthetic excellence. Thus in "Winckelmann," in the context of his discussion of Hegel's aesthetic, he notes that besides the historically conditioned in art there is also "an element of permanence, a standard of taste, which genius confesses" and that this standard "was fixed in Greece, at a definite historical period" (*Renaissance,* p. 199). The period he means is the same period Hegel has designated "classical" (ca. fifth century B.C.), and, as with Hegel, sculpture is for him the highest aesthetic expression of the beautiful (*Renaissance,* p. 209). Pater's belief in what he calls the "Hellenic ideal" is not just a "stop along the way," as it were, but something which in one form or another stays with him throughout his career so that as late as "Plato's Aesthetics" (1891-92) he is still admiring that "Dorian" or "Apollonian" sanity which reduces the "rough, promiscuous wealth of nature" to "grace and order" (*Plato,* p. 281).

The great question, however, is whether Pater believes, pace Hegel, that this Hellenic ideal can apply to aesthetic production in the postclassical period. Like Hegel he accepts that the ideal is the product of historical conditions, "a spontaneous growth out of the influence of Greek society" (*Renaissance,* p. 200). Again, like Hegel, he accepts that the rise of romantic inwardness or spirituality in the Middle Ages destroyed the balance of form and matter achieved in Hellenic art (*Renaissance,* pp. 224-25). But Pater, as I have indicated, lacks Hegel's idealist and progressivist preoccupation with the Mind's irreversible march toward some spiritual Absolute. He is far more concerned with the aesthetic expression of the Idea per se and finds it impossible to accept that such an expression is no longer possible in its highest form. Accordingly, he treats the Hellenic ideal as, mutatis mutandis, a recurring tradition in the history of art, a tradition that is in an important degree independent of time and place (*Renaissance,* p. 199). What is best about the art of the Renaissance, as Pater interprets it, is its resumption of the Hellenic spirit, after the "strange winter" of the Middle Ages, the "pagan culture awoke to life," and this theme of the reviving Hellenic ideal runs throughout Pater's comment on the art of the period.[60] For example, the "cold light" and "quaint design" of Botticelli's paintings are "a more direct inlet into the Greek temper than the works of the Greeks themselves" (*Renaissance,* p. 58); and Michelangelo's "sweetness" (as opposed to his "strength") carries his work back to the Greek system of sculpture. It is not that Pater considers that Renaissance art has simply reproduced the Hellenic ideal of the ancients; on the contrary, he is attempting to describe the new character that ideal has taken on after having been filtered, as it were, through the medieval Christian Idea.

The point of including "Winckelmann" in the *Renaissance* essays is clearly to draw attention to the parallel between the Renaissance and the Greek beauty that so fascinated the German aestheticians. At the same time, "Winckelmann" looks beyond the Greeks and the Renaissance Italians to a still more modern recurrence of the Hellenic ideal. Can we, Pater asks, toward the end of the essay, "bring down that [Hellenic] ideal into the gaudy perplexed light of modern life?" (*Renaissance,* p. 227.) His answer is to point, like Carlyle and Arnold before him, to Goethe as the model of modern aesthetic possibilities. Goethe, he says, learns from Winckelmann the "eternal problem of culture — balance, unity with one's self, con-summate Greek modelling" (*Renaissance,* p. 228), and Goethe does, to some degree, succeed in resuming the Hellenic ideal in the "perplexed" modern age. Nor is he alone, for Pater is inclined to find the high Hellenic qualities in a number of Goethe's contemporaries and immediate followers of the Romantic period, Schiller, Hegel, Heine, Blake, Keats, Wordsworth. What one calls Romanticism, he says at one point, is as much a "return to true Hellenism" as it is anything else.[61]

What Pater means in particular by the consummate union of spirit and sensuous presentation in the Hellenic idea has, I hope, already been amply suggested by my treatment above of his call for a return to the primary data and his concepts of aesthetic ideation. The question that concerns me at this point is whether this recurring Hellenic ideal which is Pater's "standard of taste" just happens or whether it is, as in Hegel, allied in some way to the nature of Zeitgeist. Is any phase of the Zeitgeist as good as any other for purposes of achieving the aesthetic ideal? The answer it would seem is no; Pater has freed the aesthetic ideal from its fixed place in ancient Greece, but he has not freed it altogether from a dependence upon historical process. Like Carlyle and Arnold before him, Pater appears to see the Zeitgeist as passing through phases of particular unity and vitality — Carlyle would have called them ages of "belief," Arnold, ages of "intellectual and moral deliverance" — and to see such phases as especially conducive to the achievement of the aesthetic ideal. Thus he writes of the Renaissance:

> There come, however, from time to time, eras of more favourable conditions, in which the thoughts of men draw nearer together than is their wont, and the many

interests of the intellectual world combine in one complete type of general culture. The fifteenth century in Italy is one of these happier eras, and what is sometimes said of the age of Pericles is true of that of Lorenzo: — it is an age productive in personalities, many-sided, centralised, complete. Here, artists and philosophers and those whom the action of the world has elevated and made keen, do not live in isolation, but breathe a common air, and catch light and heat from each other's thought (*Renaissance,* p. xiv).

Pater's concept of the poetic or aesthetic age is different in many ways from Carlyle's and Arnold's. He is not concerned, as Carlyle is, with a healthy belief in the Deity and a reverence for authority. Nor is he concerned, as Arnold is, with the rational ordering of society and the proliferation of Stoical self-containment. What concerns him, rather, is the sheer intellectual exuberance and expansiveness of the age, its many-sidedness, its testimony to the magnificent creativity of the human mind in its pursuit of the "infinite possibility of things." It is an age, which, to return to Santayana's psychological distinction, is characterized by a unity of inclusion rather than, as it tends to be in both Carlyle and Arnold, *exclusion.* At the same time Pater is continuing a tradition, continuing the assumption found in both these predecessors that aesthetic excellence depends upon a cultural unity, a shared spiritual atmosphere, which binds men together and provides them with the inspiration and emotional security, the defense from disheartening isolation and skepticism that are necessary if they are to achieve the highest aesthetic expression. Also like Carlyle and Arnold, it may be added, he is beset by an underlying consciousness that his own period has somehow lost that essential unity, is, in fact, a period of cultural and aesthetic decadence.

CONCLUSION

HISTORICISM
AND THE ENRICHMENT
OF CRITICAL THOUGHT

On the whole true statements are of more service to us than false
ones. None the less we do not and, at present, cannot order our
emotions and attitudes by true statements alone. Nor is there any
probability that we ever shall contrive to do so. This is one of the
great new dangers to which civilisation is exposed. Countless
pseudo-statements — about God, about the universe, about human
nature, the relations of mind to mind, about the soul, its rank and
destiny — pseudo-statements which are pivotal points in the organisation of the mind, vital to its well-being, have suddenly become, for sincere, honest and informed minds, impossible to believe. For centuries they have been believed; now they are gone,
irrecoverably; and the knowledge which has killed them is not of a
kind upon which an equally fine organisation of the mind can be
based.

— I.A. Richards

In my introduction I spoke of the historicist concerns that
I have been dealing with throughout as linking together the
thought of my three major figures, as giving that thought
and, in particular, the criticism that grew from it a distinctive intellectual continuity. Now, I want to review what has

246

seemed to me the main movement of mind involved, the principle element of continuity.

Carlyle, Arnold, and Pater had in common a preoccupation with historicity, a preoccupation with the spectacle of continuously changing values and beliefs through time. The spectacle was far from a reassuring one. In fact, it was by and large precisely the spiritually disorganizing experience that Richards refers to above. All man's beliefs regarding God, human nature, the soul, morality, and so on, beliefs vital to his personal well-being and to the well-being of his society, were suddenly thrown into question by the historicist spirit of the times, were seen to be not truths in themselves but merely the relative expressions of time and place. The problem all three critics faced was the problem of reconciling themselves intellectually and emotionally to the implications of this historicity. This was the essential motivating force behind their thought. The resolutions which they achieved and which I have tried to describe as fully as possible in the foregoing chapters, were all quite distinctive. Overall, however, they represented a gradual movement of mind toward an acceptance of the impossibility of belief in the traditional sense, toward the defeat of what Richards elsewhere calls "that old dream of a perfect knowledge which would guarantee perfect life."[1]

For Carlyle the historicity of belief became tolerable only insofar as the various belief-systems thrown up by the "Time-Spirit" were seen to be emanations of the Divine Mind, which was itself, of course, outside time. If the present age was one of Unbelief, of spiritual bankruptcy and social anarchy, no matter; in the Providential nature of things a hero would come, a new mythus would arise from the ashes of skepticism, and mankind would again be spiritually delivered. At the same time, Carlyle was obviously far more fascinated than a proper theist should have been by the capacity of the creative human will to participate in the making of its own belief-systems, to weave the "clothes" of symbol and myth which "body forth" the Divine Idea in the world. Insofar as Carlyle conceded this power of belief-making to the finite human mind, indeed, insofar as he tended to glory in it, just so far did he loosen the process of historically changing values and ideas from its saving anchor in the Divine or Absolute and admit the possibility of the relativity, the fundamental instability of all belief and all value. That admission he was, in the end, far too much of a religious man ever to make.

For Arnold, a quarter of a century Carlyle's junior, the spectacle of endlessly dissolving belief-systems had become still more disconcerting precisely because, unlike Carlyle but like so many of his own generation, he was unable to see this process as emanating from God. For him, if the developing Zeitgeist, the best that was known and thought in his day, had taught anything, it was that there was no transcendent Deity and no spiritual Absolute from which anything could emanate. Accordingly he accepted far more fully than ever Carlyle did that the March of Mind was a purely secular, manmade process, the product of the intellectual elite, the Aristotles, the Spinozas, the Hegels. This acceptance did not in any way lessen his longing after something constant to hold by amidst the flux of cultural relativity. Retaining a religious man's skepticism over the products of the mere intellect and the inadequacy of those products to the needs of the total man and the total community, he fixed upon a concept learned from the Stoics and from Spinoza, which is very close to what Richards means by the total psychological and moral "organization" that is "vital" to the mind's well-being. This was his concept of the harmoniously developed

Best Self. Beside this Best Self the intellectualist process of developing ideas and beliefs became virtually irrelevant; it mattered only insofar as it could, from time to time, produce the synthetic Weltanschauungen, such as Christianity, "pseudo-statements," which supported the saving organization of the mind. In all this Arnold went quite beyond Carlyle in his concept of belief. Carlyle always insisted upon the need actually to believe in the new mythus brought in by the Hero and thus never quite faced the implications of his own clothes philosophy. If one once admits that the clothes of belief go on and off with passing time, how is one ever again able to manage that total commitment to them that one had when one thought, as the Houyhnhnms did of Gulliver's outfit, that they were an organic part of the thing itself? Arnold, on the other hand, could regard the question of belief much more ironically. For him belief was a sort of illusion; it was, in Richards' terms, "objectless"; that is, it produced certain desired psychological and moral effects, but referred to no reality outside itself. Belief, in short, had ceased to be a judgment about the truth or falsity of things and become a variety of feeling, a very complex and elevated feeling to be sure, but still a feeling.

Finally with Pater the desire—so strong in both Carlyle and Arnold—to transcend or get beyond historicity ends. He accepted fully the implications of the clothes philosophy: beliefs and values are entirely man-woven and there is no spiritual reality other than that posited by the historical process. Pater's response to this state of affairs was twofold. On the negative side, the impossibility of fixed beliefs drove him back toward the basis of existence, toward unelaborated sensuous and emotional experience as the only sort of experience of which one could be certain. On the positive side, the inadequacy of this "sensuous wisdom," the desire to transcend the merely material and immediate, led him forward to embrace that "abstract secular process," that "system" of continuously developing Zeitgeist as a value in itself, as a miraculous testimony to the creativity of the human imagination and the means out of the isolation of the individual consciousness into sympathetic contact with others not only in the present but in the past and future as well. Belief, essential for Carlyle, reduced to an "attitude" by Arnold, became for Pater not only a philosophical impossibility but a positive hindrance to the expansive powers of mind in its efforts to realize the many-sidedness, the completeness of things.

The consequences of this movement of mind for poetics may perhaps best be summarized by reconsidering a problem that in one form or another has come up throughout this study, that is, the crucial problem of the relation between belief, on the one hand, and aesthetic value, on the other.

Carlyle, as I have said, rested poetic value upon the poet's power of expressing the Divine Idea. The poet penetrates behind the veil to discover the "open secret" of the universe; upon the success of this truth-seeking mission depends the value of his work. From this it followed for Carlyle that the test of aesthetic value is the test of one's ability to believe in the Idea that the poem expresses. Carlyle's notion of how one knows the Idea or truth expressed by poetry was more mystical than that of most of his Victorian contemporaries, but his preoccupation with the truth or "revelationist" criterion is still centrally characteristic of the poetics of the period. Into this view of poetic value, historicism introduced a significant qualification. A poet such as Dante, Carlyle said, penetrates into the "sacred mystery of the Universe." Yes, but the degree of that penetration is necessarily limited by historical conditions, by the spirit of the age: Dante (he continued) "emblems-forth" or "makes real" the "noblest idea hitherto" known to mankind. In that "hitherto" resided a world of difficulties for the truth criterion, for if the Idea is not absolute, once and for all, but is ever in progress, poetic value must move as well onto a sliding scale. Thus one's inability to believe in the now outmoded truth of Dante's poem becomes, as Carlyle was well aware, a serious block to accepting that poem as valuable for all time.

One way out of the difficulty was, of course, to base an estimate of poetry on something besides a capacity to believe in its truth-telling powers. Carlyle had just an inkling that this was possible. He noted that the poet's special talent lies in his "emblematic intellect," his power of figurative and symbolic expression or what Pater later splendidly described as that "complex faculty for which every thought and feeling is twin-born with its sensible analogue or symbol" (*Renaissance,* p. 138). Unfortunately, however, Carlyle could not consider this power — as Pater was to do — independently, as a basis of poetic value; he had to consider it only, as he considered everything else, in terms of its power to create belief. Another significant way in which Carlyle seems to have looked beyond the truth criterion is found in his conviction that there is a necessary causal relationship between an age of belief and aesthetic excellence. In those periods of belief which history periodically produces the poet feels himself whole and spontaneous, and in this wholeness and spontaneity he produces great poems such as Dante's. The relation thus established between belief and the poetic has only indirectly to do with truth. Carlyle was talking about a social condition produced by a viable belief-system, which by its effects on the poet's inner being conduced (somehow) to poetic excellence. Carlyle, in the end, was too little attuned to the inner self, too much preoccupied by the immediate "revolutionist" need simply to do battle with the Not-Self, to be able to work out the strictly aesthetic implications of this insight. Nor for that matter had he the critical sensitivity to define in formal terms precisely what he meant by the poetic excellence that goes with believing ages.

Arnold, who in his desire to get beyond the Zeitgeist turned inward upon the Best Self, realized possibilities ignored by Carlyle. In those great ages, which are ages for Arnold as for Carlyle in which men believe in some overall moral and intellectual interpretation of experience and are thus "delivered" from doubt and spiritual disorganization, great poetry becomes eminently possible. But Arnold, unlike Carlyle, valued the poetic expressions of such periods quite explicitly not for the truth they express but for the moral and emotional *attitudes* they produce in the reader. That the Thomistic beliefs behind Dante's "In la sua volontade è nostra pace" were in the nineteenth century untrue in any scientific sense does not matter; what does is the fact that those words activate a moral and emotional response which is analogous to the security and joyful transcendence associated with genuine belief. The value of the poetry is placed in that affective experience and, more specifically, in the aesthetic forms — architectonics and grand style — that produce it, rather than in the particular, perishable set of beliefs behind it. The principal difficulty with this position, as I have suggested, is that there must always be some question of how long the capacity to experience the sort of inner peace that Dante is talking about can exist in the absence of genuine belief in the truths that originally produced it. Be that as it may, Arnold succeeded in shifting the locus of aesthetic valuation away from the truth criterion and placing it squarely on questions of effect and of form. Where Arnold's poetic left most to be desired was in its tendency simply to exclude rather than reconcile itself to the fact of historicity. By placing value in the supposed permanent emotional and moral needs of the mind, Arnold effectively denied to the aesthetic object its power of expressing what Trilling calls the historical element, the concrete variety of the developing mind of the race, and this does seem to me a fairly significant curtailment of aesthetic experience.

For Pater the recognition of the historicity of all the higher truths of philosophy, religion, and morality, had, as I have said, the initial effect of forcing the mind back upon the primary data of experience, that is toward a sort of intellectual suicide that seems to anticipate, as Bloom has suggested, our modern "universe of death." Whatever shortcomings such a disposition may have as a philosophy of life, applied to the discussion of art it raised possibilities and interests conscientiously muted by most Victorian criticism. For Pater critical attention was redirected with unprecedented emphasis toward the discrimination of the minutiae of direct sensuous and emotional experience conveyed by art. As in the case of Keats' "negative capability," the mind was understood to see and feel the more precisely and fully just in proportion as it was able (or forced) to abandon its need for spiritual and intellectual transcendence. Pater was hardly prepared totally to abandon this need. For him, as for Kant, the very act of perception is an "inspiriting" experience in the sense that the experiential data reached one only after being transmuted or ordered by the mind "sensitive to form." Beyond this the mind builds linguistic and conceptual constructs that accumulate into the systems of belief by which men live, and art cannot be fully valuable in Pater's opinion until it is informed by this "reasonable soul" of humanity striving to articulate its own meaning. For Pater, however, as for Arnold, ideas, religious and philosophical systems care not for belief at all; they are necessary conditions on the artist's "way of seeing." Through the lenses, as it were, of his Weltanschauung the artist receives the impression of the sensible world. That impression or "soul fact" is what he imitates with the result that ideation is seamlessly incorporated in the aesthetic object as a matter of "pure perception." Aesthetic value resides, accordingly, not in truth, not in psychic balance, but in an inarticulate sensuous and formal condition, a condition of complete organic unity between idea and aesthetic expression.

The historicism that characterized nineteenth-century thought is commonly blamed for impoverishing criticism by hopelessly undermining its normative function. Historicism — it is said — by teaching that all things are to be explained and fully explained by their origins and by teaching further that all value is relative to the historical conditions in which it is posed, transformed the function of criticism from a discussion of value in art to a variety of historical discourse. This sort of objection is unquestionably justified (provided, of course, one accepts to begin with, as it seems to me one must, that the principal problem of criticism is the problem of value). From my study, it would appear that there is another side to the question as well. If historicism was from one standpoint responsible for the destruction of certain accustomed modes of valuation in criticism, from another, it was a generator of new ones. By throwing into doubt those "countless pseudo-statements" about God, the soul, and so on, and, moreover, by throwing into doubt the very concept of belief and thus limiting the mind to what Pater saw as a healthy skepticism, it did not by any means dispose of the human needs that hitherto had been satisfied by belief. Rather, it forced men to look elsewhere for that satisfaction. The situation is one in which, as Richards has said, the mind deprived of the possibility of belief is driven back to more concrete and empirical grounds to fill the psychic vacancy left by the disappearance of belief.

Richards is talking primarily about his own period, but my own view is that the awareness of the instability of truth or intellectual value and the concomitant search for alternative grounds of value set in a good deal earlier. That search tended to center itself, as it had done in the Romantic period, upon poetry and art. And, to a large degree, it amounted simply to a continuation of the Romantic effort to find in poetry and art an alternative means for doing what religion and philosophy traditionally had done, that is, provide some form of absolute revelation about the true nature of things. But with the critics I have been discussing this turning to poetry tended more and more to become, not so much a search for an alternative means of achieving belief as a substitute for the concept of belief itself. Whatever the value of this enterprise as a criticism of life, its value for criticism itself was extremely important. By undermining the concept of belief itself the historicist outlook at the same time undermined the ancient assumption that poetry is a variety of truth or knowledge, closer to philosophy than to history. In this its tendency was ever to compel critical attention back upon more specifically aesthetic criteria for the discussion of art and to liberate art from subservience to criteria more suitably applied elsewhere. I do not claim that this liberation has been entirely accomplished in the critics I have been discussing, but I do contend that it was more substantially underway than is commonly supposed and that the principal motive force behind it was, again, the historicist spirit.

NOTES

Introduction. Historicism and Criticism

1. V. F. Storr, *The Development of English Theology in the Nineteenth Century* (London: Longmans, 1913), p. 115. For more on the development of the concern with history in the nineteenth century, see E. Feuter, *Geschichte der Neueren Historiographie* (Berlin: Oldenbourg, 1911); G. P. Gooch, *History and Historians in the Nineteenth Century* (London: Longmans, 1952); K. Lowith, *From Hegel to Nietzsche: The Revolution in Nineteenth Century Thought*, trans. D. Green (New York: Holt, Rinehart, and Winston, 1964); J. W. Thompson, *A History of Historical Writing* (New York: Macmillan, 1942), II.

2. See J. H. Buckley, *The Triumph of Time* (Cambridge: Harvard University Press, 1967), chap. 2; R. Brooks, "The Development of the Historical Mind," *The Reinterpretation of Victorian Literature*, ed. J. Baker (Princeton: Princeton University Press, 1950), pp. 130, 138-148; J. W. Thompson, *History of Historical Writing,* II, 280-289.

3. *Critical and Miscellaneous Essays,* II, 84-85, in *Carlyle's Works,* ed. H. D. Trail (London: Macmillan, 1896-1899).

4. J. S. Mill, *Essays on Literature and Society,* ed. J. Schneewind (New York: Macmillan, 1965), p. 28.

5. Lord Acton, *Lectures on Modern History* (London: Collins, 1960), pp. 35-36.

6. See K. Lowith, *Nature, History, and Existentialism*, ed. A. Levison (Evanston: Northwestern University Press, 1966), pp. 131-144, for general discussion of the nineteenth-century "quest for the meaning of history."

7. See M. Mandelbaum, *The Problem of Historical Knowledge: An Answer to Relativism* (New York: Harper, 1967), pp. 88-89; K. R. Popper, *The Poverty of Historicism* (London: Routledge, 1961), p. 3; D. E. Lee, "The Meaning of Historicism," *American Historical Review*, 59 (1953).

8. Here and throughout by "idealist" I mean one who believes that the external physical world is either entirely ideal or spiritual or is informed and governed by a spiritual principle that is absolute reality.

9. G. H. Lewes, "State of Historical Science in France," *British and Foreign Review*, 31 (1844), 73, 78.

10. Popper, *Poverty of Historicism*, p. 3.

11. M. Arnold, *Complete Prose Works*, ed. R. H. Super (Ann Arbor: University of Michigan Press, 1960-), I, 20.

12. Carlyle, *Critical and Miscellaneous Essays,* III, 169.

13. F. Meinecke, *Historism: the Rise of a New Historical Outlook,* trans. J. Anderson (London: Routledge, 1972), p. liv.

14. F. Meinecke, "Values and Causalities in History," trans. J. Franklin, *The Varieties of History,* ed. F. Stern (New York: Meridian Books 1956), pp. 282-285.

15. R. G. Collingwood, *The Idea of History* (London: Oxford, 1970), pp. 113-14.

16. G. W. F. Hegel, *The Philosophy of History,* trans. J. Sibree (New York: Dover, 1956), pp.9-10.

17. See G. Calogero, "On the So-Called Identity of History and Philosophy," *Philosophy and History,* ed. R. Klibansky and H. Paton (Oxford: Clarendon, 1936), pp. 35-52.

18. B. Croce, *History as the Story of Liberty*, trans. S. Sprigge (Chicago: Regnery, 1941), p. 32.

19. J. Ortega y Gasset, *History As System and Other Essays*

towards a Philosophy of History, trans. H. Weyl (New York: Norton, 1961).

20. See W. Ferguson, "Carlyle As Historian," *Occasional Papers of the Carlyle Society,* 1 (March 12, 1966), 4-8, for an excellent account of Carlyle's achievement. Ferguson does much to dispel the myth of Carlyle's incompetence as historian.

21. Cited by G. M. Miller, *The Historical Point of View in English Literary Criticism from 1570-1770, Anglistische Forschungen,* 35 (1913), 4; my translation.

22. See ibid., chaps. 2-4, and D. M. Foerster, "Scottish Primitivism and the Historical Approach," *Philological Quarterly,* 29 (1950).

1. The Metaphysics of Will

1. A. Obertello, *Carlyle's Critical Theories: Their Origin and Practice* (Genoa: Edizioni L.U.P.A., 1948), p. 5.

2. See respectively C. R. Sanders, "Carlyle and Tennyson," *PMLA,* 76 (1961); Sanders, "Carlyle, Browning and the Nature of a Poet," *Emory University Quarterly,* 16 (1960); Lewes dedicates his biography of Goethe to Carlyle who "first taught England to appreciate Goethe"; H. Ladd, *The Victorian Morality of Art: An Analysis of Ruskin's Aesthetic* (New York: Long & Smith, 1932), pp. 72, 164, 227, 312-314; D. J. DeLaura, "Arnold and Carlyle," *PMLA,* 79 (1964); J. W. Mackail, *The Life of William Morris* (London: Longmans, 1901), pp. 219-20; A. Symons, *The Symbolist Movement in Literature* (London: Heinemann, 1899), p. 1.

3. R. Wellek, *A History of Modern Criticism: 1750-1950* (New Haven and London: Yale University Press, 1955-), III, 92.

4. Ibid., pp. 91-92.

5. I am indebted for this distinction to a very suggestive article by L. J. Starzyk, "Towards a Reassessment of Early Victorian Aesthetics," *British Journal of Aesthetics,* 11 (1971).

6. Carlyle, *Critical and Miscellaneous Essays,* I, 149, in *Works,* ed. H. D. Traill (London: Macmillan, 1896-1899). Hereafter, citations from this edition will be given parenthetically in

the text using brief titles for the particular volumes involved.

7. The empiricist or associationist aesthetic was still a significant force in early nineteenth-century English criticism when Carlyle began his literary career. The most important contemporary theorist was A. Alison (*Essays on the Nature and Principles of Taste,* 1790) whom Carlyle several times attacked publicly as above and in his notebooks. One of Alison's most influential disciples and popularizers was Carlyle's early sponsor F. Jeffrey for whom "All sensations that are . . . agreeable . . . may form the foundation of the emotions of sublimity or beauty" ("Alison on Taste," *Edinburgh Review,* 18 [1811], 7-10). It is little wonder Jeffrey eventually (1829) reacted sharply against Carlyle's increasing mysticism; see J. A. Froude, *Thomas Carlyle: A History of the First Forty Years of his Life* (London: Longmans, 1882), II, 43-44.

8. G. Saintsbury, *A History of English Criticism* (London: Blackwood, 1911), p. 452.

9. E.g., I. A. Richards, *Principles of Literary Criticism* (London: Harcourt, Brace, 1926), p. 255; W. K. Wimsatt and C. Brooks, *Literary Criticism: A Short History* (New York: Knopf, 1957), p. 429.

10. Carlyle appears to have been one of the first to bring this German term of "aesthetics" to England. The earliest *OED* listing is 1831; Carlyle first discussed the term in his biography of Schiller in 1823.

11. See W. Witte, "Carlyle's 'Conversion,' " *The Era of Goethe,* ed. H. G. Barnes (Oxford: Blackwell, 1959), pp. 181, 190.

12. *The Collected Letters of Thomas Carlyle and Jane Welsh Carlyle,* ed. C. R. Sanders et al. (Durham, N.C.: Duke University Press, 1970-), I, 129. Hereafter referred to in the text as *Letters.*

13. See K. E. Gilbert and H. Kuhn, *A History of Esthetics* (New York: Macmillan, 1939), chap. 14. Coleridge, of course, had made essentially this point in his own German-based approach to criticism in the *Biographia Literaria* (see, e.g., *Bio-*

graphia Literaria, ed. J. Shawcross [Oxford: Clarendon, 1907], I, 44).

14. B. Bosanquet, *A History of Aesthetic* (London: Swan Sonnenschein, 1904), p. 361 (Bosanquet quotes from the *Ästhetik* [Berlin: Aufbau-Verlag, 1955], p. 1105); see also M. C. Beardsley, *Aesthetics from Classical Greece to the Present: A Short History* (New York: Macmillan, 1966), chap. 9.

15. Bosanquet, *History of Aesthetic,* p. 286.

16. J. C. F. Schiller, *On the Aesthetic Education of Man,* trans. E. M. Wilkinson and L. A. Willoughby (Oxford: Clarendon, 1967), p. 189, by permission of Oxford University Press.

17. *Two Notebooks of Carlyle, from 23d March 1822 to 16th May 1832,* ed. C. E. Norton (New york: The Grolier Club, 1898), p. 188. Hereafter referred to in the text as *Notebooks.*

18. By "dialectical " I mean a concern with art as an expression of man's relation to ultimate spiritual reality. See R. Marsh, *Four Dialectical Theories of Poetry* (Chicago: University of Chicago Press, 1965), p. 15.

19. I. Armstrong's introductory essay to *Victorian Scrutinies: Reviews of Poetry, 1830-70* (London: Athlone, 1972), esp. pp. 5-6, and R. G. Cox's "Victorian Criticism of Poetry: The Minority Tradition," *Scrutiny,* 18 (1951-52), esp. sec. iii, seem to be making a similar point.

20. H. Taylor, Preface to *Philip van Artevelde* (London: Moxon, 1834), pp. ix-xi; see also an anonymous article "The Poets of our Age Considered as to their Philosophic Tendencies," *Westminster Review,* 3 (1836), esp. pp. 60-62, for another important expression of this same outlook.

21. M. H. Abrams, *The Mirror and the Lamp: Romantic Theory and the Critical Tradition* (New York: Norton, 1958), pp. 21-26.

22. Ibid., pp. 45-46.

23. After the Plotinean belief in the soul's ability to ascend to and mystically know the One (see *Enneads,* VI, 9).

24. P. B. Shelley, *Prose,* ed. D. L. Clark (Albuquerque:

University of New Mexico Press, 1954), p. 174.

25. A. Warren, *English Poetic Theory, 1825-1865* (Princeton: Princeton University Press, 1950), pp. 80-81. For similar interpretations, see Abrams, *Mirror and Lamp*, p. 131; F. W. Roe, *Thomas Carlyle as a Critic of Literature* (New York: Columbia University Press, 1910), pp. 30-34; Obertello, *Carlyle's Critical Theories*, p. 9.

26. S. T. Coleridge, *Letters of Samuel Taylor Coleridge*, ed. E. H. Coleridge (London: Heinemann, 1895), I, 352.

27. H. W. Piper, *The Active Universe: Pantheism and the Concept of Imagination in the English Romantic Poets* (London: Athlone, 1962), pp. 135-36; for complete discussion of this issue, see chap. 6 of Piper's book.

28. B. Russell, *History of Western Philosophy* (New York: Simon and Schuster, 1945), p. 828.

29. For Carlyle's characteristic scorn for the English Romantics' lack of *will*, see, e.g., *Letters*, II, 229-30, 299-300; III, 85, 233-34; Byron was the only important exception here.

30. See *Notebooks*, pp. 51, 55-56, 65-66, 149; *Schiller*, p. 13; *Critical & Miscellaneous Essays*, III, 90-91; T. Carlyle, *Reminiscences*, ed. C. E. Norton (London: Dent, 1932), pp. 7, 13.

31. See W. E. Houghton's account of Carlyle in *The Victorian Frame of Mind, 1830-70* (New Haven: Yale University Press, 1957), pp. 198, 206.

32. C. F. Harrold has produced the single most complete study of Carlyle's relations with Germany, *Carlyle and German Thought: 1819-1834* (London: Archen, 1963). Later writers have developed some of the most important intellectual implications for Carlyle of this involvement with German idealism: notably, E. Cassirer, *The Myth of the State* (New Haven: Yale University Press, 1946), chap. 15; A. J. LaValley, *Carlyle and the Idea of the Modern: Studies in Carlyle's Prophetic Literature and Its Relation to Blake, Nietzsche, Marx, and Others* (New Haven: Yale University Press, 1968); M. Peckham, *Victorian Revolutionaries: Speculations on Some Heroes of a Cultural Crisis* (New York: Braziller, 1970), chap. 2. In my subsequent discussion, I have drawn on all

these writers, and I trust I have not repeated any of them, in an effort to interpret the specific effect of German thought on Carlyle's attitude toward poetry.

33. See F. Copleston, *A History of Philosophy* (New York: Doubleday, 1962-1967), VII, i, 45.

34. See R. Wellek, *Immanuel Kant In England, 1793-1838* (Princeton: Princeton University Press, 1931), p. 200, for Carlyle's limited knowledge of Kant.

35. R. Wellek, "Carlyle and the Philosophy of History," *Philological Quarterly,* 23 (1944), 69.

36. H. Shine, "Carlyle and the German Philosophy Problem during the Year 1826-27," *PMLA,* 50 (1935), 818-826; Harrold, *Carlyle and German Thought,* pp. 161, 164-65, 171-173; *Sartor,* p. 156.

37. F. Küchler ("Carlyle und Schiller" [*Anglia,* 26 (1903)]) is the best study on the subject, but though Küchler recognizes that Carlyle took from Schiller (and Goethe) "a new life view" (p. 5), he says precious little about what that life view amounted to.

38. I. Kant, *Critique of Practical Reason,* trans. L. W. Beck (New York: Bobbs-Merrill, 1956), p. 3.

39. R. D. Miller, *Schiller and the Ideal of Freedom* (Oxford: Clarendon, 1970), p. 20; see also D. Regin, *Freedom and Dignity: The Historical and Philosophical Thought of Schiller* (The Hague: Nijhoff, 1965), p. 49.

40. Schiller, *On the Aesthetic Education of Man,* p. 11.

41. Ibid., p. 45; see also p. 37.

42. Ibid., pp. xx, 334.

43. Ibid., pp. 27, 25.

44. Ibid., p. 57.

45. "Revolutionist" in Sartre's sense of one who actively projects his subjective will outward against the resisting reality of the world around him for the purpose of changing that reality and who in so doing progressively defines the nature of the human spirit (*Les Temps Modernes,* July 1946), p. 24.

46. *On the Aesthetic Education of Man,* pp. 49, 59.

47. J. G. Fichte, *Sämmtliche Werke,* ed. J. H. Fichte (Berlin:

von Veit, 1845), I, 440.

48. J. G. Fichte, *On the Nature of the Scholar,* trans. W. Smith (London: Chapman, 1845), p. 135-36. My quotes are from works Carlyle almost certainly read.

49. J. G. Fichte, *The Characteristics of the Present Age,* trans. W. Smith (London: Chapman, 1847), p. 16.

50. Ibid., pp. 195-96.

51. Ibid., p. 244.

52. *Scholar,* p. 147.

53. Ibid., p. 135.

54. Ibid., p. 145.

55. Ibid., p. 147-149.

56. LaValley, *Carlyle and the Idea of the Modern,* p. 85.

57. Ibid., p. 85.

58. Fichte, *Characteristics,* p. 5.

59. F. W. J. von Schelling, *Werke,* ed. M. Schroter (Munich: Verlagsbuchhandlung, 1958), II, 603; my translation.

60. G. F. W. Hegel, *The Philosophy of History,* trans. J. Sibree (New York: Dover, 1956), pp. 17-19.

61. Froude, *Carlyle,* II, 82.

62. See also C. Moore, "Carlyle's 'Diamond Necklace' and Poetic History . . . ," *Studies in Philology,* 33 (1936).

63. K. R. Popper, *The Poverty of Historicism* (London: Routledge, 1961), p. 3.

64. The influence of Schiller is, again, important here. Carlyle admired Schiller for his ability to transcend mere historical data and arrange it in "a more philosophical order" (*Schiller,* p. 85). Cf. Schiller's own distinction between the mere chronicler and the writer of philosophical history in "Was heist und zu welchem Ende studiert man Universal- geschichte." This influence would have been supplemented by his later reading of Fichte, of F. von Schlegel's *Über die neure Geschichte* (in 1823, *Notebooks,* p. 37), and Herder's *Ideen* (in 1826, *Notebooks,* p. 72).

65. D. Forbes, "Historismus in England," *Cambridge Journal,* 4 (1957), 289.

66. D. Forbes, *The Liberal Anglican Idea of History*

(Cambridge, Eng.: Cambridge University Press, 1952), esp. chap. 3.

67. R. Preyer, *Bentham, Coleridge and the Science of History* (Langandreer: Pöppinghaus, 1958), chap. V, pt. i.

68. The source of the concept of alternating epochs of belief and unbelief is Goethe (Harrold, *Carlyle and German Thought,* p. 174). The concept of palingenesis probably comes from J. G. Herder (see *Ideen zur Philosophie der Geschichte der Menscheit* [Berlin: Aufbau-Verlag, 1965], I, 28), and H. Shine "Carlyle . . . and Herder . . . ," in *Booker Memorial Studies,* ed. Shine (New York: Russel and Russel, 1950).

69. L. M. Young, *Thomas Carlyle and the Art of History* (Philadelphia: University of Pennsylvania Press, 1939), p. 71.

70. Carlyle's Hero-doctrine begs comparison with Hegel's concept of "World-Historical Individuals," the "great men" who are the "agents of World-Spirit," the "clear-sighted ones" who are driven by their "unconscious" "energy of will and character" and whose "whole life [is] labor and struggle" (Hegel, *Philosophy of History,* pp. 20-34). I can find no evidence, however, that Carlyle ever read Hegel. Rather, the resemblance is probably owing to a common source in Fichte).

71. See Houghton, *Victorian Frame of Mind,* pp. 27-33.

72. Young, *Carlyle and the Art of History,* pp. 10-12.

73. See, e.g., Macaulay's *Essays* (London: Longmans, 1885), p. 322, where he proclaims characteristically that English history is "emphatically the history of progress."

74. See Houghton, *Victorian Frame of Mind,* pp. 28-33, for more on contemporary faith in progress.

75. For Coleridge as philosopher of history, see R. Preyer, *Science of History,* esp. pp. 19-20; for Coleridgean or the "Liberal Anglican" tradition in philosophy of history, see ibid., chap. 4, and Forbes, *Liberal Anglican.*

76. Copleston, *History of Philosophy,* VII, i, 29.

77. For Carlyle's relation to mystical tradition, see C. F. Harrold, "The Mystical Element in Carlyle . . . ," *Modern Philology,* 29 (1931).

78. The most intelligent discussions of Carlyle's religious position are found in B. Willey, *Nineteenth Century Studies: Coleridge to Matthew Arnold* (New York: Columbia University Press, 1949), chap. 4; G. B. Tennyson, *Sartor Called "Resartus"* (Princeton: Princeton University Press, 1965), pp. 313-318.

79. M. H. Abrams, *Natural Supernaturalism: Tradition and Revolution in Romantic Literature* (New York: Norton, 1971), pp. 95-121.

2. Poetry and the Gospel of Freedom

1. A. Obertello, *Carlyle's Critical Theories: Their Origin and Practice* (Genoa: Edizioni L.U.P.A., 1948), pp. 19-25.

2. For Schlegel and myth, see F. W. Schlegel, *Dialogue on Poetry and Literary Aphorisms*, trans. E. Behler and R. Strue (University Park, Pa.: Pennsylvania State Park Press, 1968), pp. 81-82; for Jean Paul and humor see J. W. Smeed, "Thomas Carlyle and J. P. Richter," *Comparative Literature*, 16 (1964), 233, and Carlyle, *Critical and Miscellaneous Essays*, I, 17, in *Works*, ed. H. D. Trail (London: Macmillan, 1896-1899); for Novalis and the unconscious, see C. F. Harrold, *Carlyle and German Thought: 1819-1834* (London: Archen, 1963), p. 173, and Carlyle, *Critical and Miscellaneous Essays*, II, 32-34.

3. J. C. F. Schiller, *Aesthetical Essays and Letters* (London: Bohn, 1875), p. 154; see also p. 367.

4. Cited by C. R. Sanders, *Emory University Quarterly*, 16 (1960), 204.

5. *Lectures on the History of Literature or the Successive Periods of European Culture Delivered in 1838 by Thomas Carlyle*. From the Anstey MS. in the Library of the Bombay Branch, Royal Asiatic Society, ed. R. P. Karkaria, based on Anstey's notes of the lectures (Bombay: Curwen, 1892), p. 30. Hereafter referred to in the text as *Lectures*.

6. H. Tennyson, *Alfred Lord Tennyson, A Memoir* (London: Macmillan, 1897), p. 213.

7. Cited by Sanders, *Emory University Quarterly,* 16 (1960), 205.

8. See, e.g., J. Spedding, "Poems by Tennyson," *Edinburgh Review* 77 (1843), 282-287; C. Kingsley, "Recent Poetry and Recent Verse," *Frasers,* 39 (1849), 570; C. Patmore, "The Strayed Reveller . . . ," *North British Review,* 19 (1853), 213; J. A. Froude, "A's Poems," *Westminster Review,* 5 (1854), 154-54. By the sixties and seventies, Arnold, Swinburne, and Pater in their different ways had begun to counter with an "aesthetic" call for "sweetness" in place of strength.

9. J. G. Fichte, *On the Nature of the Scholar,* trans. W. Smith (London: Chapman, 1845), p. 217.

10. Ibid., pp. 218-19.

11. E.g., Lewes, "Hegel's Aesthetic and the Philosophy of Art" (1842); Ruskin, *The Stones of Venice* (1851-1853); D. Masson, "Theories of Poetry" (1853); Arnold, "The Function of Criticism at the Present Time" (1864); Pater, "Winckelmann" (1867); S. Colvin, "English Painters and Painting in 1867" (1867); J. Morley, "Byron" (1870); J. A. Symonds, *The Renaissance in Italy* (1875-1881).

12. L. Stephen, *English Literature and Society in the Eighteenth Century* (London: Duckworth, 1904), pp. 4-5.

13. Schlegel, *Dialogue on Poetry and Literary Aphorisms,* pp. 81-82. There is just a chance that Carlyle knew this work. His notebooks and letters contain several passages indicating that he both read and admired Schlegel (*Notebooks,* 37, 104, 135; *Letters,* IV, 22, 235, 424).

14. R. Wellek, *Concepts of Criticism* (New Haven: Yale University Press, 1963), p. 188.

15. This is certainly true of Schlegel, for whom the basis of the new poetic myth was to be Schelling's *Naturphilosophie* with its view of an objective Idea in nature (*Dialogue on Poetry,* pp. 82-87).

16. H. Taine, *Histoire de la littérature anglaise* (Paris: Libraire Hachette, 1892), V, 280; my translation.

17. J. Holloway, *The Victorian Sage* (New York: Norton, 1953), p. 41.

18. E. Cassirer, *An Essay on Man* (New York: Bantam, 1970), p. 26.

19. Cited in R. P. Pankhurst, *The Saint-Simonians Mill and Carlyle* (London: Lalibela Books, n.d.), p. 34.

20. *Last Words of Thomas Carlyle* (London: Longmans, 1892), p. 96; my italics.

21. J. Bentham, *Works,* ed. J. Bowring (Edinburgh: Tait, 1843), pp. 253-54.

22. S. T. Coleridge, *Biographia,* ed. J. Shawcross (Oxford: Clarendon, 1907), II, 107.

23. M. H. Abrams, *Natural Supernaturalism: Tradition and Revolution in Romantic Literature* (New York: Norton, 1971), pp. 122-134.

24. See Buckley, *The Victorian Temper: A Study in Literary Culture* (Cambridge: Harvard University Press, 1951), chap. 3.

25. *The Letters of Thomas Carlyle to J. S. Mill, et al.,* ed. A. Carlyle (London: Unwin, 1923), p. 71. Cf. Carlyle's criticism of Scott's historical interpretations as "living," but in the end simply "amusement," not truth (*Critical and Miscellaneous Essays,* IV, 75-77).

26. For this tendency in Victorian poetry, see *Victorian Poetry,* ed. M. Bradbury and D. Palmer (London: Arnold, 1972), a book whose theme is the concern of Victorian poets with history.

27. See M. Gent, " 'To Flinch from Modern Varnish': The Appeal of the Past to the Victorian Imagination," ibid.

28. H. Tennyson, *Memoir,* II, 127.

29. Schlegel, *Dialogue on Poetry,* pp. 82-87.

30. Abrams, *Natural Supernaturalism,* p. 96.

31. C. C. Gillispie, *Genesis and Geology: A Study in the Relations of Scientific Thought, Natural Theology, and Social Opinion in Great Britain, 1790-1850* (New York: Harper, 1959), esp. chaps. 5 and 6.

32. A. L. G. de Staël-Holstein, *De la littérature* (Paris: Minard, 1959), p. 17; my translation. Carlyle probably did not

read this, but the principles I have quoted underlie Mme de Staël's later *De l'Allemagne* which he knew very well (*Letters,* I, 109, 164, 360, 367).

33. Cited by G. A. Wells in "Herder's and Coleridge's Evaluation of the Historical Approach," *Modern Language Review,* 48 (1953), 170; my translation.

34. For this outlook, see L. Whitney, "Primitivist Theories of Epic Origins," *Modern Philology,* 21 (1924); D. M. Foerster, "Scottish Primitivism and the Historical Approach," *Philological Quarterly,* 29 (1950).

35. T. Macaulay, *Essays* (London: Longmans, 1885), p. 4.

36. Carlyle's position here should be related to contemporary research into the origins of mythology and epic poetry. In England in the 1830s and 1840s there was a growing awareness that the popular notion that the bard somehow creates religious belief or myth was scientifically untenable. E.g., the year before Carlyle published Sauerteig's comments above, Milman, basing himself on Vico and German philology, argued in a prominent article that one must read the Homeric poems as "part of the national religion," as the theological teachings of a religion which already existed and not as the source of that religion (*Quarterly Review,* 44 [1831], 130-133). Four years later Thirlwall, using similar sources to Milman's, published the first volume of his *History of Greece,* in which he refuted the belief that Homer and Hesiod effected a revolution in the religion of their countrymen. They were, he said, simply the "organs and interpreters of the popular creed" (*A History of Greece,* [London: Longmans, 1835], I, 187). Carlyle would not have depended on either of these English historians to come to his conclusions; he had been to many of the same sources they had: J. A. Wolff, J. Müller, J. E. Eichhorn (see the German literature essays of 1831) and, above all, Niebuhr, whom he claims to have "laboriously perused" (*Lectures,* p. 35). The essay on the *Nibelungenlied* in *Heroes* may, in fact, be taken as his own contribution to this contemporary discussion of the historic rather than poetic origins of myth.

37. T. S. Eliot, *The Sacred Wood* (London: Methuen,

1960), pp. 157-58; *Selected Essays, 1917-32* (London: Faber, 1951), pp. 400-01.

38. For other significant examples, see J. Sterling, *Essays and Tales*, ed. J. C. Hare (London: Parker, 1848), I, 197-98; A. De Vere, *Edinburgh Review*, 90 (1849), 388-407; Ruskin, *Works*, IX, 27-32; C. Kingsley, *Frasers*, 49 (1854), 140-41.

39. R. Fry, *Vision and Design* (Harmondsworth: Penguin, 1937), p. 11.

3. History and the Best Self

1. T. Arnold, *Introductory Lectures on Modern History* (Oxford: Parker, 1842), p. 392.

2. See E. Cassirer, *The Philosophy of the Enlightenment*, trans. F. Koelln and J. Pettegrove (Princeton: Princeton University Press, 1951), p. 209.

3. D. Forbes, *The Liberal Anglican Idea of History* (Cambridge, Eng.: Cambridge University Press, 1962), p. 17.

4. T. Arnold, *The Miscellaneous Works* (London: Fellowes, 1845), p. 82.

5. G. Vico, *The New Science* (3rd ed.), trans. T. G. Bergin and M. H. Fisch (Ithaca: Cornell University Press, 1948), p. 18.

6. *Miscellaneous Works*, pp. 81-82, 109.

7. Ibid., p. 104.

8. Ibid., p. 109.

9. Vico, it may be noted, was saying precisely the same thing a hundred years before (*New Science*, pp. 371-373).

10. *New Science*, p. 302.

11. Ibid., p. 371.

12. Ibid., pp. 380-81.

13. A. P. Stanley, *The Life and Correspondence of Thomas Arnold* (London: Murray, 1881), I, 266.

14. Ibid., II, 159; the translation is A. de Selincourt's from his edition of Herodotus, *The Histories* (Harmondsworth: Penguin, 1972), p. 583 (ix. 16).

15. *Life and Correspondence of Thomas Arnold*, I, 182-186.

16. See, e.g., R. K. Biswas, *Clough: Towards a Reconsider-*

ation (London: Oxford University Press, 1972), pp. 27-31.

17. Arnold, *Lectures on Modern History,* pp. 394-95; the paraphrase of Herodotus here should be apparent.

18. See P. W. Day, *Matthew Arnold and the Philosophy of Vico* (Auckland: University of Auckland Press, 1964), Bulletin 70, English Series 12. Day has discussed certain points of connection but has left out some crucially important aspects of Dr. Arnold's influence and misinterpreted others; e.g., Day fails to recognize that Matthew, like his father, regards Vico's *modern* age, not his heroic age, as the intellectual and poetical ideal that men must seek. What follows I hope is a rather more exact account of the nature of Vico's influence on M. Arnold.

19. M. Arnold, *Poems,* ed. K. Allott (London: Longmans, 1965), p. 569. Hereafter referred to in the text as *Poems.*

20. Arnold, *Complete Prose Works,* ed. R. H. Super (Ann Arbor: University of Michigan Press, 1962-), I, 1. Hereafter referred to in the text as *Prose Works.*

21. Arnold worked on this tragedy from 1845 to 1849, when he stopped to work on *Empedocles* and took it up again in 1855-1858 (*Poems,* pp. 585-86).

22. See K. Tilloston, "Matthew Arnold and Carlyle," *Mid-Victorian Studies* (London: Athlone, 1965), pp. 222-224.

23. Something of the great importance of Lucretius' influence on the early poetry has been suggested by Allott in the notes to *Poems* (pp. 24, 90) and by W. D. Anderson, *Matthew Arnold and the Classical Tradition* (Ann Arbor: University of Michigan Press, 1965), pp. 19, 39, 42, 146-47.

24. Lucretius, *On the Nature of Things,* trans. R. E. Latham (Harmondsworth: Penguin, 1951), bk. II, ll. 7-14.

25. C. Aytoun, *Blackwoods,* 66 (1849), 340; C. Patmore, *North British Review,* 19 (1853), 210; C. Kingsley, *Frasers,* 39 (1849), 579.

26. L. Trilling, *Matthew Arnold* (New York: Norton, 1939), p. 28.

27. F. Kermode, *Romantic Image* (London: Collins, 1971), pp. 13, 18, 31.

28. *The Letters of Matthew Arnold to Arthur Hugh Clough,*

ed. H. F. Lowry (Oxford: Clarendon, 1932), p. 123; my italics. Hereafter referred to in the text as *Letters to Clough.*

29. Arnold's interest in Schiller during this period may be reasonably inferred from *Prose Works,* I, 2, 59.

30. Arnold, "Numbers," *Contemporary Review,* 15 (1884).

31. Arnold, "Emerson," *Macmillans Magazine,* 50 (1884), 2.

32. See C. Sanders, *Coleridge and the Broad Church Movement: Studies in S. T. Coleridge, Dr. Arnold of Rugby, J. C. Hare, Thomas Carlyle and F. D. Maurice* (Durham, N. C.: Duke University Press, 1942).

33. F. Copleston, *A History of Philosophy* (New York: Doubleday, 1962-1967), IV, 253.

34. B. de Spinoza, *Opera,* ed. C. H. Bruder (Leipzig: Bernh. Tauchnitz, 1846, III, 93-94; the translation is Arnold's own *Prose Works,* III, 176, Super's notes, p. 449).

35. Ibid., I, 346, 345, 344, 317 (*Prose Works,* III, 450); Arnold's translation (*Prose Works,* III, 176; Arnold's translation of the Latin is not entirely accurate, but the meaning is essentially the same as in the original).

36. Arnold, "The Bishop and the Philosopher," "*Tractatus Theologico-Politicus,*" "Dr. Stanley's Lectures . . ." (all written between December 1862, and February 1863). For more on the mid-Victorian reaction to the Higher Criticism, see B. Willey, *More Nineteenth Century Studies: A Group of Honest Doubters* (New York: Columbia University Press, 1956), chap. 4; O. Chadwick, *The Victorian Church* (London: Adams and Black, 1966-1970), II, chap. 2.

37. Spinoza, *Opera,* I, 344: ". . . virtus . . . nihil aliud est, quam ex legibus propriae naturae agere, et nemo suum esse conservare conetur, nisi expropriae suae naturae legibus." Spinoza of course, is describing the nature of virtue, not, as Arnold is, God. Super makes the connection with Spinoza in *Prose Works,* VI, 423-24.

38. Cited by W. Armytage, "Matthew Arnold and T. H. Huxley," *Review of English Studies,* 4 (1953), 350.

39. F. H. Bradley, *Ethical Studies* (New York: Bobbs-Merrill, 1951), pp. 149-151.

40. For a very different account of the relationship between Carlyle and Arnold, see David DeLaura's "Arnold and Carlyle," *PMLA*, 79 (1964).

41. L. Stephen, *The Science of Ethics* (New York: Putnam, 1882), pp. 144, 188.

42. Cf. Aristotle, *Nicomachean Ethics*, trans. J. A. K. Thomson (Harmondsworth: Penguin, 1955), p. 209 (X, 9); and see Carlyle's *Notebooks*, p. 81.

43. Ibid., pp. 51, 122.

44. E. Cassirer, *An Essay on Man* (New York: Bantam, 1970), pp. 9-10.

45. Spinoza, *A Theologico-Political Treatise and a Political Treatise*, trans. R. Elwes (New York: Dover, 1951), pp. 177, 180.

46. Ibid., pp. 180, 186.

47. Ibid., p. 185.

48. F. D. E. Schleiermacher, *On Religion: Speeches to Its Cultured Despisers*, trans. J. Oman (New York: Harper, 1965), p. 40.

49. M. Christensen, "Thomas Arnold and the Background to *Literature and Dogma*," *Modern Philology*, 55 (1957), 14-17; Christensen makes the important point that Thomas Arnold followed the "mediating" German theologians and critics who sought to reconcile the "barren learning" of the more rationalistic critics (represented pre-eminently by Strauss) with the emotional fervor of the less-informed pietists.

50. Arnold, *Prose Works*, III, 61; Spinoza, *Tractatus Theologico-Politicus* . . . , trans. R. Willis (London: Trubner, 1862), p. 14.

51. Schleiermacher, *On Religion*, pp. 14, 46.

52. Ibid., pp. 60-61.

53. Ibid., p. 48.

54. *Letters of Matthew Arnold, 1848-88*, ed. G. W. E. Russell (London: Macmillan, 1901), I, 442. Hereafter referred to in the text as *Letters*.

55. Ibid., pp. 58-59.

56. For Jowett, Hegel, and "Germanizing" Balliol in the forties, see G. Faber, *Jowett: A Portrait with Background* (Cam-

bridge: Harvard University Press, 1958, pp. 177-183; London: Faber, 1957). Arnold's early diaries (1845-46) show that he was probably reading Cousin on the history of philosophy fairly closely at this time (K. Allott, "Matthew Arnold's Reading Lists in Three Early Diaries," *Victorian Studies*, 2 [1959], 258-260); Arnold's knowledge of Guizot, Heine, Renan, and Strauss, all of them greatly influenced by Hegel, is amply attested to in his notebooks (e.g., *The Notebooks of Matthew Arnold*, ed. H. F. Lowry et al. [London: Oxford University Press, 1952], pp. 13, 561, 19, 565, 222). The notebook of 1862 lists Hegel as someone to read (*Notebooks*, p. 568). For Hegel's concept of Reason as the moving power of history, see *Philosophy of History*, trans. J. Sibree (New York: Dover, 1956), p. 9.

57. Arnold, "The French Play in London," *The Nineteenth Century*, 6 (1879), 240.

58. Anderson, *Arnold and the Classical Tradition*, pp. 6, 8, 10-14, and the *Nicomachean Ethics*, p. 55 (II, 1), respectively.

59. See T. Arnold, *Lectures on Modern History*, pp. 302-03.

60. For J. S. Mill's discussion, see *On Liberty* (London: Parker, 1859), pp. 87-90.

61. Arnold's association of "imagination" with the religious sense may well come from Spinoza, for whom the imagination is the distinctive faculty of religious knowledge and as such is opposed to the intellect or understanding (*Tractatus Theologico-Politicus*, chaps. 1 and 2); see also Arnold, *Prose Works*, III, 162.

62. Schleiermacher, *On Religion*, p. 140.

4./A Reformer in Political Matters

1. H. W. Garrod, *Poetry and the Criticism of Life* (Cambridge: Harvard University Press, 1931), p. 70.

2. T. S. Eliot, *The Sacred Wood: Essays on Poetry and Criticism* (London: Methuen, 1960), p. ix.

3. W. Wimsatt and C. Brooks, *Literary Criticism: A Short History* (London: Routledge & Kegan Paul, 1957), p. 447.

4. T. S. Eliot, *The Use of Poetry and the Use of Criticism* (London: Faber, 1964), p. 108.

5. *Unpublished Letters of Matthew Arnold,* ed., A. Whitridge (New Haven: Yale University Press, 1923), pp. 15-17.

6. Wimsatt and Brooks, *Literary Criticism,* p. 450.

7. H. James, *North American Review,* 101 (1865), 206.

8. Froude, *Westminster Review,* 5 (1854), 158-59; Roscoe, *Poems and Essays* (London: Chapman & Hall, 1860), II, 63; Aytoun, *Blackwoods,* 75 (1854), 305-06; Shairp, *North British Review,* 21 (1854), 493-496; C. Patmore, *Edinburgh Review,* 104 (1856), 341-42.

9. Roscoe, *Poems and Essays,* II, 63.

10. *The Sacred Wood,* p. xiii.

11. The expression is George Saintsbury's (*A History of Criticism* [London: Blackwoods, 1911], p. 479).

12. A. Warren, *English Poetic Theory: 1825-1865* (Princeton: Princeton University Press, 1952), pp. 152-154.

13. T. Arnold, "Rugby—the Use of the Classics," *Miscellaneous Essays,* p. 349.

14. E.g., Saintsbury, *History of Criticism,* p. 470.

15. Arnold's principal theoretical source throughout the Preface is, of course, that "admirable treatise of Aristotle" (*Prose Works,* I, 7). Cf. "Plot . . . [is] the ordering of particular actions"; "tragedy is a *mimesis* of a complete, that is, of a whole action"; "the poet should be considered a maker of plots, not verses" (*Poetics* in *Ancient Literary Criticism* (Oxford: Clarendon, 1972) ed. D. A. Russel and M. Winterbottom, pp. 97-103.

16. Arnold, *Essays in Criticism, Second Series* (London: Macmillan, 1888), pp. 115-16. Hereafter referred to in text as *Essays II.*

17. See, e.g., J. Blackie, "Homer and his Translators," *Macmillans Magazine,* 4 (1861), esp. pp. 271-274.

18. Longinus, *On Sublimity* in *Ancient Literary Criticism,* pp. 466-468.

19. Arnold's rejection of the contemporary commonplace

that Homer is a primitive or balladist very likely derives from Vico, who insists that Homer as poet is early modern although his subject matter is heroic (*The New Science*, trans. T. Bergin and M. Fisch [Ithaca: Cornell University Press, 1948], p. 275).

20. Longinus is also a likely source for Arnold's touchstone method; he constantly illustrates the grand style by citing short passages from Homer and contrasting them, in precisely the way Arnold does, to inferior lines; see, e.g., *On Sublimity*, pp. 469, 472-73, 477.

21. *Prose Works*, I, 212; *Iliad*, XXIV, 505; Arnold's translation.

22. *Prose Works*, I, 212; *Inferno*, xxxiii, 49; my translation.

23. It is worth noting that essentially the same moral sentiments may be found throughout the *Notebooks* in the prose passages Arnold was forever taking down. E.g., p. 76, "Non est alia via ad vitam et ad veram internam pacem, nisi via sanctae et quotidianae mortificationis" (Thomas à Kempis). ("There is no other way to life and true internal peace than the way of holy and daily mortification"); p. 84, "Es ist ein Artikel meines Glaubens, dass wir durch Standhaftigkeit und Treue in dem gegenwärtigen Zustande, ganz allein der höhern Stufe eines folgenden [werden] werth und, sie zu betreten, fähig werden, es sey nun hier zeitlich oder dort ewig." (Goethe). ("It is an article of my faith that in these times we become capable of achieving a higher level of value — whether merely temporal or eternal — only through constancy and truth.")

24. Shairp, *North British Review*, p. 497; see also Clough, *North American Review*, 77 (1853), esp. pp. 2, 22.

25. Contrast this statement with Wellek's view that Arnold believed in the possibility of form apart from meaning (*A History of Modern Criticism: 1750-1950* [New Haven: Yale University Press, 1955-], IV, 169). See also J. Casey's high praise for Arnold's position in *The Language of Criticism* (London: Methuen, 1966), p. 180, as "one of the subtlest statements" ever made on the relation between form and content.

26. Saintsbury, *History of Criticism,* p. 475; Wimsatt and Brooks, *Literary Criticism,* p. 442.

27. *Notebooks,* pp. 345, 346, 359-364; Arnold was reading Taine (*Notes sur l'Angleterre*) at least as early as 1873 (*Prose Works,* VII, 462).

28. H.Taine, *Philosophie de l'art* (Paris: Bailière, 1879), pp. 13, 9; my translation.

29. I am thus in substantial disagreement with Allen Tate's belief that Arnold considered poetry as primarily a "vehicle of ideas" ("Literature as Knowledge: Comment and Comparison," *Southern Review,* 6 [1941], pp. 229-231).

30. G. Santayana, *The Sense of Beauty: Being the Outlines of Aesthetic Theory* (New York: Random House, 1955), pp. 24, 52.

31. Spinoza is the one philosopher to whom Santayana was perhaps most indebted; see R. Butler, *The Mind of Santayana* (London: Kegan Paul, 1956), p. 31; see also Santayana, *Essays in Critical Realism* (New York: Macmillan, 1920), p. 168. Santayana was also a great admirer of Arnold (*Realms of Being* [New York: Scribners, 1942], p. 19).

32. I. A. Richards, *Science and Poetry* (New York: Norton, 1926), pp. 70-71.

33. This connection is partly explored by M. Krieger, "The Critical Legacy of M. Arnold . . . ," *Southern Review,* 5 (1969).

34. This critical tradition is discussed in detail by G. MacKenzie, *Critical Responsiveness: A Study of the Psychological Current in Later Eighteenth-Century Criticism* (Berkeley: University of California Press, 1949).

35. David Hume, *"On the Standard of Taste" and Other Essays,* ed. J. W. Lenz (New York: Bobbs-Merrill, 1965).

36. Santayana, *Sense of Beauty,* p. 231; for Richards, see, e.g., *Principles of Literary Criticism* (London: Harcourt Brace, 1926), pp. 249-50.

37. See Santayana, *Sense of Beauty,* p. 231; Richards, *Principles,* p. 249.

38. J. S. Mill, "What is Poetry," *Monthly Repository,* 7 (1833), 61.

39. Richards, *Principles,* pp. 275-283.

40. W. Madden, *Matthew Arnold: A Study of the Aesthetic Temper in Victorian England* (Bloomington: Indiana University Press, 1967), chap. 1.

5. Historicism as Weltanschauung

1. M. Ward, *Macmillans Magazine,* 52 (1885), 137-38.

2. *Marius the Epicurean: His Sensations and Ideas,* I, 44, from *The New Library Edition of the Works of Walter Pater* (London: Macmillan, 1910). Subsequent reference to Pater's works will be to this edition and will be indicated in the text by short titles.

3. H. Sidgwick, *Miscellaneous Essays and Addresses* (London: Macmillan, 1904), p. 60.

4. See A. W. Benn, *The History of English Rationalism in the Nineteenth Century* (New York: Russell, 1962), pp. 353-387; W. Houghton, *Victorian Frame of Mind: 1830-1870* (New Haven: Yale University Press, 1957), pp. 15-17.

5. J. Morley, *Fortnightly Review,* 13 (1873), 75-76.

6. See G. Mure, "Oxford and Philosophy," *Philosophy,* 12 (1937), 298.

7. For Pater's undergraduate reading of Mill, see W. W. Jackson, *Ingram Bywater* (Oxford: Clarendon, 1917), p. 79.

8. That Pater knew this work appears likely from his late essay, "Plato's Doctrine."

9. Other notable documents include Sir William Hamilton's *Lectures* (1860), Spencer's *First Principles* (1862), T. H. Huxley's "On the Physical Basis of Life" (1864), and J. H. Newman's *Grammar of Assent* (1870).

10. Mill means the empirical idealist tradition, not the German metaphysical one, which I discussed in Chap. One.

11. J. S. Mill, *An Examination of Sir William Hamilton's Philosophy* (London: Longmans, 1867), pp. 5-16.

12. Cf. Hume's account of "personal identity," which Pater who knew Hume's work (Jackson, *Bywater*, p. 79) may well have had in mind (*A Treatise of Human Nature* [Harmondsworth: Penguin, 1969], p. 301).

13. No comprehensive discussion of Pater's empiricist outlook exists, but his fundamental proclivities in this direction have been recognized by a few: e.g., G. Bullough, "Changing Views of the Mind in English Poetry," *Proceedings of the British Academy*, 61 (1955), 80; H. Young, *The Writings of Walter Pater: A Reflection of British Philosophical Opinion from 1860-1890* (New York: Haskell, 1965), pp. 11-15.

14. For Pater's association with the Oxford idealist tradition and the argument that he was, in fact, a real part of that tradition, see A. Ward, *Walter Pater: The Idea in Nature* (London: MacGibbon and Kee, 1966), pp. 32-42, and chap. 3; see also G. C. Monsman, "Pater, Hopkins, and Fichte's Ideal Student," *South Atlantic Quarterly*, 70 (1971).

15. After Aristippus of Cyrene, an important forerunner of Epicureanism.

16. G. Eliot, "The Influence of Rationalism," *Fortnightly Review*, 1 (1865), 55.

17. Epicurus, *The Extant Remains*, trans. C. Bailey (Oxford: Clarendon, 1936), p. 99. Pater probably first learned his Epicureanism from Jowett's lectures on ancient philosophy, although he obviously did not pick up Jowett's moral prejudices against Epicureanism. I have been through Jowett's lecture notebooks at Balliol and have found in them an ample basis for Pater's introduction to the Cyrenaic and Epicurean traditions in Greek philosophy; see especially the notebook for 1851-1853, 129 ff.

18. Cf. Mill's paraphrase of the extreme skeptic's position: ". . . [If] my Mind is but a series of feelings . . . what evidence have I (it is asked) of the existence of my fellow creatures?" (*Hamilton*, p. 238).

19. F. Copleston, *A History of Philosophy* (New York: Image Books, 1962-1967), I, i, 108.

20. Again Jowett was probably responsible for introducing Pater to both Protagoras and Heraclitus; see note 17 above.

21. Mill, *Hamilton*, p. 226.

22. H. Bloom, *The Ringers in the Tower* (Chicago: University Press, 1971), p. 189.

23. L. Stephen, "The Scepticism of Believers," *Fortnightly Review*, 22 (1877), 356.

24. This is perhaps an extension of Mill's "We have no conception of Mind itself, as distinguished from its conscious manifestations. We neither know nor can imagine it, except as represented by the succession of manifold feelings which metaphysicians call . . . Modifications of Mind" (*Hamilton*, p. 235; see also pp. 238-243).

25. Cf. Mill, *Hamilton*, pp. 364-366. Pater has not exactly followed Mill's distinction between these three modes of thought; conceptualism for Mill is not mere subjective thought; it is, rather, something close to what Pater means by a middle position between the realists and the conceptualists.

26. G. P. Gooch, *History and Historians in the Nineteenth Century* (London: Longmans, 1952), chap. 27.

27. F. Meinecke, *Historicism: The Rise of a New Historical Outlook*, trans. J. Anderson (London: Kegan Paul, 1972), p. 246.

28. E. Pattison, *Westminster Review*, 43 (1873), 639-40.

29. *The Drift of Romanticism* (London: Constable, 1913), p. 99. For other comments along similar lines, see G. Tilloston, "Arnold and Pater: Critics Historical, Aesthetic, and Otherwise," *Essays and Studies*, 3 (1956), 57; D. DeLaura, *Hebrew and Hellene in Victorian England* (Austin: University of Texas Press, 1969), p. 265.

30. See F. Stern, "Introduction," *The Varieties of Historical Experience* (New York: Meridian, 1957), pp. 20-24.

31. For discussion of the problem, see M. Mandelbaum, *The Problem of Historical Knowledge* (New York: Harper, 1967); W. Dray, *Philosophy of History* (Englewood Cliffs: Prentice-Hall, 1964), chaps. 2, 3.

32. R. Collingwood, *Idea of History* (London: Oxford University Press, 1961), pp. 248, 296.

33. Bradley in *The Presuppositions of Critical History* (1874), Croce in *Teoria e storia della storiografia* (1917), and Dilthey beginning with *Einleitung in die Geisteswissenschaften* (1883).

34. W. Dilthey, *Meaning in History: Wilhelm Dilthey's Thoughts on History and Society,* trans. and ed. H. P. Rickman (London: Allen and Unwin, 1961), p. 123.

35. Ibid., pp. 123-24; see also pp. 78-79.

36. Ibid., p. 125.

37. Ibid., p. 126.

38. Collingwood, *Idea of History*, p. 172.

39. Pater may well have taken the weaving metaphor from Carlyle; so may Dilthey have done, for Dilthey was a great admirer of Carlyle's (see his article on Carlyle in *Gesammelte Schriften* [Leipzig: Teubuer, 1914-1917], IV, 506-527).

40. Pater, "Poems by William Morris," *Westminster Review*, 34 (1868), 307.

41. Dilthey, *Meaning in History*, p. 82.

42. See Collingwood, *Idea of History*, pt. IV; Dray, *Philosophy of History*, chap. 1.

43. See M. H. Carré, *Phases of Thought in England* (Oxford: Clarendon, 1949), p. 351.

44. R. Flint, *The Philosophy of History in Germany and France* (Edinburgh: Blackwood, 1874), p. 2.

45. Dilthey, *Meaning in History*, pp. 165-66.

46. B. Croce, *History As the Story of Liberty*, trans. S. Sprigge (Chicago: Regnery, 1970), p. 36; see also pp. 28-31, 144-146.

47. See also *Renaissance*, pp. 33-35.

48. Dilthey, *Meaning in History*, p. 156.

49. Croce, *History*, p. 173.

50. Mandelbaum, *Problem of Historical Knowledge*, p. 320.

51. Dilthey, *Meaning in History*, pp. 166-168.

52. Ibid., pp. 51-53.

53. Croce, *History*, p. 30.

54. Meinecke, "Values and Causalities in History," trans. J. Franklin, in *Varieties of History,* ed. F. Stern (New York: Meridian Book, 1956).

6. Historicism and the Hellenic Ideal

1. W. J. Courthope, *Quarterly Review,* 141 (1876), pp. 132-136.

2. The best general discussion remains G. Hough's in *The Last Romantics* (London: Methuen, 1947), chap. 4.

3. R. Langbaum, *Poetry of Experience: The Dramatic Monologue in Modern Literary Tradition* (Harmondsworth: Penguin, 1974), p. 14.

4. G. Santayana, *Three Philosophical Poets: Lucretius, Dante, and Goethe,* Harvard Studies in Comparative Literature, I (1910), 196.

5. W. Wordsworth, *Literary Criticism,* ed. N. C. Smith (London: H. Frowde, 1905), pp. 13-15.

6. S. T. Coleridge, *Biographia Literaria,* ed. J. Shawcross (Oxford: Clarendon, 1907), II, 9-10.

7. J. S. Mill, *Essays on Literature and Society,* ed. J. Schneewind (New York: Collier, 1965), pp. 140-41.

8. R. Buchanan, *Contemporary Review,* 18 (1871), 335.

9. Pater, *Westminster Review,* 34 (1868), 305.

10. See his autobiographical sketch in *Miscellaneous Studies,* p. 186, from *The New Library Edition of the Works of Walter Pater* (London: Macmillan, 1910).

11. For an excellent discussion of this movement, see H. Hatfield, *Aesthetic Paganism in German Literature* (Cambridge, Mass.: Harvard University Press, 1964).

12. H. Heine, *Religion and Philosophy in Germany,* trans. J. Snodgrass (Boston: Beacon, 1959), pp. 76-77. Pater knew this work at least as early as 1866 when he drew on it for his discussion of Coleridge (*Westminster Review,* 29 [1866], 118).

13. Pater's knowledge of Hegel is discussed in detail below; for his knowledge of Schiller, see *Appreciations*, p. 18, where he quotes from *Über die Ästhetische Erziehung*.

14. See T. H. Huxley's signal essay in *Fortnightly Review*, 5 (1869).

15. *Westminster Review*, 28 (1865), 78, 101.

16. Cited by Houghton, *Victorian Frame of Mind: 1830-1870* (New Haven: Yale University Press, 1957), p. 71.

17. Notably, M. Praz in *The Romantic Agony*, trans. A. Davidson (London: Oxford University Press, 1970).

18. A. Swinburne, *William Blake* (Lincoln: University of Nebraska Press, 1970), p. 95.

19. *Swinburne as Critic*, ed. C. Hyder (London: Routledge & Kegan Paul, 1972), p. 30.

20. Cited in *Letters of Walter Pater*, ed. L. Evans (Oxford: Clarendon, 1970), p. 74.

21. See W. K. Wimsatt, "The Structure of Romantic Nature Imagery," *The Verbal Icon* (Lexington: University of Kentucky Press, 1954), and H. M. McLuhan, "Tennyson and Picturesque Poetry," *Essays in Criticism*, 1 (1951).

22. Baudelaire, *L'Art romantique, Oeuvres Complètes*, ed. J. Crépet (Paris: Conard, 1925), p. 297; my translation.

23. M. Hamburger, *The Truth of Poetry* (Harmondsworth: Penguin, 1972), p. 7.

24. Cited by M. Raymond, *From Baudelaire to Surrealism* (London: P. Owen, 1957), p. 360.

25. G. Orsini, *Benedetto Croce: Philosopher of Art and Literary Critic* (Carbondale: Southern Illinois University Press, 1961), p. 44. Orsini fails to note, however, that Pater places a quite un-Crocean emphasis on the artist's need to work and re-work his art object into conformity with his original intuition. In this way Pater avoids the kind of difficulty one has with intuitionist theories such as Croce's, namely, the tendency, as W. Charleton points out, to regard "any object of conscious intuition [as] a kind of work of art" (*Aesthetics* [London: Hutchinson, 1970], p. 85). Pater assumes that to his native intuition of reality the artist

adds his peculiar ability to accommodate the art object to the vision within by "many stages of refining."

26. Pater may have had in mind either the *Prolegomena Logica* (Oxford: Graham, 1851) or the *Metaphysics* (Edinburgh: Black, 1860). Both would have supplied him with his views of the relation between form and matter expressed in "Style" (see *Prolegomena*, chap. 7; *Metaphysics* pp. 52-66). For Mansel's debt to Kant, see *Prolegomena*, p. x, where he notes that he is obliged to Kant at almost every step of his argument.

27. Kant, *Critique of Pure Reason*, trans. J. Meiklejohn (London: J. M. Dent, 1969), pp. 41-42. The connection between Pater's view of form and Kant's transcendental aesthetic seems to me to be further evidenced in his Oxford lectures on philosophy (*Plato and Platonism*) where speaking the "unconscious constituent tendencies of mind," he notes the mind's possession of an innate principle: "Truth of number: the essential laws of measure in time and space: — Yes, these are indeed everywhere in our experience: must as Kant can explain to us, be an element in anything we are able so much as to conceive at all" (*Plato*, p. 52). See also *Westminster Review*, 29 (1866), 120; *Renaissance*, pp. 181-82; *Plato*, p. 28; *Miscellaneous Studies*, p. 11, for other significant references to Kant.

28. Cf. Kant's belief that in a "pure judgment of taste the delight in the object is connected with the mere estimate of its form." (*Critique of Judgment*, trans. J. Meredith [Oxford: Clarendon, 1952], p. 146.) There is no evidence, however, that Pater knew this work.

29. R. Child, *The Aesthetic of Walter Pater* (New York: Octagon, 1969), pp. 55-61.

30. Wilde, *Intentions, Collected Works*, ed. R. Ross (London: Dawsons, 1969), p. 165.

31. L. Trilling, *The Liberal Imagination* (New York: Anchor, 1953), p. 179.

32. Pater, *Westminster Review*, 29 (1866), 123.

33. G. H. Lewes, "Hegel's Aesthetics and the Philosophy of

Art," *British and Foreign Review*, 13 (1842).

34. See Pater, *Westminster Review*, 31 (1867), 80, 83, 94, 97, 99, 102-105.

35. B. Fehr has written the best account to date of Hegel's influence on Pater's criticism, but has pretty well limited himself to tracing echoes of the *Ästhetik* in "Winckelmann." From these he concludes, I believe correctly, that Pater had read deeply in Hegel's *Ästhetik* ("Pater und Hegel," *Englishe Studien*, 50 [1916], p. 305). Accounts of Hegel's influence in L. Rosenblatt (*L'Idée de l'art pour l'art* [Paris: Champion, 1931], pp. 188-89); R. Child (*Aesthetic of Walter Pater*, pp. 19-21, 61-66); and G. d'Hangest (*Walter Pater* [Paris: Didier, 1961], I, 90, 147-48) are too generalized to be of much use. A. Ward (*Walter Pater: The Idea in Nature* [London: MacGibbon and Kee, 1966]) and W. Shuter ("History As Palingenesis in Pater and Hegel," *PMLA*, 86 [1971]) are better on Hegel's influence on Pater's thought in general but say virtually nothing of his influence on Pater's specifically critical thought.

36. G. F. W. Hegel, *The Philosophy of Fine Art*, trans. F. Osmaston (London: Bell, 1920), I, 11.

37. Ibid., I, 9.

38. Thus Goethe writes, "high works of art are . . . like the highest works of nature, produced by men according to true and natural laws" (cited by F. Will, "Goethe's Aesthetics: the Work of Art and the Work of Nature," *Philological Quarterly*, 6 [1956], p. 57; my translation), and Coleridge constantly employs the metaphor of natural or vegetable growth to explain the nature of aesthetic creation (see M. H. Abrams, *The Mirror and the Lamp: Romantic Theory and Critical Tradition* [New York: Norton, 1958], pp. 167-177).

39. Hegel, *Fine Art*, I, 36.

40. This preoccupation of Pater's with craftsmanship has been frequently noticed by critics. But it has almost always been connected with France, that is, with Gautier and Flaubert. These connections are valid and important. But at least as much so—

and I should think probably more so as far as the earliest formation of Pater's critical approach is concerned — is the influence of
Hegel.

41. *Fine Art*, I, 9.

42. Pater, *Westminster Review*, 31 (1867), 94.

43. R. Child, *Aesthetic of Walter Pater*, pp. 31-32.

44. *Fine Art*, I, 107.

45. Ibid., pp. 97, 98.

46. Compare Pater's discussion here (*Renaissance,* pp. 209-
211) with Hegel's (*Fine Art*, I, 98 ff.).

47. Pater, *Westminster Review*, 90 (1868), 305.

48. The inspiration throughout appears to be quite specifically Hegelian. Cf. Hegel's discussion of the breakup of Greek
serenity under the influence of Christian inwardness (*Innerlich-
keit*) and the consequent development of the "Romantic" type of
art. (*Fine Art*, I, 107 ff.) Pater has made this notion of developing
inwardness, which he first discusses in "Winckelmann" with regard to Angelico and others (*Renaissance,* p. 205), the principal
theme of his interpretation of Renaissance art.

49. L. Stephen, *Hours in a Library: Third Series* (London:
Smith, Elder, 1879), p. 118.

50. For another relevant contrast with Pater on this question, see his fellow interpreter of the Renaissance and Hegelian, J.
A. Symonds. Unlike Pater, Symonds never really managed to take
Hegel's point about the sensuous presentation of Zeitgeist; see,
e.g., his treatment of Leonardo's "Last Supper" in the *Renaissance in Italy: The Fine Arts* (London: Smith, Elder, 1909), p.
238.

51. W. Dilthey, *Meaning in History: Wilhelm Dilthey's
Thoughts on History and Society,* trans. and ed. H. Rickman
(London: Allen and Unwin, 1961), p. 166.

52. See Hough, *Last Romantics*, pp. 159-161; R. V. Johnson, *Walter Pater: A Study of his Critical Outlook and Achievement* (Melbourne: University Press, 1961), pp. 12-13; M. Shmief-
sky, "A Study in Aesthetic Relativism: Pater's Poetics," *Victorian
Poetry*, 6 (1968), 108.

53. Pater's concept of the emergence of an "informing reasonable soul" in Hellenic art almost certainly owes something to Hegel's account of the development of "soul experience" in classical art (see, e.g., *Fine Art*, I, 105 ff.; II, subsect. ii, esp. 183 ff.).

54. Pater is commonly and erroneously regarded as having removed art to a sphere where moral categories have little or no relevance (see, e.g., Rosenblatt, *L'Idée de l'art*, pp. 169-70). Even the view that he was art-for-art in his early works and became "moralistic" in later ones (see Child, *Aesthetic of Walter Pater*, pp. 22-23) is untenable, as my quote from "Winckelmann" above indicates. Eliot's passing observation that Pater was "always primarily the moralist" (*Selected Essays, 1917-32* [London: Faber and Faber, 1951], p. 438) is much closer to the truth.

55. *Fine Art*, I, 98.

56. Ibid., I, 107.

57. Ibid., I, 106.

58. Ibid., I, 107.

59. *Aesthetic As Science of Expression and General Linguistic*, trans. D. Ainslie (London: Macmillan, 1922), pp. 302-03.

60. Pater, *Westminster Review*, 29 (1866), 115.

61. Ibid., 34 (1868), 300.

Conclusion. Historicism and the Enrichment of Critical Thought

1. I. A. Richards, *Science and Poetry* (New York: Norton, 1926), p. 78.

INDEX

Absolute, the, 4, 5, 7, 20, 21, 22, 29, 45, 87, 117, 128, 129, 168, 180, 210, 224, 241, 243, 248

Acton, J. E. E. D., Lord, 3, 4

Aeschylus, 61, 82

Aesthetic value: in Carlyle, 83-86; in Arnold, 152-165; in Pater, 236-245

Aestheticism, 8, 174, 214-217, 224-225

Affectivism, 18, 159-165, 252

Alison, Archibald, 18, 162

Architectonics, 144-148, 222

Aristippus, 182, 209

Aristotle, 11, 76, 93, 118-119, 130

Arnold, M., 1, 8-12; on history, 5, 97-104, 125-129; 152-165; on modern age, 5, 14, 104, 154-55; and Spinoza, 12, 72, 112-118, 121-125, 159; and Carlyle, 63, 72, 103, 112-114, 126, 245; and Goethe, 63, 113-115, 116, 119; and Heine, 63, 113-114; and T. Arnold, 91, 97-100, 106, 143; and Vico, 97, 106, 108-09, 153; on aesthetic withdrawal, 101-104; and Lucretius, 101-02, 106, 108; and Clough, 104, 119, 144, 145, 153; and Epicureanism, 111; and Stoicism, 111,115;

and religion, 114-118, 120-129, 165-168; and Epictetus, 118-120; on ideal of the Best Self, 118-138, 238, 249, 252; and Schleiermacher, 123-125; and Hellenism, 124, 130; and Pater, 126, 156, 168, 172, 224-225, 245; and Hegel, 127-28; and Marcus Aurelius, 133-135; and J. S. Mill, 133-34, 166-67; summarized, 248-49, 252-53

Poetry and Poetics: on poetry and belief, 85-86, 165-168; his classicism, 141-152; on architectonics, 144-148, 222; on grand style, 148-152; on touchstone method, 148; the Best Self and poetry, 152, 163; on poetry and history, 155-165; affectivist principle of poetic value, 159-165; and Romanticism, 167-68

Works discussed or quoted from: Poetry: "Cromwell," 100, 113; *Empedocles,* 77, 79, 98, 99, 103, 104-05; *juvenilia,* 97; *Merope,* 153; "Obermann," 100, "Resignation," 98, 100, 101;

Index

Index

aesthetical thought, 12, 16, 18-22, 59, 60-61, 62-63, 66; standing as literary critic, 15-16; on "aesthetic" criticism, 16-24; on artistic form, 17; on the Idea in poetry, 24-30; his Neo-Platonism, 26-28; on history of German Literature, 48; on poetry and history, 62-66, 79-86; on poetry and myth, 67; on poetic language, 70-75; on poetry as rhetoric, 71-73; poetry as unreal, 73-75; on poetry and religious belief, 81-83, 85; on poetic value, 83-86, 238

Works discussed or quoted from: "Biography," 60, 75, 76, 81, 84; "Characteristics," 37, 49, 51, 52, 56, 85, 86, 154; *Chartism,* 49; "Corn Law Rhymes," 62; "Count Cagliostro," 49; "The Diamond Necklace," 50; *French Revolution,* 31, 49, 76; "German Playwrights," 17; "Goethe," 63, 71, 80; *Heroes and Hero Worship,* 27, 32, 39, 42, 49, 53, 54, 55, 56, 70, 82, 96, 118; "Historic Survey of German Poetry," 64; "Jean Paul Richter" (I), 27; "Jean Paul Richter" (II), 27; *Latter Day Pamphlets,* 49; *Lectures on the History of Literature,* 49, 61, 82, 84; *Notebooks,* 46, 49, 62, 69, 80; "On History," 3, 72; "On History Again," 6, 50; *Past and Present,* 87; *Sartor Resartus,* 31, 37-39, 41, 43-44, 46-48, 49, 52, 62, 63, 67, 69, 73-74, 79, 118, 229; "Schiller," 22, 51; *Schiller,* 33, 35, 43, 60-61, 73; "State of German Literature," 18, 19, 20, 21, 79; *Sterling,* 49;

"Voltaire," 17; *Wilhelm Meister,* 63; *Wotton Renfried,* 72
Cassirer, E., 69, 120
Chapman, G., 149
Cicero, 106
Classicism, 141, 152
Clough, A. H., 78, 104, 119, 144-145, 172
Coleridge, H., 16
Coleridge, S. T., 15; as Romantic theorist, 26, 28-29, 56, 73, 85, 98, 207-08, 210-11, 241; and Idealism, 28-29, 179; and Carlyle, 54, 58, 85; and Arnold, 85; and Pater, 207-08, 210-11, 228
Collingwood, R. G., 6, 7; and Pater, 185; as historical relativist, 190-91, 202; and aestheticism, 204, 205
Colvin, S., 65
Comte, A., 51
Courthope, W. J., 206-207, 208
Cousin, V., 127
Cowper, W., 235
Croce, B., 7, 8, 169; and Pater, 185, 191, 236; his concept of history, 197, 203, 204; and aestheticism 205, 220; and Hegel, 242
Cromwell, O., 100-101

Dante Alighieri: Carlyle's view of, 61, 82, 84, 250-251; Arnold's view of, 113, 131, 135-136, 252; and grand style, 148; and Hegel, 240
Decadent movement, 213-215
Descartes, R., 92
Dilthey, W., 7; and Pater, 185, 191; as complete historicist, 192-195, 197, 203, 236; and aestheticism, 204, 205
Dowson, E., 215

Eichthal, G. d', 69-70
Eliot, G., 173, 182

Index

Eliot, T. S., 84, 140-142
Elliot, E., 61
Empedocles, 99
Empiricism, 17, 165, 174-184, 207, 220-221
Epictetus, 118-120, 139
Epicureanism, 111, 180-183
Epicurus, 182, 183
Euripides, 61, 82

Fichte, J. G.: and Carlyle, 21, 25, 29, 30, 33; on will, 39-44; and historicism, 45, 46, 48, 55, 68; on literature, 62-63
Figurative language, 68-72
Flint, R., 196
Formalism, 17, 86, 140-152, 222-225, 228-229
French Revolution, 44, 127
Froude, J. A., 142, 172
Fry, Roger, 86

Gautier, T., 174
Genius, 43, 82, 155, 229
Gerard, A., 162
German Idealist movement, 32-34, 45-48, 55, 103, 117, 179-180
Gibbon, E., 48, 54
Giotto di Bondone, 233
Goethe, J. W. von: and Carlyle, 19, 20, 33, 63-64; and poetic language, 67, 70; and Arnold, 113, 114-116, 119; and form, 145, 148; and Pater, 174, 209, 210, 243-44
Grand style, 109, 148-152
Gray, T., 154, 158
Green, T. H., 179, 226
Guérin, Maurice de, 151, 208
Guizot, F., 127

Hamilton, W. R., 175-76
Hare, J., 51
Hartley, D., 176

Hazlitt, W., 15
Hebraism, 130
Hegel, G. W. F., 6-7, 9; and Carlyle, 19, 20, 21; as part of German Idealist movement, 25, 33, 46; as philosopher of history, 48, 50, 192, 193; and Arnold, 127-28; and Pater, 174, 179, 189, 209; on art, 210, 226-232, 236, 239, 240-242, 244
Heine, H.: and Arnold, 63, 113-14, 133, 159; and Hegel, 127; and Pater, 174, 209, 210; as Romantic, 217-18, 244
Hellenic ideal, 124, 237, 240, 242, 243
Hellenism, 130, 133
Heraclitus, 183, 197-98
Herder, J. G., 2, 13, 19, 46, 57, 80
Herodotus, 93, 96
Historicism: as dominant concern of nineteenth century, 1-11; defined, 3-8; in Hegel, 6-7, 46, 47, 127-28, 226-236; complete, 7-8, 58, 185-205, 225-236; as revelation of truth, 7-8, 48, 78, 200-204; influence on nineteenth-century criticism summarized, 8-11, 254-55; in Schiller, 33-39, 45, 62-66; in Fichte, 39-45, 62; in Carlyle, 45-58, 62, 157; as Victorian poetry's "high argument," 75-79; in T. Arnold, 91-97; in Vico, 91-94; in M. Arnold, 97-104, 126-129, 155-160, 168; in Pater, 185-205, 225-236; in Dilthey, 192-203
Home, H., Lord Kames, 162
Homer, 82, 84, 109, 139, 149
Horace, 93, 106
Hume, D., 18, 53, 162, 176, 177, 184
Huxley, T. H., 117, 173, 212-213

Idea, the: as spiritual truth in poetry, 24-26; in Carlyle, 26-27, 51-52, 53, 55, 57, 62-63, 66-68, 70-72, 76, 250; in Arnold, 113-117, 127-129; in

292

Index

Pater, 217-236, 240-245; in Hegel, 228, 230-31, 240-41

James, H., 142
Jeffrey, F., 48
Johnson, L., 215
Johnson, S., 31
Jowett, B., 86, 127, 131, 179, 226, 230

Kant, I.: and Carlyle, 19, 25; and Coleridge, 26, 28; on freedom, 33, 34; and relativity of knowledge, 176, 178; and Pater, 184, 204, 220, 221-22, 224
Keats, J., 73, 78, 145, 151, 208, 244

Lecky, W. E., 189
Leonardo da Vinci, 233
Lessing, G. E., 2
Lewes, G. H., 4, 16, 65, 86, 173, 209, 226
Livy, 93
Locke, J., 176
Lockhart, J. G., 16
Longinus, 150, 151
Lucretius, 93, 99; early influence on Arnold, 101-02, 105, 106-07, 108, 137; as empiricist, 182

Macaulay, T. B., 16, 54, 81
Mallarmé, S. de, 218, 219
Mansel, H. L., 221
Marcus Aurelius, 120, 133
Masaccio, 233
Masson, D., 65
Maurice, F. D., 86, 114, 173
Meinecke, F., 6, 7, 8; as complete historicist, 185, 189, 204, 205
Michelangelo Buonarroti, 233-34, 243
Mill, J. S., 3, 16, 51, 76, 86; and Arnold, 133-34, 165-66; and Pater, 173, 179, 180, 186; on relativity of knowledge, 174-176, 178-79, 183,

184, 220; on general consciousness, 187; as critic, 208, 209
Milman, H. J., 16, 51
Milton, J., 82, 148, 150, 240
Modern spirit, 36, 37, 40, 91-97, 105-108, 113-116
Moore, G., 215
More, P., 190
Morley, J., 65, 173-74, 180
Morris, W., 16, 82-83, 174, 177, 208
Müller, J., 46

Naturalism, 113-118
Nature, 6, 13, 39-40, 57, 208-217, 227-228
Neo-Platonism in poetics, 25-28
Nettleship, R. L., 179
Newman, J. H., 173
Nibelungenlied, 61
Niebuhr, B. G., 51
Nietzsche, F., 45, 56
Novalis (F. L. von Hardenberg), 20, 33, 59, 114, 117

Ortega y Gasset, 7, 8
Ovid, 93

Pater, W. H., 1, 8-12; and Arnold, 126, 156, 168, 172, 225, 238, 245; and skepticism, 171-173, 177-180, 182-83; and empiricism, 173-185; and Mill, 174-179; and Epicureanism, 180-182; his historicism 185-205; and *Kulturgeschichte,* 189; and Dilthey, 185, 191-204; and Heraclitus, 197-98; and religion, 200-204; and Romanticism, 206-217; and contemporary science, 211-12; and Carlyle, 238, 245; summarized, 249-50, 253-54

  Poetry/Art and Aesthetics: and Hegel, 9, 179, 189, 226-232, 240-242; and Goethe, 64, 243-

293

Index

Index

DATE DUE

DEC 21 '92			

DEMCO 38-297